THE WAR PERIOD
OF AMERICAN FINANCE
1908–1925

BY
ALEXANDER D. NOYES

Being the continuation of
" Forty Years of American Finance "

———

G. P. PUTNAM'S SONS
NEW YORK AND LONDON
The Knickerbocker Press

Copyright, 1926
by
Alexander D. Noyes

The
Knickerbocker
Press
New York

Made in the United States of America

PREFACE

THIS book has been written in response to numerous and urgent requests that my *Forty Years of American Finance*, published in 1909, should be so extended as to cover the period of the European War. It was originally planned to add three or four chapters to the older book and publish them with the rest, under the same or an amended title; but it soon became evident that the necessary scope of the wartime narrative would not admit of that arrangement. Although, however, the present book embodies separate and independent treatment of the period, it also provides an unbroken historical continuation of the preceding work—as indeed it was bound to do, since examination of the country's financial history between 1908 and 1914 was indispensable in order properly to explain the remarkable economic experiences of the United States in the war itself. Similarly, it appeared to me that the War Period of American Finance must logically include the extraordinary

episodes of inflation and deflation which immediately followed return of peace.

The immense complexity of interlocking events
in war-time finance has made it necessary, especially in describing the period when the United
States was itself at war, to treat the subject in
broad perspective. A narrative which should
undertake to discuss exhaustively every economic
incident and expedient of the war would require a
book of many volumes; probably a good many
separate books. I believe, however, that there is
need for a book of moderate length which will tell
the story in its larger outlines, describing and
discussing those economic events, financial movements and governmental policies which primarily
determined the history of the period. For the
same reason, I have not indulged in discussion of
the controversial theories that surround many of
the financial occurrences during and after war-
time, except so far as was necessary to make the
sequence of events plain to the reader. The
limitation placed many years ago on the *Forty
Years of American Finance*, that it was not an
economic treatise but a financial history of our own
times, may frankly be applied to this volume.

The narrative contained in this book is based on

original sources. Published description or interpretation of events by other writers has been utilized only when it expressed the view of active participants in the events described. For first-hand personal information regarding certain facts not generally known or of public record I owe acknowledgment to Senator Carter Glass, author of the Federal Reserve Law in its existing form; to Bernard M. Baruch, chairman of the War Industries Board, and to Benjamin Strong, governor of the New York Federal Reserve Bank. But my conclusions regarding the facts in question are my own.

If I shall succeed in making clear to the reader the true relation of events in the bewildering economic chapter from 1914 to 1920 inclusive, the actual operation of economic cause and effect, and the reason for a change in the American financial position which was beyond the conception of human imagination in the days before 1914, I shall be satisfied.

A. D. N.

May, 1926.

CONTENTS

Contents

Industrial revival of 1922 and 1923—The decline in money rates—Negotiations over Europe's war debt to our government—Accumulation of gold in America —Reserve banks' policy—The agricultural problem— Conclusion.

THE WAR PERIOD
OF AMERICAN FINANCE

1908–1925

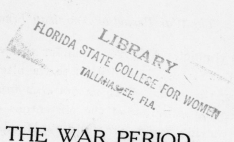
THE WAR PERIOD
OF AMERICAN FINANCE

CHAPTER I

ON THE EVE OF THE WAR

THE purpose of this book is to describe and examine the economic events which either shaped or reflected transition from the America of days before the great European war to the America of today. In a period whose economic phenomena were absolutely world-wide in their scope, our own financial history was of necessity closely interwoven with the movement of events in Europe. Those events, however, I shall discuss only so far as they directly affected at a given moment the particular incidents in American finance. That the war itself should have been the paramount influence on the course of affairs outside of Europe, followed inevitably from the unprecedented cost and destructiveness of

3

the conflict. Yet the manner in which the
United States adapted itself to the altered conditions, the actual effect on our own financial and
industrial structure of the portentous changes in
the outside world, are fully explainable only in
the light of events and tendencies within the
United States itself and independent of foreign
influences. It is those events and tendencies to
which my narrative will be primarily directed.

Many financial phenomena of the time, notably
the rise of prices and the magnitude of financial
transactions in this country during the period
of war and afterward, merely repeated the world's
previous experience in such episodes. All great
wars of the past have disclosed, as this one did, an
unimagined economic power in the possession of
every nation. If our own public loans, public
expenditure, national taxes and industrial production came to be measured in 1917 and 1918 in
terms of billions, where a few hundred millions
would have startled the markets of pre-war days,
not only had Europe in 1915 and 1916 set the
pace for that while the United States was neutral,
but financial resources equally unsuspected at
the time had been called into play during England's wars with Napoleon, for instance, and

during our own War of Secession. When, however, long before this war was ended, the United States became the financial centre of the world, the dispenser of credit even to Europe, a picture was presented wholly distinct from that of any other country. As in the period of actual warfare, so on return of peace. Our own markets and the rest of the world had emerged from other wars when the world's economic machinery was almost brought to a stop. Most of the financial and political consequences of the Great European War—the widespread abandonment of the gold standard, the attitude of labor, the disintegration of the Austro-Hungarian Empire, the capture of Russia by Communist dictators, the sweeping of Germany into a maelstrom of currency depreciation beyond all experience of previous economic history—were changes no more unpredicted and no more epoch-making than those which had followed such other conflicts of the past as the Thirty Years' War or the campaigns of Frederick and Napoleon. But the shifting of balance in the world's economic relations which followed 1914 was something new in history.

That the United States was then a borrowing community, largely dependent on European capital for the development of its industries, everybody recognized in 1914. The country was vitally influenced in its own finance by the course of Europe's markets. It paid so great a yearly tribute as interest on its obligations to European banks and investors, the accumulation of more than half a century, that a very large surplus of merchandise exports over imports was necessary to balance the account, and we were always likely to be drained of our gold supply when foreign markets sold back part of their holdings of our stocks and bonds. The change to the position of 1923 and 1925 was complete in every particular. With our Treasury in 1922 stipulating terms for England's refunding of $4,000,000,000 indebtedness to the United States Government, contracted in only two years; with New York subscribing in 1924 for a billion and a quarter in new securities of foreign governments and companies, including half a billion to Europe,[1] whereas $100,000,000 to $150,000,000 was the maximum of our takings of European bonds in any year before 1915;[2] with the British government avow-

[1] *Balance of International Payments in 1924*, U. S. Department of Commerce, April, 1925, pp. 13–20.
[2] *Forty Years of American Finance*, p. 282.

edly leaning on our Federal Reserve to effect its own resumption of gold payments in 1925;[1] with an import of gold which, notwithstanding repurchase of Europe's holdings of our own securities, had brought into our bank vaults before the end of 1924 half of the world's available stock of gold,[2] including all of the old Russian State Bank's accumulations, most of the German Reichsbank's original reserve, and practically the whole Transvaal gold output since 1920—with all this series of events, which the wildest imagination of 1914 could not have pictured as possible, it is within the facts to describe the outcome of the war as reversal of the old economic order. These changes did not occur at once in 1914, but most of them came with extraordinary suddenness very shortly afterward, and all the basic causes for the new economic situation will be found in the history of the twelve months after war began in August, 1914. I hope to show in what way and by what special influences that dramatic economic transformation was effected.

To do this, it will be necessary to review cer-

[1] Speech of W. S. Churchill, Chancellor of British Exchequer, announcing gold resumption to Parliament, April 28, 1925.
[2] *Balance of International Payments in 1924*, p. 6.

tain incidents of our financial history before the
war. There was nothing in the country's economic situation, on the eve of the European war,
to suggest to financial imagination the possibility of such achievement. It is true that there
had been a moment, at the climax of the windfall of American prosperity in 1900, when New
York began to talk of "displacing London as the
world's money centre."[1] But the course of events
had soon seemed to relegate that idea to the limbo
of discarded economic illusions. The financial
dependence of the United States on Europe had
again become as plainly visible as in the eighties
and nineties. The brief and disappointing revival
of trade in 1909, following the panic of 1907 and
the depression of 1908, was itself followed in this
country by what seemed to indicate an enfeebled
economic condition. Our railways, sometimes
even our cities, were compelled to place large
loans both at London and Paris during 1910,
admittedly for the reason that the American
investment market was itself in an unsatisfactory
condition and suspicious of the situation in American industry.[2]

[1] *Forty Years of American Finance*, p. 283.
[2] *Financial Chronicle*, "Retrospect of 1910," Jan. 7, 1911, p. 7.

For a time, during 1909, all the familiar indices of trade recovery had appeared to be in evidence. From 9,018,000 tons in the second half of 1908 the country's iron production had increased to 14,-773,000 in the second half of 1909, the larger figure surpassing all previous records. Exchange of bank checks in the United States had risen 25 per cent above 1908; the stock market had moved as if the country was back again in 1906. But the equally familiar "secondary reaction" came, as it had come after 1895 and 1875, quickly and with discouraging completeness. The higher protective tariff installed by the Payne-Aldrich Bill of 1909 was as futile for stimulating trade or restoring prosperity as it turned out to be politically unpopular. It did not even serve its avowed purpose of checking import of foreign goods, which in the calendar year 1910 was $139,000,000 greater even than in 1907, representing the largest total on the record, while exports were reduced by $57,000,-000. Whereas imports of gold had exceeded exports by $88,100,000 in 1907, the surplus of gold exports in 1909 was $88,700,000, and this was accepted as another sign of weakened economic strength. The price of iron fell from $19 to $15.50 per ton during 1910, of steel from $27.50 to $23, and the steadily slackening activity in general trade, of which this was an indication, occurred as an unmistakable result of declining industrial demand. Reaction in trade found its natural reflection in decreasing railway earnings. The companies, alleging that transportation rates at the existing level were in many cases unremunerative, undertook to raise them; but the advances were promptly suspended by the Interstate Commission under the larger powers conferred on it by Congress in 1910.[1] A great decline ensued on the investment markets; it was presently aggravated by partial failures of the harvests of 1911, when a long drought cut down the wheat crop to the smallest yield since the very short crop of 1904.

As has often happened under such circumstances in our history, discouragement over the business situation found expression in politics, and the political result on this occasion deserves special attention, because it had direct and important influence on the nature of our unconscious preparation for the war-time economic strain, and

[1] Annual Report Interstate Commerce Commission, Dec. 20, 1911, p. 2. *Financial Chronicle*, "Retrospect of 1911," Jan. 6, 1912, p. 7.

probably on our national policy during the period of war itself. Even in 1910 the Congressional elections voiced the popular feeling of unrest and discontent. New York, Massachusetts, Connecticut and New Jersey, all of which the Republicans had carried in 1908, went over to the other party. In some usually doubtful states, such as Ohio, the Democrats won sweeping victories; a Republican majority of 47 in the existing House of Representatives was replaced by an elected majority of 63 Democrats in 1910. The wave of political opposition to the ruling powers—the most familiar of all phenomena at such times of industrial depression—did not abate until the Democratic party had elected Woodrow Wilson president in November, 1912. Although no one then foresaw the coming European conflict, that election had a very distinct bearing on it, through determining personnel and party affiliations of the Executive and Congress by whom this country's policies were directed, during our period of neutrality and, when supplemented by the election of 1916, during our own participation in the war.

How far those policies might have differed and with what results on the course of the war, if Mr. Roosevelt or Mr. Taft had been elected presi-

dent in 1912, will always remain a matter of historical controversy. That Mr. Roosevelt, with
his political intuition and his individual prestige
in the field of international diplomacy, might conceivably have restrained the German government
from its fatal step of July, 1914, or, having failed to
accomplish that, might have brought the United
States into the war in 1915, thereby shortening
the conflict, is at least a debatable proposition.
Yet it cannot be overlooked that, on the outbreak
of the war, Mr. Roosevelt publicly declared that
"neutrality may be of prime necessity to preserve our own interests," especially "to conserve
our influence for helping towards the re-estab-
lishment of general peace when the time comes,"[1]
and that when his attitude had changed in 1915
it was an open question (which contemporary
expression of public opinion did not settle)
whether the West and South would then have
followed even Roosevelt's lead into armed intervention. Nor can the fact be dismissed from
consideration that President Wilson's insistence
on the enactment of the Federal Reserve Law during 1913 turned out to be a matter of paramount
importance in the financial relations of this coun-

[1] Article in *The Outlook*, N. Y., Sept. 23, 1914.

try to the war, whereas there is little reason to suppose that a banking and currency-reform law would have been enacted in that year if Mr. Taft or Mr. Roosevelt had occupied the White House. To both the opportunity had come for pressing such legislation during their own respective tenure of office, and neither had taken any aggressive stand regarding it. The political reasons for their attitude, in view of the proposals to which their party was committed, would almost certainly have been as strong in 1913 as in 1909 or 1908.

As a matter of political history pure and simple, the election of Mr. Wilson in 1912 has frequently been described as accidental. That it was actually an Opposition victory is often denied. Although the Democratic candidate carried all but eight states in the Union and polled a vote in the Electoral College larger by 347 than the next strongest candidate, whereas even in 1904 Roosevelt's electoral plurality was only 196, nevertheless that sweeping success was admittedly made possible by the breach in the Republican party and the candidacy of ex-President Roosevelt on an independent ticket. The popular vote for Mr. Wilson was more than 2,000,000 greater than the vote for either President Taft or Mr. Roosevelt, but it was smaller by 1,309,836 than their combined vote. If all the votes polled by the two Republican candidates had been cast for either one of them, he would have carried enough of the states in which neither actually won a plurality to have overtopped Mr. Wilson by more than 100 votes in the Electoral College. This does not, however, mean that 1912 should normally have witnessed a Republican victory. The result of a "three-cornered contest" can never be accurately accounted for in that way. A popular independent candidate like Roosevelt always draws votes from both regular tickets; it is impossible to know exactly how much he has drawn from either, or what would have been the division of votes without his candidacy. The essential fact remained that the Opposition party had carried the election, for the first time since the Republicans won the presidency under not altogether dissimilar economic conditions in 1896, sixteen years before, and that the voters had unconsciously decided who was to guide the country's political destinies through the European conflict. Since the feud in the Republican party had been carried so far as to nominate opposing candidates not only for the presidency but for Congress, another result of the election was that the Democratic House majority of 66 in the preceding Congress now rose to 145, while the Senate, which the Republicans had previously controlled by a majority of 6, now became Democratic by a majority of 10. Thus the new president had behind him a party in full control of both houses; a consideration which played an important part, both in the pre-war legislation and in the conduct of the war.

The year in which Mr. Wilson was elected, almost the month of his election, witnessed what was recognized in after years, but not at the time, as premonition of the Great European War and of its immediate financial consequences. In many respects the year 1912, notwithstanding the atmosphere of depression and discouragement carried over from 1911, had presented indications of normal trade revival in the United States. The circumstances were not entirely unlike those which had preceded returning prosperity in 1879 and 1897.[1] Readjustment of American prices had been drastic; it was followed by increased exports. With Europe's grain reserves exhausted by the previous season's short production, American harvests as a whole surpassed every previ-

[1] *Forty Years of American Finance*, pp. 53–58 and 270–275.

ous record for magnitude; wheat nearly matching the famous crops of 1901 and 1906, cotton far exceeding its largest yield of other years and nearly all agricultural products selling at good prices.   Our export of such products in the twelve months after the harvest of 1912 was valued by the Department of Agriculture at $1,123,000,000, as against only $871,000,000 two years before and a previous maximum of $1,054,000,000.[1]   It was supplemented by increase of more than $100,000,-000, or 16 per cent, in export of manufactured goods.   We imported on legitimate commercial account in 1912 more gold than had entered the United States in any calendar year since we were buying gold from Europe at a premium in the panic of 1907.[2]   Our monthly iron production at the end of 1912 was wholly unprecedented; the industry was working at 95 per cent of capacity, with prices rising and unfilled orders greater by nearly 60 per cent, than at the end of 1911.[3]   According to all precedent of American financial history, these economic weather-signs should have preceded genuine industrial recovery.

[1] Yearbook, U. S. Department of Agriculture, 1913, p. 507.
[2] *Forty Years of American Finance*, p. 375.
[3] *Iron Age* estimates; U. S. Steel Corporation, monthly reports of unfilled tonnage.

But nothing of the kind ensued. On the contrary, what might be described as a flicker of hopefulness on all the markets was followed, during the period between 1912 and the outbreak of war in 1914, by relapse into business uncertainty, unsettled markets, and financial discouragement. On Wall Street, this disappointment of what had seemed to be reasonably-grounded hopes was commonly ascribed to the Tariff Reduction Bill of 1913, to the vetoing by the Interstate Commerce Commission of freight rates which the railways asserted to be necessary for a living profit, to the so-called "radical tendencies" of the new administration at Washington. These factors in the political situation may have had their influence; but very similar circumstances had existed at other times when financial prosperity was in full career (in 1902 and 1906, for instance) and, furthermore, the financial and industrial reaction which followed 1912 in the United States occurred simultaneously in all other countries.

A far more convincing explanation will be obtained by considering when and how the movement of economic recovery came to a halt. It was visibly and with great suddenness terminated in October, 1912; not because of any disturbing turn

of affairs in home finance or politics, but by the
outbreak of the Balkan War. It might no doubt
have been argued (and, indeed, was argued at the
time) that a quarrel between half a dozen states
of the second or third rank in the Southeastern
corner of Europe gave no reason for business reaction and collapse of financial confidence in America. But in the light of what happened two
years afterward, the Balkan episode of 1913 bears
a very different aspect nowadays on the pages of
history. We know today, what was then only
a matter of vague surmise (except perhaps in
the inner circles of European diplomacy), that
Austria was even then considering military intervention in the Balkans, that Germany was ready
then, as in 1914, to abet her, and that Russia
was watching both of them.[1] If our own financial
markets did not in 1912 and 1913 understand the
larger menace of this Balkan War, there is convincing evidence that the European markets did.

Although none of the greater Powers was at
any time engaged in the Balkan conflict, those
markets instantly moved as if in preparation for
such a turn in the situation. On October 17,

[1] Speech of ex-premier G. Giolitti in Italian Parliament, Dec.
5, 1914.

Turkey accepted the challenge of war from Bulgaria, Servia and Montenegro. On the same day the Bank of England's discount rate rose from 4 to 5 per cent, the highest since the world-wide panic period of 1907, and, in quick succession, the German bank rate rose from 4½ to 5 and the Austrian from 5 to 5½. European capitalists began to realize on their investment securities. French government bonds fell to the lowest price since 1890 and British consols to the lowest in their history. In the last five months of 1912 we had imported $37,000,000 gold, mostly in payment for our large grain shipments; in the first half of 1913 our gold exports were $63,000,000, of which the greater part went to France. Gold was in fact already being drawn from European bank reserves by the European people for hoarding purposes; it was estimated by the statisticians that in 1913 not less than $250,000,000 was already hidden away by the French, German and Austrian people.[1] This apprehension of an immediate and world-wide diplomatic crisis ceased abruptly late in 1913, when a conference of responsible ministers of the great European powers settled the Balkan conflict and terminated the

[1] London *Economist*, May 10, 1913, p. 1100.

struggle in Southeastern Europe with a formal peace. As we shall see, that settlement was immediately followed by reaction of sentiment to a spirit of political confidence and reassurance which provided very extraordinary background for the actual outbreak of war between the greater powers in 1914. Nevertheless, it is impossible to doubt that the grave political and financial possibilities which surrounded the Balkan War itself must have reacted on the American economic situation of 1912 and 1913. It is equally noteworthy that, while financial markets recovered abruptly on conclusion of the Balkan peace, nowhere did trade and industry revive from their depression.

During this confused and troubled pre-war period two questions of the first importance— each a source of grave financial uneasiness and each a disturbing influence in American economic history—were solved by the national authority. The action by which their solution was achieved was destined in the case of one to have immediate bearing on the country's financial interests; in the case of the other, its influence on the war period in American finance was vital. These problems concerned the Anti-Trust Law and the banking and currency system. It is difficult for people of a later generation to realize the confusion into which legitimate plans of industry had been thrown in the three or four years before 1911, not by the law against combination in restraint of trade but by the erratic and bewildering application of it. The useful and wholesome general purpose of the Law of 1890 has never been seriously denied; it had been enacted to suppress manifest evils, injustices and dangers in the industrial practices of the day, which were equally recognized by all impartial observers.[1] But the law was framed in general terms, and judicial interpretation of it began about 1907 to take wide and confusing range. Many of such judgments, in the lower federal courts, seemed to embody sweeping condemnation of any and every kind of agreement or understanding between competing producers, as to policy regarding prices or even regarding methods of doing business.

One eminent federal judge, who avowedly disapproved the law itself but who applied it according to his own construction of it, pronounced the formal opinion that any combination whatever in business enterprise was repugnant to the Act.

[1] *Forty Years of American Finance*, p. 349.

Under the Anti-Trust Law, he stated from the bench, "two individuals who have been driving rival express-wagons between villages in two contiguous states, who enter into a combination to join forces and operate a single line, restrain an existing competition."[1] They had violated the Anti-Trust Act, in his judgment, even if they had merely formed a partnership. This interpretation of the law was commonly regarded as absurd, but it was stated in a serious judicial opinion; it at least paraphrased certain actual decisions of the lower courts, and it left in doubt the question whether even such a case could be surely excluded from the scope of the prohibitory statute. Business men who went to the federal attorney-general to ask his judgment as to the lawfulness of contracts of the sort, which they offered to submit to his opinion, were informed that they would have to take the risk and await decision by the courts.

It is true that a different interpretation than Judge Lacombe's had been placed on the law by other men who spoke with high authority. Justice Brewer, whose concurring vote had ensured a majority in the Supreme Court for the Northern

[1] Judge Lacombe, opinion in U. S. *vs.* American Tobacco Company, U. S. Circuit Court of Appeals, N. Y., Nov. 7, 1908.

Securities decision of 1904, had himself dissented
from the application of the Anti-Trust Law to
"minor contracts in partial restraint of trade."[1]
The author of the law, Senator George F. Edmunds, declared much later that the law's prohibitions could not properly apply to "just, fair
and wholesome business arrangements," because
"such conduct is not restraining but on the other
hand is promotive of and beneficial to the public
interest."[2]   Justice Brewer's personal opinion
was merely the unsupported judgment of one
member of the Court, and Mr. Edmunds's interpretation had no necessary judicial force.   The
principle was now, however, finding its way more
definitely into court decisions.   The Federal
Court of Appeals, before which the government's
suit against the Standard Oil Company was first
argued in 1909, put the case formally.   The
court's decision was against the company, but it
coupled that decision with the opinion that
monopolies of "part of inter-State and international commerce by legitimate competition, however successful, are not denounced by the law."[3]

[1] *Forty Years of American Finance*, p. 348.
[2] *North American Review*, December, 1911.
[3] Opinion of Justice Sanborn, U. S. *vs*. Standard Oil Co.,
November, 1909.

Yet even this judicial ruling was manifestly vague. It did not indicate the basis for determining what agreements or combinations were to be held lawful, and what were not. Evidently the question could not be settled except by an unmistakable ruling of the United States Supreme Court on the main point at issue. In May of 1911, the leading case against the Standard Oil Company came up for decision before that Court. The Supreme Court of that period, under the leadership of a jurist of high distinction, Chief Justice White, had already achieved repute for decisions nearly or wholly unanimous, in contrast with the close divisions which had for many previous years surrounded its judgments (as in the case of the Income Tax decision of 1894[1] and the Anti-Trust Law decision against the Northern Securities in 1904[2]) with an atmosphere of uncertainty. The Court's decision of 1911 was unanimous to the effect that the Standard Oil combination was illegal, and its dissolution was therefore ordered. But the formal opinion of the Court went further.

It was delivered by the Chief Justice himself, and

[1] *Forty Years of American Finance*, p. 227.
[2] *Ibid.*, p. 348.

it did not stop with recital of the form of organization and the corporate acts which were in that case considered to have fallen under the ban of the Anti-Trust Law. That law, the Chief Justice set forth, was plain in declaring the illegality of "every contract, combination in form of trust or otherwise, or conspiracy, in restraint of trade and commerce." But the interpretation of the law, Justice White proceeded, must nevertheless be "guided by the principle that, where words are employed in the statute which had at the time a well-known meaning at common law or in the law of this country, they are presumed to have been used in that sense unless the context compels the contrary." Now judgment as to what constitutes restraint of trade, so the opinion proceeded to point out, had been defined in a long series of older court decisions; which the opinion cited. The principle recognized in such judicial precedent was that contracts or actions were in restraint of trade only when they "had not been entered into or performed with the legitimate purpose of reasonably forwarding personal interest and developing trade but, on the contrary, were of such character as to give rise to the inference or presumption that they had been entered into or done with the intent to do wrong to the general public and to limit the right of individuals."

The Anti-Trust Law, the Chief Justice argued, must be presumed to have been drawn with full knowledge of this body of interpretative precedent; whence, in the opinion of the Court, it followed inevitably that application of the law "called for the exercise of judgment" to determine "whether the prohibitions contained in the statute had or had not in any given case been violated." This, he went on, required some standard, and that standard could only be "the standard of reason which had been applied in the common law and in this country, in dealing with subjects of the character embraced by the statute." When, therefore, it had to be decided in a given case whether a contract or combination was or was not in restraint of trade under the Anti-Trust Law, "then of course the rule of reason becomes the guide." The Standard Oil Corporation, the opinion proceeded, had manifested since its earliest days "an intent and purpose to exclude others," that purpose having been proved by repeated actions whose necessary motive was to drive such competitors from the field "and thus accomplish the mastery which was the end in view." But every other case must equally be decided on its own merits, under the principle set forth in the Court's decision.

The order for dissolution of the $100,000,000 Standard Oil Company was followed by a decision, based on similar grounds, for dissolution of the $40,000,000 Tobacco combination. But it was soon apparent that the establishment of the "rule of reason" by the Supreme Court had cleared up the obscurities of the Anti-Trust Law. Subsequent decisions under that statute were plainly based on the Supreme Court's criterion, and the bringing of a suit against the United States Steel Corporation, a short time after the Court's decision of 1911, had no such unsettling effect on investors as it would have had if the doctrine of intent to restrain freedom of contract had not been thus defined. The application of the "rule of reason" determined the decision in that leading case, when the highest Court reaffirmed on appeal the lower court's decision of June 3, 1915, in favor of the company, on the ground that the purpose of the organization "was not monopoly, but concentration of efforts with resultant economies and benefits."[1]

[1] Opinion of Justice McKenna, March 1, 1920.

Even in the actual dissolution of the oil and tobacco combinations into their constituent companies, the courts rejected the contention that the mere fact of a constituent company controlling larger business than its outside competitors required dissolution of that company also into smaller units. The importance of the Supreme Court decision of May, 1911, became strikingly evident when the war period began. The immense concentration of industrial energy which the war made necessary in the United States would have been surrounded with obstacles and achieved with the greatest difficulty if the Anti-Trust Law had still been administered under the judicial interpretations of 1908. When the United States emerged from war, almost the first important statute was one which recognized and asserted that large-scale combinations of the railways, controlled and supervised in the public interest, should be promoted and not proscribed by Acts of Congress.

The second financial problem which was solved in this period between 1907 and 1914 constituted a far more important landmark in our financial history. Discussion of plans for a sounder banking system and a more efficient currency originated in the discovery, after the first two decades of the old national banking system, that the admitted virtues which that system possessed, as contrasted with the state banks of issue prior to the Civil War, were offset by very grave defects. The requirement of the National Bank Act of 1864, on which our banking and currency system had for nearly half a century been based, was that each bank should independently keep on hand or (to a limited extent) on deposit in other city banks, a cash reserve of 15 to 25 per cent against its deposits. This meant that in an emergency of the Treasury, in a sudden demand on our gold for export, or in a great financial panic, the country's reserve of gold and other money would be scattered in the vaults of six or seven thousand separate institutions, hundreds of miles away from one another and each acting for itself. The chaotic circumstances which prevailed in the relations between banks and government during 1894, and between banks and the general market during 1893 and 1907, were an inevitable consequence.[1]

In the matter of national bank circulation, through which the Law of 1864 had intended to

[1] *Forty Years of American Finance*, pp. 183–4, 193–5, 371–5.

provide circulating money for the expanding needs
of trade, it had long been evident that those
note issues, far from creating a truly "elastic
currency," increased or decreased from causes
wholly unconnected with business requirements.
They were based entirely on the pledge, by the
issuing banks with the Treasury at Washington,
of a virtually equivalent sum in United States
government bonds. The history of the Great
European War has shown the peculiar hazards of
that system, purely from the viewpoint of potential currency inflation and depreciation; for the
continental belligerent states of Europe paid their
war expenses, after 1914, largely through borrowings from a central bank, against which borrowings the government pledged immense amounts
of its own war-time obligations, and in return for
which it received an equivalent in new paper
money issued by the bank. Since gold payment
on such bank notes had been suspended when the
war began, those war-time currency issues were
in actual fact only a left-handed output of fiat
money by the government itself. When in Germany, for instance, the rapid post-war depreciation of the currency caused an uncontrollable
further inflation, the result was not only a rise of

prices to monstrous heights, but ruin of the thrifty savings investor and eventual repudiation of the currency itself.

This could not have happened, it is true, if gold redemption of the paper currencies had been maintained in Europe; but the national bank currency of the United States was never explicitly redeemable in gold. In 1913, such possibilities as Europe's later experience indicated seemed altogether remote to the American public mind. But it had nevertheless been evident that our bank circulation was entirely ill-contrived for the varying needs of the country's industry.[1] It was a matter of record that in one decade of our history, when trade as measured by the country's exchange of bank checks was increasing 54 per cent, bank circulation, in consequence of redemption of the government bonds behind it, decreased 53 per cent, and that in another four-year period, when trade activity similarly measured decreased 26 per cent but when the government was putting out new bonds, the bank notes actually increased 18 per cent.[2] In 1907 the ab-

[1] *Forty Years of American Finance*, pp. 109–111.
[2] "History of the National Bank Currency"; National Monetary Commission, 1910.

solute ineffectiveness of the national bank note issues as a means of meeting the "money-hoarding panic" was clearly proved.[1]

This lack of any machinery for expanding the money circulation in response to urgent needs of trade, even at a moment of panicky money-hoarding, and the highly unpleasant actual results in all directions, had caused nation-wide reconsideration of the problem. The successive investigations of the subject had reached different conclusions as to the exact lines on which the machinery of banking and currency reform should be shaped, but three requirements had been recognized by all proposals of competent experts as indispensable. The first was centralization of the country's gold reserve; the second, establishment for that purpose of some central organism which could lend its credit, on prescribed security, to private banks when resources of those banks should be under pressure; the third, replacement of the national bank circulation by a currency issued from such a central institution—a currency which should be supported by the centralized gold reserve, which should be based on the pledge of qualified short-term paper arising from actual

[1] *Forty Years of American Finance*, p. 376.

commercial obligations and which, therefore, would increase or decrease according to the actual state of trade. It had also become evident that the crux of a practical scheme for such reform would be its attitude on the questions, who should control and administer the central banking organism, the government or the private banks; who should issue the currency, the government itself or a central banking institution; what should be the nature of the loans to be "rediscounted," and what should be the character and percentage of the cash reserve maintained against circulating notes.

Numerous proposals of such legislation had been submitted, in and out of Congress, during the ten years prior to the panic of 1907; none of them effected anything except to hold public attention to the subject. In March of 1908, with the events of 1907 fresh in mind, the problem was taken in hand aggressively by Nelson W. Aldrich, then chairman of the United States Senate's Finance Committee. Senator Aldrich of Rhode Island was widely known as leader and organizer of the Republican party in the Senate, a recognized master of political strategy and, in considerable measure, a dictator of party policies. To the general public, he had been chiefly familiar as

the advocate in Congress of the protected industries and was regarded, not altogether with kindly
feelings, as an expert in legislative bargaining
when a tariff bill was before the Senate. But, as
with many other statesmen whose careers had
previously been identified with purely partisan and
ephemeral legislation, the ambition of his later
years appeared to be to associate himself with
enactment of a public policy so important as to
give him a name in history. In the light of what
had occurred in 1907, reform of the banking and
currency system appealed to Aldrich's imagination; his mind became absorbed in it. The practical details of the plan were outlined with the
collaboration of Paul M. Warburg, a New York
private banker who had long made special study
of the subject, both in Europe and in America;
Aldrich applied himself to the political side of it.
Through public discussion of the problem, through
personal speeches in and out of Congress and
through the drafting of proposals for legislation, he
devoted to promotion of that reform the remainder of his official life.

The first endeavor of Senator Aldrich was to
obtain enactment of a law designed to provide,
with a view to a future "money-hoarding crisis"

such as those which paralyzed the markets of 1893
and 1907, a temporary but instantly available
"emergency currency." The statute to that
effect was passed in May, 1908, in the face of
strong Congressional opposition and of something
like indifference on the part even of the business
public.[1] We shall find this statute playing an
unexpectedly important part, half a dozen years
after its enactment. Next, he persuaded Congress to appoint a so-called Monetary Commission, made up from members of both House and
Senate, to investigate the whole problem of banking and currency and submit recommendations.
This commission's life was to last four years, until
March, 1912; in the interval the commissioners
examined in great detail, often through personal
inquiry in foreign countries, all the important
banking and currency systems of the world, and it
submitted what is perhaps the most voluminous
report on the subject ever published.

In January, 1911, Senator Aldrich made public
in behalf of the Monetary Commission his plan for
what he described as The Reserve Association of
America. It was in substance, though not in

---

[1] *Congressional Record*, May 29, 1908; *Financial Chronicle*,
May 16, 1908, p. 1186, May 30, p. 1305.

name, a proposal for the creation of a central bank. Briefly summed up, the plan contemplated a central institution, its capital stock of $300,000,000 to be subscribed and owned by the national banks. That institution was to have 15 branches, operating in the 15 districts into which the country was to be divided. The directors of each branch were to be chosen by the "member banks" of its respective district. The central bank was itself to be governed by 45 directors, of whom 6 should be made up of officers of the bank and members of the United States cabinet, 15 chosen by the branches, 12 elected by the shareholding national banks, and 12 more appointed by the other directors. The executive committee of 9 was to consist of the governor of the association, his two deputies, the United States Comptroller of the Currency, and five other members elected by the general board. It will readily be perceived that these provisions meant control and management of the entire organization by representatives of the private banks.

In this outline of the plan, and more fully in a carefully drawn bill given out nine months later, detailed provision was made for rediscounting the loans of national banks which should become members of the Reserve Association. The central institution was also to issue circulating notes, covered one third by "gold or other lawful money" and two thirds by "United States bonds or approved commercial paper or both." Further issue of notes was to be forbidden "whenever the lawful money so held shall fall below one third of the notes outstanding."[1] Three months later, a final revision of the proposed bank statute changed the organization's title to The National Reserve Association of the United States and stipulated a 50 per cent cash reserve against both notes and deposits, though permitting continued issue of notes subject to a graduated tax if the ratio of the reserve to the total note issue should fall below 50 per cent but not below 33⅓ per cent. When the reserve percentage should be less than 33⅓, it was provided that "no additional circulating notes shall be issued." Note issues in excess of $900,000,000, unless wholly covered by a reserve of lawful money, were to be taxed 1½ per cent per annum; issues in excess of $1,200,000,000, unless similarly covered, were to be taxed 5 per

[1] *Outline for a Tentative Plan for the Revision of our Banking Legislation*, Washington, Jan. 16, 1911. *Suggested Plan for Monetary Legislation*, revised edition, Washington, Oct. 14, 1911.

cent. Private banks in the system were required
to keep against their own deposits "the same
percentages of reserve as are now required" by
the National bank law—which were 25 per cent
for city banks and 15 per cent for country banks.
But "the deposit balance of any subscribing bank
in the National Reserve Association, and any notes
of the National Reserve Association which it
holds, may be counted as the whole or any part
of its required reserve." [1]

I have reviewed thus at length the proposals of
Senator Aldrich's bill, because the Federal Reserve
Law which now exists was in some respects (notably in the provision for rediscounts) unmistakably
based upon it, though in other and vitally important
provisions the two measures presented absolute
contrast. [2] But the Aldrich bill itself was not
destined to pass into the statute books. Whatever its economic merits or demerits may have
been, its basic theory of a central bank, not only
owned by private banking institutions but controlled by them through a clear majority both in
the directorate and in the executive board, was

[1] "A Bill to Incorporate the National Reserve Association of
the U. S." Report of the Monetary Commission, Jan. 8, 1912.
[2] H. R. Speech, Carter Glass, Sept. 7, 1916.

recognized as politically impossible. It was proposed at the very moment when Congress was beginning to investigate the so-called "Money Trust," in an atmosphere surcharged with legislative hostility. As a result of the incidents preceding 1907,[1] alleged manipulation of the banking system by powerful capitalists, with a view to serving their own selfish purposes, had become the constant text of Congressional speeches, political declarations, and newspaper controversy.

To this political trend the Aldrich bill was an uncompromising challenge. Furthermore, in addition to the political attitude of the day there existed, in the American public mind, a deeply-rooted hereditary tradition opposed to a "central bank." Voters who had never heard of the clash between President Jackson and the old United States Bank in 1832 had unconsciously absorbed much of the feeling of those earlier days. The Aldrich bill of 1911 was hopelessly blocked by this powerful underlying sentiment. It was never pressed in Congress, never endorsed in a political convention platform, never seriously urged even by friendly Administrations at Washington. Its place in history is merely, as its author originally described

[1] *Forty Years of American Finance*, pp. 333–341.

it, that of a "tentative plan." The plan as it
stood was passively rejected; but much of the
framework, so readjusted to remove political distrust, survives in our present Federal Reserve Law.

No such result was in any respect indicated at
the time. In the presidential nominating con-
ventions of June and July, 1912, which followed
by only a few months the final promulgation of the
Aldrich currency plan, the Republican party had
refrained from any explicit endorsement of the
legislation thus proposed, confining itself to the
vague declaration that "we need measures which
will prevent the recurrence of money panics and
financial disturbances." The Democratic convention had positively opposed "the so-called Aldrich
bill or the establishment of a central bank" and
had merely proposed, with similar vagueness and
with similar absence of any sign of serious purpose, "such systematic revision of our banking
laws as will render temporary relief in localities
where such relief is needed, with protection from
control or domination by what is known as the
Money Trust." The election of Mr. Wilson in
November could hardly, therefore, be considered
to mean continued effort at currency reform. Mr.
Wilson's legislative policy was announced as revi-

sion of the tariff. The extra session which he summoned to meet on April 7, 1913, was called expressly for that purpose; banking and currency reform was not mentioned in the call. On that question, indeed, his party was believed to be divided into irreconcilable factions.

But Mr. Wilson, although he had not made currency reform an issue in his campaign and although his natural bent was not in the direction of finance, appears to have had positive ideas on the need of such legislation. Less than a fortnight after the election of November, 1912, he wrote to the leading member of the House Banking and Currency committee that "the question of the revision of the currency is one of such capital importance that I wish to devote the most serious and immediate attention to it."[1] On June 23, 1913, before the tariff bill had passed, the President notified Congress in a second special message that reform of the currency and banking system was "absolutely imperative," that "we must act now," and that "the committees of Congress to which legislation of this character is referred have devoted careful and dispassionate study to the means of accomplishing these objects." An early

[1] Letter to Carter Glass, Nov. 14, 1912.

and satisfactory result of this sudden change in
the legislative program, involving a question of
such intricacy, would ordinarily have been impossible at the beginning of a new Congress and
a new administration, elected to displace a party
which had held power during the sixteen preceding years. It was made possible in 1913 by one of
those curious political accidents of which our history is full, and which have often shaped our
national legislation.

The so-called "Money Trust investigation," to
which I have referred, had been undertaken in
1912 in compliance with a resolution urged in the
House of Representatives by ultra-radical Congressmen. The manifest purpose of that resolution, adopted in February and drastically
amended in April, was to expose alleged abuses of
power on the part of the "banking interest" and
to frame legislation for suppression or punishment
of such abuses. The original proposal was to
entrust the investigation to a special committee,
but this encountered so much opposition that the
task was placed in the hands of the regular Banking and Currency committee of the House. The
debate on the resolution gave no evidence whatever that the House expected scientific study of

the currency system or a serious report on plans of currency reform.   The chairman of the Banking committee himself described it as "a Pandora's box," quoting the opinions of members that "the investigation would be a farce"[1]—as, indeed, in many respects it turned out to be.

But it so happened that the resolution had also instructed the committee, not only "to obtain full and complete information on the banking and currency conditions of the United States" but to do so "for the purpose of determining what legislation is needed."[2]   That clause of the legislation was scarcely mentioned in the House debate; nevertheless, in view of the definite instruction, the Banking and Currency committee had divided itself into two sub-committees, of which one was to investigate banking abuses, the other to frame proposals for currency legislation.   The sub-committee on legislation was under the chairmanship of Carter Glass of Virginia, a statesman of character and decision and of positive convictions on the subject, who was re-elected to the House in November, 1912, and who became in the next Congress chairman of the full Bank-

---

[1] H. R. Speech, Arsène Pujo, April 25, 1912.
[2] H. R. resolution, Feb. 24, 1912.

ing and Currency committee. The investigating Sub-committee finished its task with its report of February, 1913, on the wrongdoings of the Money Trust,[1] and the public promptly lost interest in the subject. But the other sub-committee held that its work had only begun and that, under the resolution, its opportunity and duty were to prepare at once a scheme of banking and currency reform. The preliminary work on the present Federal Reserve Law was therefore well under way before Congress met in extra session.

Thus singularly did a great constructive achievement in financial legislation result from a blind and futile effort at political agitation. The Pujo committee's "Money Trust report" has long been forgotten; but the work of the Glass committee as embodied in the banking and currency statute was destined to have so great a part in determining the country's financial history, after 1914, that it is difficult to construct an imaginary picture of what that history would have been without it. Into the full particulars of the discussion which ensued, beginning with the drafting of a tentative outline of the banking and currency bill in January, 1913, and reaching completion

[1] Report of Pujo committee, Feb. 28, 1913.

with the enactment of the Federal Reserve Law on December 23 of the same year, I shall not undertake to go. The discussion was complicated, on the one hand by opposition from the banking community to any plan which departed from the Aldrich formula of a single central institution and majority control by bankers, on the other by proposals, from responsible sources in the administration party itself, for a reserve system which the government should not only supervise but administer in all its functions. For the surmounting of these formidable obstacles, and for the enactment of the Reserve law within six months of the introduction of the Glass bill—notwithstanding the frequent amendments urged to favor certain classes of borrowers, and notwithstanding also the demand that the whole legislation be postponed to another session—the credit must fairly be divided between Chairman Glass, whose courage, energy and personal grasp of the principles at stake swept aside factious opposition, and President Wilson, who gave full support to the House committee, held back the inflationists of his party, and insisted peremptorily on prompt enactment of the law.

The original House bill was itself repeatedly

amended, in nearly all instances to its advantage. Its essential variation from the Aldrich plan, however, and its distinctive theory in banking and currency legislation, appeared in the first draft of the measure and was incorporated without dispute in every alternative proposal of the session. That was the creation, not of a central bank with branches as in the Aldrich plan, controlled by elected bankers, but of a designated number of separate and independent "regional reserve banks," themselves conducted by practical bankers but supervised and controlled by a central board. In its preliminary draft the House bill had proposed for such supervisory duties a large commission with mixed representation, partly of government officers or appointees and partly of delegates of the various regional banks; that commission to appoint the Federal Reserve Board. But this idea, with its cumbrous machinery, was soon abandoned for a Reserve Board of seven, made up of two designated government officers, the rest of its membership to be named by the President of the United States, thereby removing the political objection of a central banking organization directly or indirectly controlled by private bankers.

It was at first proposed that circulating notes, issued to the regional Reserve banks "at the discretion of the Federal Reserve Board," should "purport on their faces to be the obligations of the United States," but in the final bill it was stated that they "shall be obligations of the United States," redeemable both at the Reserve banks and the Treasury Department. In the first drafts of the bill the Federal Reserve Board was itself to establish at intervals the "rate of discount, which shall be mandatory upon each Federal Reserve Bank," but the final bill left the fixing of such rates to each Reserve Bank, "subject to the review and determination of the Federal Reserve Board." The original draft prescribed that every private bank in the system should maintain a reserve of at least 15 per cent against its deposits in the case of country banks and 25 per cent in city banks. These were the same percentages as in the National Bank Act and the Aldrich bill; but only 5 per cent in the one case and 10 per cent in the other were required to be held in cash, the rest to be made up of deposits in a Reserve Bank or in private banks at the Central reserve cities. In the law as enacted in 1913, the percentage of reserve required from private member banks against demand deposits was so far reduced that it ranged from 12 per cent to 18 per cent, similarly divided between actual cash and banking credits. The requirement therefore extended widely the possible credit facilities as compared either with the previous law or the Monetary Commission's plan.

As for reserves to be kept by the Reserve banks themselves, the first draft prescribed that each Reserve Bank should keep on hand, "in gold or the equivalent thereof," at least 25 per cent of its combined deposits and note circulation, but that this must also amount to 50 per cent of its circulating notes. When introduced in the House on June 26, the Glass bill restricted the system's note issues to $500,000,000 plus the amount in which outstanding national bank notes should thereafter be canceled, and it required every Reserve bank to maintain in "gold or lawful money" a reserve of 33⅓ per cent against both its deposits and its outstanding notes.

It will be perceived that this minimum reserve ratio was less than the untaxed limit prescribed by the Aldrich plan, which in its final revision stipulated 50 per cent. In its enacted form, however, the Law of 1913 placed a Reserve Bank's minimum percentage against deposits at 35 per cent in "gold or lawful money," fixed no limit on the note issue, but on the other hand required against outstanding notes a reserve of 40 per cent in gold alone, not in "gold or lawful money" as in the earlier drafts and in the Aldrich plan. It also incorporated the highly important proviso that, when notes of one reserve bank should be received in its deposits by another reserve bank, "they shall be promptly returned for credit or redemption to the Federal Reserve Bank through which they were originally issued"; the penalty for paying out such notes of another Reserve bank being 10 per cent of their face value. The number of separate Reserve banks was fixed in the law at 12, as against 15 proposed in the original draft and the 15 branches named by the Aldrich plan.

In this form the Reserve law was enacted in Christmas week of 1913, and that unexpectedly prompt result of a legislative situation which had long seemed alternately dangerous and hopeless settled the problem of banking and currency reform. After the bill had been finally enacted, by a vote of 43 to 25 in the Senate and of 298 to 60 in the House, the opponents of the plan accepted the result philosophically.   Little enthusiasm was displayed, however.   The banking community did not relinquish its mistrust of a system whose central administrative board was not to be controlled by representatives of banks.   The stock market made no response.   The comment of the leading New York financial journal was that "the practical considerations possibly standing in the way of successful establishment of the system overshadow everything else."[1]   No one who had participated in that notable discussion imagined for a moment what in retrospect was subsequently recognized by everybody—the supreme importance of having placed precisely that measure on the statute book before the end of 1913.

[1] *Financial Chronicle*, Dec. 27, 1913, p. 1855.

CHAPTER II

THE OUTBREAK OF THE WAR

THE suddenness with which the European War broke out in the middle of 1914, the total absence of popular belief in the possibility of any such event, up to the very week in which it came, are familiar history. It is true, as I have shown in the preceding chapter, that the Balkan War of 1912 and 1913, enlisting on the one side or the other the sympathies of the greater European powers, had been regarded at the time as a formidable danger-signal. But the fact that those antagonistic interests had been brought into seeming harmony, that the delegates of the larger governments had conducted jointly and successfully the complicated peace negotiations, occasioned very striking revulsion in general sentiment, especially when that result was achieved without any of the conditional threats and warnings which had accompanied the Algeçiras incident of

1911. This reversal of feeling is the only possible explanation for the course of the financial markets, which, in the first half of 1914, not only did not give the slightest premonition of the approaching crisis, but pointed in exactly the opposite direction.

The year began in all markets of the world with falling money rates; a perfectly plain reflection of relief that the apprehensions created by the Balkan War had been removed by the settlement of that conflict.   In January the Bank of England reduced its discount rate from 5 per cent to 3; the Bank of Germany followed its example. Rates on the New York market fell so rapidly that, in February, loans running until August were made on Stock Exchange collateral at 3½ per cent. A vigorous advance, with much speculative excitement, occurred on the London and New York stock markets.   That picture is all the more impressive in retrospect from the fact that the rising markets did not result from a favorable industrial situation.   As a matter of fact, our own foreign trade decreased, the customary surplus of exports disappeared early in 1914, and in the five months beginning with April there occurred the largest excess of merchandise imports since 1895. Gold was exported to the extent of fifteen to fifty millions monthly. But no one, in or out of Wall Street, ascribed this to misgiving over foreign politics, except in so far as the crisis in England's Irish relations might be mentioned, or our own dispute with Mexico.

When financial markets are forewarned of war, they prepare for its outbreak in a manner prescribed by long experience. Investment securities are sold on the stock exchanges so that capital may be released for war loans—in quantity, to be sure, but with careful effort to avert a panicky collapse. Gold reserves of state banks are enlarged as a basis for expanded credit. Anticipating heavy borrowing by governments, money rates rise, but with violent changes avoided so far as may be possible. The price of wheat advances, having in view possible interference with production and ocean trade. Output of war material is immediately speeded up; production of other material slows down. During the month or two before every other great war of our time, these preparatory adjustments had occurred more or less deliberately in every market of the world, including the United States. They had always mitigated the shock of the actual outbreak of hostilities.

Nothing of the kind preceded Germany's

declaration of war. The financial markets failed
so completely to foreshadow coming events that
on July 4, a week after the Austrian Archduke was
assassinated at Sarajevo and barely three weeks
before the beginning of hostilities, it was reported
from the London Stock Exchange that "the
tragedy in the House of Hapsburg has had no
effect."[1]   As late as July 16, it was remarked at
Paris that "large numbers of members of the
Stock Exchange are absent in the country."[2]

This meant complete absence of financial apprehension. At Berlin itself, on July 9, watchers of the
financial markets reported that "the Norway visit
of the Kaiser marks the beginning of the dead
season in German politics."[3]   Money rates on the
principal European markets, which had been
reduced at the beginning of the year to the lowest
since 1912, had not moved up at all.   Less than a
week before Germany invaded Belgium, bank
rates stood as low as 3 per cent at London, 3½
at Paris, 4 at Berlin, and private discount rates
were considerably lower.[4]   On Wall Street, until

[1] *London Economist*, July 4, p. 36.
[2] *Ibid.*, Paris correspondence, July 18, p. 125.
[3] *Ibid.*, Berlin correspondence, July 11, p. 73.
[4] *Ibid.*, July 25, pp. 158, 200.

the last week of July, European war was not even
mentioned among possible financial influences.
When prices weakened, the stock market talked of
Mexico, just as London talked of Ulster. Demand loans on the New York Stock Exchange,
whose rate is always and instantly advanced
by apprehension of a strain on credit, commanded only 2 per cent five days before war
broke out.

The first consequence of this economic unpreparedness, when Germany sent its ultimatum of
July 31 to France and Russia, and England
followed with declaration of war on August 5,
was not so much financial and commercial panic as
complete and world-wide financial paralysis. I
shall not undertake to discuss the course of events
on Europe's markets—the 10 per cent Bank of
England rate in the first week of war, the moratorium on debts, the prohibition of gold exports, the
recourse of every European government to paper
money. Neither is it my purpose to describe,
except in so far as they bore directly on the
American position, the "emergency expedients"
adopted in the credit market by all belligerent
states and imitated by non-combatants.[1] We

[1] *Financial Chapters of the War*, pp. 30, 31, 32.

are here concerned with the story of American finance, American trade, American currency and the American credit system, in what was unquestionably the most formidable crisis of the world's financial history.

In every financial crisis, great or small, it is the stock exchanges which first have to face the shock. They met it this time by closing their doors in every market of the world. That recourse was adopted at Brussels, Paris and St. Petersburg three or four days before Germany's ultimatum; it was adopted in the next few days in every other great city of the Eastern and Western hemispheres. The London Stock Exchange, which had never before suspended business, even in the Napoleonic wars, shut down indefinitely on the morning of July 31, 1914; the double motive for that action being, first to prevent such throwing-over of investment securities as should create financial panic, second, to forestall what was indeed already in sight, the "unloading" of international stocks and bonds on London by other markets, possibly in the enemy's country.[1] None of these European stock exchanges resumed

[1] H. Withers, *War and Lombard Street*, p. 20. W. R. Lawson, *British War Finance*, pp. 54-56.

business until long after the end of 1914. Half an hour before the time for opening business on Friday, July 31, the board of governors of the New York Stock Exchange declared the purpose of not following Europe's example;[1] but before the regular opening hour of ten o'clock they changed their mind, announcing through the Secretary that the Exchange would "be closed until further notice." It was not reopened to unrestricted trading until April, 1915. Never in its previous history, even in the panic of 1873, had the New York Stock Exchange shut down for longer than ten consecutive days.

This reluctant decision was induced by knowledge that, with every foreign stock exchange already closed indefinitely, the panicky effort of Europe to turn its investments into cash at any price would converge on the only stock exchange which was still doing business and that, with securities thrown in a mass on our market for whatever they could bring, New York would find it impossible to raise the money for payment. On July 30, the day before the Exchange suspended business, a long list of important securities had fallen to prices 20 or 30 per cent below those of a very few

[1] New York *Evening Post*, July 31, 1914.

weeks before; they were selling, in fact, for less than the lowest prices reached in the panic of 1907.[1]   Yet, before the Stock Exchange governors decided to close on the morning of July 31, they had obtained definite information of a wholly unprecedented array of selling orders cabled overnight from Europe to New York banking houses, for execution at any price obtainable when the market should reopen.[2]

This was the first indication of the economic chaos created by the war.   It is not possible, even now, to say precisely what would have happened if the New York Stock Exchange had kept open. We know what occurred on the "panic day" of older economic crises—collapse in the value of investment securities, so sudden and sweeping as to compel the wholesale closing-out of loans against which such securities were pledged; an agonized money market; rapid shrinkage of bank assets and therefore widespread failures of banks and banking houses.   In the middle of 1914 outstanding loans of the national banks, secured by stocks or bonds and repayable on demand,

---

[1] New York *Evening Post*, July 31, 1914.

[2] *Financial Chronicle*, Aug. 1, 1914, p. 314, N. Y. *Evening Post*, July 30 and 31, 1914.

amounted in the whole United States to
$1,036,976,000, of which $372,091,000 were outstanding in New York.[1] The closing of the Stock
Exchange, which stopped the quotation of falling
prices and made it impossible to sell this collateral on the open market, removed the most
urgent necessity for closing out such loans; the
Treasury, a month after the Stock Exchange had
shut down, reported that "not a single national
bank of New York City had, according to the
sworn statement of the banks, either sold or
ordered sold the collateral held as security for any
call loan."[2] Since no sale of securities could now
be made an official record, it was also possible to
continue appraising assets or collateral on loans
at the values of July 30. Therefore the question
of how great the decline of prices would have been
with the market open, the whole world in a panic,
Stock Exchange prices crumbling and the banks
calling loans and throwing the collateral on the
market, is a matter of pure conjecture. If New
York had continued to provide an open stock
market during financial Europe's bewilderment and
consternation of August, 1914, when even London's

[1] Treasury Report for 1914, p. 494.
[2] Statement of Comptroller Williams, Sept. 12, 1914.

banking business was suspended for two successive days by proclamation of "special holidays,"[1] it is not impossible that foreign selling would have driven down to all but nominal figures the already very low prices of securities. That might very possibly have forced the closing-out of the great mass of loans secured by the depreciating Stock Exchange collateral, with resultant wide-spread insolvency of private bankers or of the banks themselves.

Nevertheless, it was easy to understand that the immunity of August, 1914, rested on an entirely artificial basis. Even with the Stock Exchange closed (a condition which could not last indefinitely) the visible situation which had required that action threw alarming light on the question, what would happen when the market should reopen. Subsequent careful estimates, based on official data obtained from American companies whose stocks and bonds were held abroad, placed the total market value of such foreign holdings, in July of 1914, at $2,400,000,000.[2] This was less than some previous

---

[1] *Financial Chapters of the War*, pp. 43, 44.
[2] Report of L. F. Loree, June 28, 1915. *Financial Chronicle*, July 3, 1915.

estimates had figured, but it left the question open, how could the American market buy back such a sum if Europe insisted on selling? Furthermore, while the closing of the Stock Exchange had averted for the moment the overwhelming of our markets from that quarter, it could not stop recall of European capital loaned or deposited on the open New York market. The banks necessarily continued to do business; they were subject to cabled drafts on such credits for immediate remittance to the hard-pressed European markets, and the amount which New York had engaged to pay on demand had reached enormous figures. At the outbreak of war, so the Secretary of the Treasury stated on the basis of information gathered from the New York banks, our merchants and bankers were "indebted to London in the sum of approximately $450,000,000 maturing by January 1, 1915," with "$80,000,000 additional owed London and Paris by the City of New York" and shortly to fall due.[1]

We shall presently see what consequences actually ensued in the money market. But it was also perceived at the beginning of August that a good deal more was involved in this world-wide

[1] Secretary McAdoo, Treasury Report for 1914, p. 17.

crisis than international credit and the solvency of
banking institutions. Banking was not the only
American enterprise which seemed, on August 1,
1914, to be confronted with ruin. Some of
our largest industries were stricken with not at all
unwarranted panic on their own account. During
the twelve months ending with June, 1914, exports
of merchandise from the United States to Europe
had amounted to $1,486,000,000, and of this huge
sum $344,000,000 had been taken by Germany
alone and $815,000,000 by England, France
and Belgium. The question arose immediately
whether this trade, mostly conducted in British
and German vessels, could continue. German
merchant steamers had ceased to navigate the
sea as soon as war had been declared at Berlin,
but German war-ships were still in action, one
of them claiming to have sunk thirteen British
merchantmen in the first few weeks of hostilities.
Under such circumstances few American exporters
ventured in August to undertake consignments
to the ports of any belligerent, and the greater
part of our export trade came to a stop. The
President of the New York Chamber of Commerce
declared of the situation, in a speech at a special
emergency meeting convened by the Chamber

on August 13, that "Europe has placed an embargo on the commerce of the world."[1]

It was soon made plain what such an embargo, if continued and enforced, would mean to American industry. The grain trade was heard from first. One fifth of the wheat crop raised in the United States is habitually exported, Europe being its principal destination. In the very week when war began, our Agricultural Department estimated our wheat harvest of 1914 as larger by 163,000,000 bushels, or 21 per cent, than the highest previous yield of our agricultural history. Since consumption of wheat and flour at home did not change greatly from year to year, this meant that a proportionate increase in grain exports was necessary to market the crop. But the grain-exporting season had hardly begun when war broke out, and wheat sold by the farmers of the early-harvest districts was already, in August, crowding the facilities of seaboard storage markets. To Germany alone we had shipped 2,637,000 bushels in July; we sent none at all in August.[2]

---

[1] Speech of Seth Low. Annual Report N. Y. Chamber of Commerce, 1914–15, Part I, p. 48.

[2] Monthly summaries of U. S. Foreign Trade, Department of Commerce, 1914.

"Not in the memory of any living member of the trade," one New York grain market review asserted, "has such a situation ever before existed."[1] Instead of the traditional rise in wheat on news of war the cash price at Chicago, which had gone to 95½ cents per bushel on July 30, fell to 85¼ by August 3, reflecting the grain trade's apprehension that the crop could not be marketed.

The crisis in the cotton trade was still more formidable. In the first place cotton is not, like wheat, a necessary of life; on the contrary, it was at once inferred not only that transport of cotton to Europe might be stopped, but that introduction of forced war-time economies by Europe's people would dispense with all expenditure for clothing that could possibly be spared. In the full year 1913 we had exported 8,609,000 bales of cotton—60 per cent of that year's crop and valued at $575,000,000. Half of this total cotton export, or 4,377,000 bales, had been taken in 1913 by four of the belligerent countries; England, France, Belgium and Russia. More than one-fourth of the total, or 2,561,000 bales, had gone in 1913 to Germany, whose market now appeared to be

[1] *Financial Chronicle*, "Grain Trade Review," Aug. 18, 1914, p. 421.

entirely cut off. Stated in another way, the
foreign country which a year before had consumed
18 per cent of our cotton production of 1913 could
no longer buy from us at all, and other countries
which had taken 30 per cent were suddenly thrown
into the chaos of war. In the face of these two
gravely disquieting circumstances, the United
States had produced in 1914 a cotton crop greater
by nearly 20 per cent than the largest previous
yield in its agricultural history.

In August, 1913, we had exported 257,172 bales
of cotton; in August, 1914, we sent out only
21,219. In September not a bale went to France,
Germany, Belgium, Russia or Austria, which
collectively had taken 457,013 bales from us in
the same month of 1913, worth more than
$32,000,000.[1] A condition seemed to be fore-
shadowed for midwinter in which more than half
of our 16,000,000-bale crop of 1914 would be left
unsold and unsalable on the hands of producers
who were in debt for the money spent to raise and
harvest it. At the end of July, cotton had sold
for $62.50 per bale; in December it brought only
$36.25, which was below the average price of any

[1] Monthly Summaries of Foreign Commerce, 1914; U. S.
Department of Commerce.

year since 1901 and much less than the 1914
estimated cost of production. Even so, a further
decline was thought to be inevitable. Absolute
ruin of the Southern cotton-planter was predicted;
the cotton trade, in fact, fell into a condition
which can only be described as hysterical. A
Southern "cotton congress" demanded by resolution the issuance of Federal Reserve currency to
cotton-producers, on the security of cotton valued
at 75 per cent of the average price of the five
preceding years.[1] When Congress brushed aside
the amendment to the Reserve Law formally submitted to authorize that transaction, another bill
was submitted guaranteeing preference to cotton-
producers in all loans of emergency currency.

This also being voted down, two well-known
Southern senators proposed an amendment to the
federal tax law requiring the Treasury to issue
$250,000,000 in government bonds, to be advanced
to planters on the pledge of cotton valued at $50
per bale.[2] In the South Carolina legislature, the
plan was seriously discussed of prohibiting under
penalty the planting of any cotton whatsoever in

[1] Proceedings at Washington, Aug. 14, 1914.
[2] Senate speeches Hoke Smith of Georgia and L. S. Overman of
North Carolina; *Congressional Record*, Oct. 17, 1914.

1915, with a view to forcing up the price.[1] In the end a conference of responsible bankers, merchants and cotton-producers, called at Washington by the Secretary of the Treasury, drew up in October a plan levying subscriptions on banks in all parts of the country, whereby $135,000,000 cash was pledged to lend against cotton at the valuation of 6 cents a pound, or $30 per bale.[2] No one who lived through 1914 will have forgotten the frantic appeal for every one in the ranks of sympathizing American citizenship to "buy a bale of cotton." The example for such individual philanthropy was set by the President of the United States.[3]

These two notable industries give a picture of the consternation which in fact spread throughout the entire field of industrial production, paralyzing the market for such other export products as copper, steel manufactures, meat, oil.[4] The market for copper was completely demoralized; only drastic curtailment of production stopped the fall in prices. Mills of the United States

[1] *Financial Chronicle*, Oct. 24, 1914, p. 1181.

[2] Annual Report Federal Reserve Board for 1914, pp. 14, 206–209.

[3] *Financial Chronicle*, Sept. 26, 1914, p. 869; Oct. 3, p. 945.

[4] U. S. Department of Commerce, Monthly Summary of Foreign Commerce, January, 1915, pp. 579, 580, 583, 585, 587.

Steel Corporation reduced their output in the face
of the rapid decline of orders until the company
was turning out barely 30 per cent of capacity.
Some foreign materials indispensable for steel
production, notably ferro-manganese, became
almost unobtainable except at prohibitive prices.[1]
The dry goods trade found itself suddenly shut
off from German dyes, from wool, flax and jute.

At the same time, so great was popular apprehension regarding the probable consequences of
that war that, even in the dry goods trade and
despite the lower cotton prices, purchases at the
retail stores were stopped as suddenly as in the
older panic years and wholesale trade, as reported
in a year-end retrospect, was practically stifled.[2]
Nothing in the history of that extraordinary
period proved more conclusively than did the
profound depression which seized on the business
community in the summer and autumn of 1914,
the failure even of experienced observers to foresee what was actually in store for the American
producer, as a direct result of the European war.
Most of them followed the reasoning of the

[1] Annual Report, N. Y. Chamber of Commerce, Part II.,
p. 109.

[2] *Ibid.*, p. 96.

British foreign minister, to the effect that a war conducted with four great European states in arms "would be accompanied or followed by a complete collapse in European trade and industry,"[1] and they assumed that American industry and trade would go down with Europe's.

Even aside from an expected paralysis of foreign trade, it became instantly evident that technical insolvency of the banking community in the foreign world was unavoidable. In practically every important market outside the United States, the closing of the stock exchanges had been followed by government decree of a "moratorium" on debts. This was formal admission that, if payment at the due date were to have been required, downfall of the great London and Continental banking houses must have ensued, as in the Overend-Gurney panic of 1866; for all these houses had immense sums due and non-collectible from enemy countries. Such open insolvency had been averted, but only through general suspension of payments under government decree. The British government's order of August 6 had declared that payments already due or falling due within

[1] Sir Edward Grey to British Ambassador at Vienna, July 23, 1914.

a month, "in respect of any bill of exchange which was drawn before the beginning of the fourth day of August, 1914, or in respect of any contract made before that time, shall be deemed to be due and payable on a day one calendar month after the day on which the payment originally became due."[1] This extension of the due date was twice repeated, so that payment of debts maturing on August 4 was eventually put off to November 4, and no one could be sure beforehand how much further the suspension of credit would be carried. It affected payments due by London bankers or merchants to the American business community.

Necessarily, this extraordinary situation in the London market caused quick demand for return of the large sums of capital standing to London's credit in our market and payable on demand. In foreign exchange, Europe's call upon its New York credit balances had some spectacular results. Normally the New York rate could not rise above $4.88 or $4.89, the "gold-shipping point"; at those rates we had already exported $117,000,000 gold during 1914 before the war

[1] Postponement of Payments Act, Aug. 6, 1914; Lawson, *British War Finance*, pp. 103, 104, 105.

broke out, of which $84,000,000 had gone to
France and $27,000,000 to England.[1] But the
rate for cable remittances rose on August 1 to
$7 per pound sterling, whereas the highest figure
in the memory of living men was the $4.91 of the
panic of 1907.[2] New York exchange on Paris,
for which the gold parity is 19⅛ cents per franc,
rose to 23½; even the rate on Berlin rose to 26
cents per mark, although parity was 23⅞. These
wholly unprecedented rates, a singular prelude
to what happened later on, undoubtedly measured
in part the impracticability of shipping gold with
hostile cruisers on the seas, but they also reflected
foreign demands which were converging on New
York for recall of European capital invested here,
under expectation that the United States, like
Europe, would presently suspend gold payments.
As the situation presented itself to most people on
August 1, 1914, the American markets were confronted with complete collapse of credit in the
outside world, with financial and commercial panic
at home (which had apparently been obscured only
by the closing of the stock exchanges), with block-

[1] *Monthly Summary* of U. S. Foreign Commerce for July, 1914,
p. 65.

[2] *Forty Years of American Finance*, p. 375.

ade of international commerce, and with a "run" by Europe on the gold supply of every other country which did not protect its own position (as the European belligerents had done at once) by an outright embargo on gold exports.[1]

It was impossible that so absolute a breakdown of the foreign credit system should not have its repercussion on the New York bank situation. Yet the course of events was not altogether what the magnitude of the crisis might have suggested. The American business community was undeniably in a state of bewilderment and consternation, but it showed few signs of outright panic. There was no run of depositors on any depository institution; none of the "rumors," such as circulated in October of 1907 and August of 1893, that this or that concern was "in danger"; no crippled or threatened bank had to be "helped out" by its associates. For this immunity the closing of the Stock Exchange, and the consequent absence of any recognized further impairment in the value of stock or bond collateral against outstanding bank loans, were no doubt important influences. But there were certainly other reasons; among them absence of speculation or inflated credit

[1] *Financial Chronicle*, August 1, 1914, p. 292; Aug. 22, p. 499.

during the preceding year with its falling markets and inactive trade, the admitted soundness of the banking position and, perhaps more than all, the knowledge that the influences which had tied up credit were directly at work in Europe, not in the United States.

It is true, $80,000,000 cash was drawn from the New York banks in the last week of July and the first week of August, 1914, and $73,000,000 of the withdrawal was in gold; bringing down the New York bank reserve from a surplus of $27,127,000 above requirements at the end of July to a $47,992,000 deficit three weeks later, which was not far short of the $54,103,000 maximum deficit of 1907. Many of the banks as a consequence refused to lend at all, and Wall Street rates for merchants' paper rose to 8 per cent, the high figure of the 1907 panic. But the withdrawal of cash was made in an orderly way. Individual depositors were more stunned than excited by the war news and, although the New York savings banks applied the "sixty-day notice clause" against all but the smallest withdrawals, the sequel proved that action to have been hardly necessary.

The Treasury reported, four months afterward, that "at no time since the war broke out has there been to the knowledge of this Department, with the exception of a few isolated cases, a failure on the part of any solvent national bank to honor its checks in currency or money, or to meet its obligations."[1] As against the 158 national American bank suspensions of 1893 and the 22 of 1907, with a long list of insolvencies among private bankers on both occasions, there were practically no failures of private bankers or Stock Exchange houses in the war panic of 1914, and only 6 national banks, with an aggregate capital of $550,000, stopped payment during the five months after July.[2]

Nevertheless, no banker could know what turn would be taken next in the bewildering situation, and money was unquestionably being withdrawn and hoarded by depositors, as in the older panics. The banks therefore, on August 3, resorted to the expedient used on other similar occasions and issued clearing-house loan certificates, whereby balances owing by one bank to another should be discharged, not with cash but with certificates of debt.[3] The amount of such certificates

[1] Treasury Report, 1914, p. 1.
[2] *Ibid.*, pp. 484 and 535.
[3] *Forty Years of American Finance*, pp. 192 and 373.

outstanding reached towards the end of September a maximum of $109,185,000 at New York, or more than in either 1907 or 1893, and $211,788,000 in the country as a whole, compared with $238,000,000 in 1907.[1] Left to themselves, with the suspension of free cash payments to depositors which had always followed that expedient, the loan certificates would undoubtedly have brought the consequences that came with them in the two preceding panics—depreciation of bank checks in terms of actual money and, therefore, a "premium on currency" which could not have been removed in 1914, as it was in 1907 and 1893, by automatic shipment of European gold to us in response to that premium.[2] On those occasions New York was the "panic market," London and Paris had hardly felt the shock; this time Europe itself was in the grip of panic. The foreign gold which New York imported, later in the war, would not have come in August or September, 1914, when the outstanding problem was our own market's repayment of its gold obligations to Europe. If the withdrawal and hoarding of money had

[1] Report of N. Y. Clearing House Loan Committee, Dec. 21, 1914; Treasury Report 1915, p. 576.
[2] *Forty Years of American Finance*, pp. 195, 375.

been long-continued—as might have happened even in 1907, but for the almost immediate import of $90,000,000 gold from Europe with sterling above $4.90[1]—and if no recourse outside of clearing-house loan certificates had been available, automatic suspension of all gold payments at New York in the autumn of 1914 and a depreciating makeshift currency would at least have become possibilities.

That no such results ensued was not primarily a consequence of the Federal Reserve Law; the rather prevalent impression to that effect is erroneous. Although that law was on the statute-books with its provision for an elastic paper currency, its machinery had not been erected when the war broke out and the Reserve banks had not been established, whereas relief for such banking crisis as existed had to be immediate. The Reserve Board which was to direct the system had, it is true, been appointed early in the summer of 1914 and was formally organized on August 12. The twelve reserve districts and reserve banks prescribed by the law had been designated as early as April by the committee named for that purpose in the law, comprising the

[1] *Forty Years of American Finance*, p. 375.

Secretary of the Treasury, the Comptroller of the Currency, and the Secretary of Agriculture. But the organization of the districts, the subscription to the Reserve Banks' capital and the rearrangement of reserves, necessitated much slower procedure. With all the stimulus of financial and commercial crisis, the new federal banks were not able to open their doors for business until November 16; they could not, therefore, meet the August panic. But in the meantime another and a highly practical agency of immediate relief was for the first time in our history made available.

We have seen in the preceding chapter how the promoters of the Aldrich currency bill in 1908, while recognizing that enactment of a complete currency reform law would involve prolonged study, delay and investigation, had convinced Congress that an "emergency currency law" ought to be prepared at once to bridge the interval, and had induced it to pass, on May 30 of that year, the so-called Aldrich-Vreeland Emergency-Currency Act. The purpose of that statute was "to render available under the direction and control of the Secretary of the Treasury, as a basis for additional circulation, any securities, including commercial paper, held by a national banking association." National banks were empowered by it to organize groups called "national currency associations" which might in an emergency apply for additional note circulation through depositing, not only the United States bonds prescribed by the National Bank Act but other qualified securities or commercial paper, against which circulation would be issued up to 75 per cent of their face value, or qualified state, city, town, county and municipal bonds, on which notes would be obtained up to 90 per cent.

The currency thus provided was not to be guaranteed by the United States, but supervised and regulated by the government. The Treasury was to pass on the collateral and to hold it as security or for redemption purposes. The total issue of such notes was to be limited to $500,000,000. To restrict its use wholly to an actual emergency, there was imposed on the bank to which such currency should be issued a tax of 5 per cent per annum during the first month in which it should be outstanding, such tax rate to rise thereafter by 1 per cent monthly until 10 per cent was reached. The "emergency notes" had been actually printed in advance; the law of 1908, mindful of the panic of 1907 and of the run on the banks which had caught the New York banking community wholly off its guard, expressly stipulated that emergency currency "in blank, registered and countersigned," should be at once prepared and kept ready in the Treasury "to an amount equal to 50 per cent of the capital stock of each national banking association," and long before August, 1914, the Treasury Department had on hand the full $500,000,000 of this unissued currency.[1] Not a dollar of the emergency notes, however, had actually been issued at any time between the law's enactment, at the end of May, 1908, and the outbreak of war in 1914. So little expectation had there been of sudden recourse to this currency that the only comment of the leading New York financial weekly on the usefulness of the law, when it was enacted, was that "quite possibly it may prove more serviceable than is generally supposed."[2] The statute itself had in fact stipulated in its text that it should cease to be a law on June 30, 1914, but the Federal Reserve Act of December, 1913 (again long before the war was dreamed of), had provided that the life of the "Emergency Currency Law"

[1] Treasury Report for 1915, p. 577.
[2] *Financial Chronicle*, June 6, 1908, p. 1375.

should be extended to June 30, 1915; by which time, it was expected, the machinery of the Reserve Law would be in full operation. Curiously enough, the party which had voted for the original Emergency Currency Law, in 1908, voted in 1913 against its extension as an amendment to the Federal Reserve Act.[1] Very rarely has financial or legislative history witnessed so purely accidental but so extremely fortunate an adjustment of dates to future emergencies which could not possibly have been foreseen.

This law of 1908 was invoked at once when the run of bank depositors began in August, 1914. Under its provisions, nearly $68,000,000 of the new emergency notes were issued to the national banks in the second week of August, on the pledge of merchants' paper from the banks' portfolios. By the third week of October the outstanding total had reached $363,632,080, which was the highest point; the currency being circulated by banks in 39 states of the Union, and in Alaska and the District of Columbia.[2] Of the total authorized issue 57½ per cent was secured by merchants notes, 28 per cent by miscellaneous securities, 14

[1] H. R. Speech of Carter Glass, Sept. 7, 1916.
[2] Treasury Report for 1915, p. 586.

per cent by state and municipal bonds, and the small balance by warehouse receipts[1]; the banks had found no difficulty in providing the requisite collateral. On the hoarding panic, the effect was immediate. The new "emergency notes," which differed only in their inscription from the familiar national bank notes, were accepted without demur for use in hand-to-hand circulation. The result was that hoarding of money ceased, as it was bound to do when every depositor could readily obtain all the cash to which his bank account entitled him. The emergency currency could not be used in bank reserves, and total reserve money in the vaults of the New York banks had decreased heavily during the first week of August; but $11,400,000 of that was redeposited before September. As we shall see, both the loan certificates and the "emergency notes" were promptly absorbed and retired when the full machinery of the Federal Reserve began to operate, after which the Emergency Currency Law went quietly out of existence.

Thus was the immediate money crisis met and overcome. But the "emergency currency" could not help to meet the $500,000,000 or more in

[1] Treasury Report for 1915, p. 531.

immediately maturing gold obligations of America to Europe, and the unprecedented premium on sterling exchange, which continued into the autumn months, indicated Europe's purpose of collecting them. What was to be done about these obligations? It was now evident that belligerent Europe, and with it all neutral governments except the United States, were suspending to a future date the payment of their own current indebtedness even to the New York market. Therefore, and not wholly unreasonably, the opinion began to spread among New York bankers that, for purely protective reasons, the American market ought to resort to a similar "moratorium" on its own account.[1] The entire gold reserve of all banks reporting to the government in June, 1914, was less than double the immediately maturing foreign obligations[2] and, judging by the foreign exchange market, Europe would draw on that gold fund against all future maturing obligations, if permitted.

On August 7 the Secretary of the Treasury

[1] Jacob H. Schiff, speech at N. Y. Chamber of Commerce meeting Aug. 13, 1914; Annual Report Chamber of Commerce 1914–15, Part I, p. 54.

[2] Comptroller of the Currency's Statements, Treasury Report 1914, p. 539.

called a meeting of the most important bankers
and merchants to consider this urgent problem.
At that moment, even the New York banks were
divided in opinion as to what policy ought to be
pursued. With probably the majority of bankers,
the proposal to continue gold payments was
opposed vigorously; in some instances even
angrily. Against that opposition the most powerful private banking houses urged the advantages of
such action to the country's future international
prestige, insisted that it was feasible if taken with
due precaution, and laid great stress on the argument that an $80,000,000 New York City loan,
placed in London and Paris during the troubled
home finance of 1910, would fall due on January 1,
1915, and that, unless provision for its payment in
gold were to be arranged, the largest American
city would have defaulted on its obligations.[1]

In the end, that argument turned out to be convincing. Before the meeting at Washington could
be held, the New York bankers had been persuaded that the harm which failure to meet our
gold obligations would inflict on American credit
and on the American financial future would be far
more dangerous than the risk incurred by agreeing

[1] Speech of Jacob H. Schiff.

to meet such obligations punctually in gold.   On
September 4 the committee of bankers which had
taken the task in hand reported to the Treasury,
not only that payment of New York City's foreign
loan in gold had been provided for, but that the
country's banks had been asked to contribute
$150,000,000 more in gold, on which a permanent
committee of eminent bankers would draw to meet
our external payments as the obligations matured
and were recognized. The amount was subsequently reduced to $100,000,000 and, with the
Treasury's concurrence, the plan was made
effective.[1]   The Bank of England agreed to
receive all remittances of gold at its newly-estab-
lished branch in Ottawa, Canada, as if they had
been delivered at London; thus avoiding the risk
of war-time ocean transit.

It will be observed that the gold fund thus
accumulated was much less than the sum total
of maturing foreign liabilities; which, as we have
seen, the Treasury estimated at $530,000,000;[2] but
the bankers reasoned that display of willingness
to pay in gold, if required, would lead at once to
willingness on the part of foreign creditors to

[1] Annual Treasury Report 1914, pp. 4–7, 71–74.
[2] See p. 61.

extend the obligations, and the result proved in a very impressive way the correctness of that judgment. Something over $108,000,000 gold was pledged by the banks participating in the "gold pool," but only one fourth of this subscription, or $27,000,000, was ever called up, and even of this amount only $10,000,000 was actually shipped by the managers to Canada for account of the Bank of England. On the 22nd of the ensuing January the gold pool formally wound up its operations, on the ground that its continuance was no longer necessitated by the situation. The balance of gold deposited by the subscribing banks was returned to them; this remarkable operation, so the managers reported, having been conducted at a total expense of $16,542.67.[1] This decision for maintenance of gold payments had not influenced the "gold pool's" activities alone. It had also resulted in resumption of gold exports to Canada under ordinary banking auspices, so that between August 1 and the end of the year, $104,900,000 gold was exported from the United States, of which $102,300,000 went to Canada.[2] With December,

[1] Statements of Gold Fund Committee, Jan. 22 and Mar. 12, 1915.

[2] Monthly summaries 1914, U. S. Department of Commerce.

however, even the gold-export movement to Canada became negligible; a moderate return flow of gold had in fact begun before the year was ended. The rate for sterling exchange, which in the August war panic had reached $7 and which ranged only a trifle below $5 during September, had fallen to parity by November 12 and ran strongly in favor of New York in the last week of 1914.

The importance of that decision to maintain gold payments, in the face of suspension of such payments and of resort to inevitably depreciated money in practically every other country of the world, it would be difficult to exaggerate. It is not too much to say that, as a matter of financial history, the United States stood during those two or three weeks of August at the parting of the ways. In the light of what happened after 1914 and with the Federal Reserve, anchored as it was by law to the gold-standard basis, about to appear on the scene, it is not easy to suppose that a lapse to depreciated money in the United States could have been permanent. But on the other hand, it is impossible to be sure that a decision in August, 1914, to suspend gold payments, even with the purpose of subsequently resuming them, would not have given to at least our immediately subsequent financial history a different turn from that which it actually took. The magnificent courage of the American decision played no small part in the chapter of financial prestige and reversed international position which actually followed. Every one knew in a very few months to what extent the decision had been justified by events; but in August and September of 1914 those events could not be foreseen.

It should not be forgotten that the financial outlook for the United States seemed desperate, even to a great part of the banking community, at the time when maintenance of gold payments was agreed on. The counsel of timidity had not been lacking; the argument had become familiar that the American market not only had the right to protect itself as London and the European continent had already done, but that such self-protection was a duty. The promptness of the decision, the clear-cut distinctness with which the American banking community pledged its resources to the task of standing single-handed against the expected requisitions of the whole outside world, had as much to do with the subsequent amazing financial strength and prestige of the United States as did the turn in Europe's conduct of the war which eventually, but not in 1914, created an abnormally large foreign demand on our productive resources. The action of our bankers, in short, provided the plainest possible evidence to the outside world that the United States was at the moment, and would be during the war and for an indeterminate period after peace, the one locality in which the world's floating capital could be safely lodged without fear of depreciation in its value. Many of the remarkable incidents of the ensuing decade, notably the capacity shown by the United States, during and after the war, to lend on a wholly unprecedented scale to other countries while redeeming its own foreign debt by the thousands of millions, must be judged in the light of this momentous decision to maintain gold payments, whatever might be the incidental difficulty or hazard.

Necessarily, and almost immediately, it made New York the banking centre of the world; which meant that the "working balances" of neutral markets, and to a great extent of the belligerent markets also, were deposited in American banks as they had been habitually deposited in British banks before the war. But this in turn had two

other consequences, also familiar in the previous
history of London. Having become, in steadily
increasing measure, the banking depository for the
outside world, New York was at once equipped
as a lender of capital to such foreign markets and,
at the same time, the remittance of this foreign
capital to the United States naturally caused a
strong movement of foreign exchange in favor of
New York. From the rate of $7 to the pound
sterling, reached on August 1 and representing a
premium of 43 per cent against the American
market, New York exchange on London declined
to $4.95 in September, to $4.89 in October and at
length, on November 12, reached normal parity
of $4.86⅝. The New York rate on practically
all other foreign markets moved similarly.

The task of the "gold pool" had been achieved
when sterling was back at par, and it is interesting
to observe that the rate had reached that normal
level four days before the Federal Reserve began to
operate. The Reserve banks opened for business
on November 16. On November 20 the Reserve
Board reported for the twelve banks of the system
a gold reserve of $203,415,000, turned over by
member banks in subscription to Reserve Bank
stock, and a note circulation of $1,215,000. By

the end of the year outstanding notes were
$16,027,000; by the following April they were
$65,612,000 and the cash reserve against notes
and deposits was 93⅓ per cent. All of the clearing-house loan certificates had been canceled in
the middle of December,[1] and on July 1, 1915, it
was officially stated that all of the "Aldrich-
Vreeland" emergency currency had also been
retired except $200,000 issued to a single bank
which had subsequently failed, but whose security
for the notes was ample.[2]   Two weeks before
the Reserve banks opened, the deficit in reserves at
the New York private banks had been changed to
a surplus of $15,900,000; even their gold reserve
was larger than it had been at the beginning of the
year.   Discount rates had come down from the 8
per cent rate of early autumn to the normal figure
of 4 per cent.   In the last week of December,
sterling exchange had reached a rate, $4.84¾,
actually more favorable to New York than had
been quoted at any time in the first half of 1914
or in December of 1913.   Gold exports had ceased;
there were even gold importations of twelve or
thirteen millions, before the year had ended,
across the Canadian border or across the Pacific

[1] Treasury Report, 1915, p. 576.   [2] *Ibid.*, p. 577.

from Japan. What would be the next turn in events seemed now to depend on circumstances which could not be foreseen.

Revival of confidence had been very real on the American financial markets; it was believed that our own position was at all events safeguarded. But whether anything more was to be anticipated than the rescue of American finance from the cataclysm which had shaken Europe, few bankers or financiers ventured to predict. If the banking and foreign exchange position had been restored to equilibrium, home and foreign trade remained at a standstill. The ground most commonly assigned for confidence in the longer future was early termination of the war, from economic exhaustion of the fighting governments if from no other cause. It is entirely probable that, even at the end of 1914, actual foreknowledge that the conflict was destined to last four years longer would have occasioned profound despondency over the financial fortunes of America.[1] We have now to see in just what way, and by just what sequence of events, the subsequent great change came in this view of the situation.

[1] N. Y. *Evening Post*, Dec. 31, 1914; "Forecasts."

CHAPTER III

OUR PERIOD OF NEUTRALITY

IT would not correctly describe the state of affairs to say that the American business community entered 1915 with confidence restored. Panic, indeed, was ended. The fear of immediate wreck of the American financial organism, as a result of Europe's moratorium on debts, had been dispelled. The bold experiment of maintaining American gold payments had apparently achieved success. Foreign exchange was moving in favor of the United States; the central banking system was established. But it did not yet enter the mind, even of experienced financiers, that anything more had happened than the averting of a crisis; prediction at the beginning of 1915, that the United States was on the eve of perhaps the most remarkable period of financial and industrial expansion that had been witnessed in history, would not have been taken seriously.

When the question, How will the American financial situation be affected if the war continues
through 1915? was put by a New York newspaper
at the end of 1914 to a list of well-known Eastern
and Western bankers, it elicited such replies as
that "the effect would be detrimental," that its
influence on all investments would be "powerful
and unfavorable," that it was doubtful if, under
such circumstances, our manufacturers "could continue even the present activity."[1]   In a forecast
published on the first day of 1915 by the leading financial weekly of New York, the prediction
that normal conditions could not be restored "for
a considerable time to come" was supported by
reference to the "deadening paralysis which has
settled over many of the country's industries."[2]
The annual report of the New York Chamber of
Commerce, published as late as May in 1915,
remarked on the evidence that "the hopes early
entertained by American steel manufacturers,
that they would profit by the conflict through an
expansion of exports, were ill-founded."[3]

[1] N. Y. *Evening Post*, Dec. 31, 1914.
[2] N. Y. *Financial Chronicle*, Jan. 2, 1915, p. 2.
[3] N. Y. Chamber of Commerce, annual report for 1914–15,
part II, p. 110.

This attitude of doubt and despondency reflected the very unusual character of the situation. All past experience, it is true, had proved that a foreign war was apt to enrich neutral countries which were large producers of necessaries of life and war supplies; that fact was as well known in January, 1915, or in August, 1914, as at any other time. But in no previous war had a neutral state been confronted with what appeared to be the financial insolvency of the entire outside world. The defeat of the Germans at the Marne in September of 1914 ended the peril of quick and sweeping victory of the Central Powers, but it indicated also the possibility of a long war which might be, and was then expected to be, a conflict of complete economic exhaustion. The United States had surmounted in the autumn of 1914 the crisis of gold payments; yet it was still indebted on an immense scale to belligerent Europe, it was doubtful regarding the purchasing power even of the Entente Allies, and it was cut off almost completely from export trade with several countries, notably Germany, which had previously been among its largest customers.

Furthermore, at the beginning of 1915 there was no sign of recovery in our manufacturing indus-

tries from the shock of 1914. The Secretary of
the Treasury had called conferences of eminent
business men and bankers during August, 1914,
to consider the problems of the export trade, of
"war-risk insurance" and of the cotton industry,
and in all these directions prompt and energetic
measures had been taken during the next few
months, sometimes with supplementary legislation
by Congress.[1] Nevertheless, trade depression
increased. The country's steel plant was working
in January, 1915, at only 50 per cent of its
producing capacity; in the two first months of
1915 the United States Steel Corporation's earnings did not cover the period's interest on its
bonds.[2] Cotton had just sold at 7¼ cents a
pound, the lowest price in fifteen years, barely
one-half the average price of the two preceding
seasons and far below cost of production. Purchases by Continental Europe were only 50 per
cent of the season's normal quantity. What the
transportation industry looked for was shown by
the fact that new railway construction in the
United States had fallen to the lowest mileage in

[1] Treasury Report for 1914, pp. 5–17, 64–78.
[2] U. S. Steel Corporation, quarterly earnings statement, April,
1915.

half a century.[1] Bank checks drawn in the whole country during the first quarter of 1915 were the smallest in half a dozen years; they were less in amount by $4,000,000,000, or nearly 10 per cent, than in the same months of 1914, when trade was described as unfavorable.[2] On the average and despite the rise in wheat, prices of goods were lower than they had been in the first month after war broke out.[3] In April, 1915, it was estimated by the United States Bureau of Labor that in New York City alone 398,000 workmen were unemployed, or $16\frac{1}{4}$ per cent of the laboring population; the estimated percentage in other cities being $11\frac{1}{2}$.[4] As late as the middle of the year, the Federal Government was working on plans for relief of unemployment.[5]

There had come into view, however, two indications of a change. Not only had Europe's graingrowers been drafted by millions into the belligerent armies, but the Continental wheat harvest

[1] *Railway Age*, estimate for 1914.

[2] N. Y. *Financial Chronicle*, April 10, 1915, p. 1233.

[3] "Wholesale Prices, 1890 to 1923," U. S. Bureau of Labor Statistics, p. 17.

[4] U. S. Bureau of Labor Statistics, reports for April and May, 1915.

[5] National conference to consider unemployment, San Francisco, Aug. 3–6, 1915, *Financial Chronicle*, Sept. 4, 1915, p. 746.

of 1914 turned out in the autumn to have run heavily short of preceding years. Even this was not the whole story. While France had raised 38,000,000 bushels less than in 1913 and Italy 45,000,000 less, the entry of the Ottoman Empire into the war on the German side at the end of October completed the blockade of Russia, from whose farms the wheat-consumers of Central and Western Europe had usually drawn in a single year upwards of 150,000,000 bushels. No more food supplies could be relied on from that source, and at the same time the requisitions of the fighting states, on grain-surplus markets to which they still had access, were made increasingly urgent by the possibility that a turn in the fortunes of war might cut off even existing avenues of importation.

Under these circumstances the British navy had in October, 1914, finally cleared the transatlantic highway of the German warships, and immense European orders converged at once on the abundant American wheat supply. During the four months beginning with December, 1914, the United States exported 98,000,000 bushels of wheat, as compared with 18,000,000 in the same months of the preceding season. By the end of

June, 1915, the exports of the fiscal year footed up 259,600,000 bushels, against 92,300,000 and 91,600,000 one and two years before. The largest export of any previous twelvemonth had been 157,200,000 bushels, in 1892. At Chicago the price of wheat, which was 85 cents per bushel on August 3, 1914, had risen at the beginning of 1915 to $1.31 and in February to $1.67; the higher price not having been matched on the American market in thirty-eight years, except in the temporary and purely artificial "wheat corners" of 1898 and 1888. As a consequence, the money value of our wheat export in the twelve months ending with June, 1915, reached $333,500,000. It had been only $88,000,000 and $89,000,000 respectively in the two preceding seasons,[1] and not even after the celebrated "European famine years" of 1897 and 1879 had a season's wheat export come within $140,000,000 of the figure. Thus rapidly was dispelled one of the misgivings of the 1914 war-panic.

Another was shaken in the early weeks of 1915. The closing of the Stock Exchange during the four months after July, 1914, with a view to preventing disastrous realizing sales by Europe, had put an end to large-scale buying or selling of

[1] U. S. Commerce Department, monthly summaries.

stocks and bonds, whether by home or foreign
investors or by speculators endeavoring to antici-
pate the investors' action.   But it could not stop
sales between individuals and, after the first few
weeks of wholly suspended business, a group of
unofficial brokers began to assemble every day
on the Wall Street sidewalk to deal in stocks, for
their own account or for that of outside customers
who were anxious to invest their idle money or
turn their securities into cash.   The Stock Exchange denounced the experiment and forbade
its own members to take part in it.   Some of the
banks went so far as to threaten newspapers which
reported the sidewalk prices.   Wall Street, which
is fond of descriptive metaphor, christened it
"the outlaw market."   This hostile attitude
resulted clearly from an uneasy feeling that, if
the "outlaw brokers" should come to transact a
business of real importance, the crash of prices
which had been narrowly averted by shutting up
the Stock Exchange might begin in earnest, with
all of its possible consequences in the field of
credit.

But the banks and the Stock Exchange overlooked two essential facts—first, that the period
of outright financial panic had ended; second,

that the actual situation in American finance and banking was, as we have seen, taking very different shape from what had been anticipated in August. The "outlaw market" did not attract great attention until October, when a few of the sidewalk brokers began to publish typewritten sheets of daily closing prices. They were much discussed; after a while, even the banks which had denounced the innovation asked for these daily reports and filed them. The prices caused surprise. When the "outlaw market's" sheets were first put out in the middle of October, well-known railway and industrial shares were quoted for the most part only 2 to 5 per cent below the closing prices of July 30 on the Stock Exchange. Later in the month, further declines of 2 to 4 per cent occurred; Union Pacific Railway shares, for instance, had then fallen 7½ points from the last Stock Exchange quotation of July, New York Central 5, Chicago, Milwaukee & St. Paul 8, General Electric 5, United States Steel 12. But this was a far less formidable shrinkage than had been predicted and, what attracted much more interest, the recovery in the field of general credit during November, with the turning of the foreign exchanges in favor of New York, was instantly reflected in the "outlaw market." On December 11, the last day on which prices were formally quoted in that market, most of the standard investment shares were selling practically at the prices of July 30; some of them considerably higher.[1]

The reason why the "outlaw market" then went out of business was that the Stock Exchange itself reopened for restricted trading on December 12. Dealings in bonds alone,—with minimum prices prescribed so that a panicky break should be impossible, and with the requirement that the origin of sales based on foreign orders should be declared by brokers executing them—had already been resumed on November 28 and the bond prices, after a momentary decline, had gone above the final July quotations. When transactions in stocks were resumed on December 12, it was positively required by the Stock Exchange authorities that all sales should be made for cash; "short selling" or "future contracts" were prohibited. An advance at once occurred, beyond the stipulated minimum prices and beyond the highest "outlaw market" quotations. Several

[1] N. Y. *Financial Chronicle*, Dec. 26, 1914, page 1866; "Stock Prices during the Period when the Stock Exchange was Closed."

important railway and industrial shares rose 5 to 10 per cent above the closing prices of July. Notwithstanding much subsequent irregularity, occasioned by the bad reports of January and February from home trade and industry, this movement of recovery continued. On April 1, 1915, the Stock Exchange, now completely reassured, removed all restrictions and a very rapid advance occurred in every kind of shares, with unusually large transactions. In another month it had run into what Wall Street called an "old-fashioned bull market."

This was for two reasons an incident of high importance in the return of financial confidence; first, because the bidding for railway and industrial shares was recognized as expressing the financial community's belief in the soundness of the American situation and in the prospect of industrial recovery, but second, because the action of prices disposed of the idea that Europe, once it had the chance, would submerge the Stock Exchange with its $2,000,000,000 of American stocks and bonds, forced upon a declining market. It did not by any means signify, however, that Europe had decided not to part with those investments; on the contrary, the advance occurred in the face of evidence that selling of American stocks by European investors was actually in progress, on a very substantial scale. Subsequent investigation of the accounts of railway share-transfer offices proved that, even in the first half of 1915, nearly $500,000,000 American stocks and bonds, out of $2,704,000,000 estimated to have been held abroad at the end of 1914, must have been sold back by foreign holders.[1] The United States Steel Corporation reported at the end of 1915 that $53,000,000 worth of its shares had been transferred in the year from foreign to domestic names.[2] But panic being now ended, all such sales by foreign holders of American investments were made in orderly fashion; with a view, not to "forcing" the market but to getting the highest possible price. How the American buyers were able to take and pay for such a mass of returning securities in a rising market was a question which brought up other considerations.

Before the war, it was calculated by economic experts that the annual payments due by the

[1] Reports and estimates of L. F. Loree, based on railway share transfers and federal income tax returns, June 28, 1915; Dec. 23, 1915. N. Y. *Evening Post*, June 28, 1915; N. Y. *Times*, Dec. 24, 1915.

[2] Statement of U. S. Steel Corporation, Jan. 10, 1916.

United States to European and other foreign
countries for interest on our large foreign borrowings, for ocean freight charges by foreign carriers
and for remittances against American tourists'
expenditure or money sent home by immigrants,
were barely covered by our annual surplus of
merchandise exports over imports.   Those annual
payments were then commonly placed somewhat
above $500,000,000,[1] whereas the annual merchán-
dise export surplus had ranged, in the decade
prior to 1914, between the $252,000,000 of the
calendar year 1909 and the $691,000,000 of 1913.
When the export surplus did not cover the "invisible debits," the American market either shipped
gold or sold its own securities to Europe.   If Europe for any reason chose to re-sell any large amount
of its holdings of our securities, New York had to
balance the account by increased shipment of gold.[2]

Events had proved the prediction of August,
1914, that American securities would return in a
sudden and overwhelming avalanche, to have been
wrong; but we have also seen that the sales of 1915,
although deliberate, were of very large aggregate

[1] "Balance of Trade of the United States," *Harvard University
Review of Economic Statistics*, June, 1919.

[2] *Forty Years of American Finance*, pp. 217, 246, 307.

amount. At the beginning of 1916, indeed, the British government itself took steps to acquire, in exchange for its own securities, all foreign stocks and bonds in the hands of British investors, and used them either for actual sale in the American market or as collateral for a similar amount raised through loans at New York.[1] Those loans were of wholly unprecedented magnitude; the Allied European governments sold one issue of $500,000,000 bonds to our investors in October, 1915 (the largest loan until then ever taken in this country on a single offering), and in 1916 they borrowed in various loans upward of $750,-000,000 more. It is true, the proceeds of the loans were mostly used to pay for American grain or merchandise; but the transaction none the less increased the debit column on the season's international account. No such transactions would have been conceivable at any time before the war without exhausting our gold supply in payment. Yet New York did not export gold at all while these huge advances of capital to Europe were being made.

[1] London *Economist*, Jan. 8, 1916, p. 52; May 13, p. 858; June 3, p. 1057; June 24, p. 1193. "The Financial Review," 1917, N. Y. *Financial Chronicle*, p. 105.

Events moved with such bewildering swiftness in that first year of the war that the capacity for astonishment, over any occurrence which would once have been deemed impossible, seemed to be exhausted. Nevertheless, even with the visible phenomena of the day before its eyes, Wall Street itself often wondered in 1915 what had so suddenly equipped the United States with resources adequate to meet these enormously increased requisitions. After the war, the usual answer to the question was, our export of war material to Europe. But that, as we shall see, is far from explaining all that happened, notably our country's subsequent extraordinary position as the dispenser of credit to the entire outside world and the possessor of nearly half of the world's stock of gold. There were other influences at work.

In the first place, with the British government's suspension of gold payments in August, 1914, and with the Exchequer's formal announcement of January, 1915, that British loans "for undertakings outside the Empire will not be allowed,"[1] London necessarily ceased to be the money centre

[1] Treasury "Order in Connection with the Reopening of the Stock Exchanges," Jan. 19, 1915. London *Economist*, Jan. 23, 1915, p. 135.

of the world. Since gold payments were at the same time being maintained in the United States, alone of all the great markets, New York necessarily took London's place. London itself described the Exchequer's order as "temporary abandonment of our historic claim as an international money centre"; making it inevitable that "much of the international business we have been accustomed to do should pass to the only other country, the United States, which is capable of doing it."[1]

This meant that, in the long run, foreign merchants would discount their bills in Wall Street; but its immediate significance, which had much greater bearing on the American position of 1915, was that New York was becoming the depository for those immense sums of foreign capital which, until August, 1914, had been habitually placed with London, but whose lodgment there under existing circumstances would expose the principal to shrinkage if sterling exchange, no longer linked with gold, should have depreciated heavily when the foreign owner of the deposit wished to draw on it. To estimate the total amount which came to New York as a consequence is impossible,

[1] London *Times*, Jan. 20, 1915.

but it must have been immensely large. It represented not merely actual transfer of capital for safe-keeping to the United States, but the leaving in New York of capital accruing to foreign merchants from their trade with America, which in pre-war days would have been forwarded to London. The financial prestige and resources derived by the new money centre of the world from this altered situation were precisely similar, though on a vastly greater scale, to that which a banking institution acquires when a multitude of important and highly profitable deposit accounts, previously placed with other institutions, have been transferred to it.

This was the first and in some respects the most important influence in creating the new position of the United States. It is an influence much too commonly overlooked in the summary of causes. The other and more plainly visible influence was the expansion of our export trade, which is a story by itself. I have already described the increase in wheat shipments when transatlantic trade began again in the autumn of 1914. During 1915, Europe's purchases of American food products of all kinds became so large that the calendar year's total exports in that category footed up $428,000,000 more than in 1914. Payment for those exports alone went a considerable distance towards balancing what our market had to pay Europe for returning American securities. But it did not wholly cover that requisition, not to mention our $500,000,000 loan to Europe; and, moreover, except for grain the exports increased only slowly during the first months of 1915. In particular, the influence of Europe's requirements of war material seemed then to be inconsiderable. Shipments of war munitions were reported in the monthly official trade returns mainly under the heads of explosives, fire-arms, brass products, barbed wire and miscellaneous iron and steel products. Even as late as February, 1915, total shipments of such goods from the United States were only $6,700,000, which was less than twice as much as in the same month of 1914, a period of world-wide peace. Large foreign purchases had been made of blankets, cloth for uniforms and all kinds of hospital supplies,[1] but this was bringing a monthly increase of only a few million dollars. During the first half of 1915 our monthly export trade on all acounts exceeded only slightly the

[1] N. Y. Chamber of Commerce, Annual Report for 1914–15, Part II, p. 96.

figures reached in several months of 1913 and 1912.

But in this respect the situation changed very suddenly. On March 15, 1915, Lord Kitchener told the British House of Lords that England's output of war munitions "is not only not equal to our necessities, but does not fulfill our expectations." The army staff was pressing urgently for high explosives; "want of an unlimited supply" of such munitions, it was publicly asserted, "is a fatal bar to our success."[1] One of the members of the British ministry of the day, describing the situation many years afterward, told how there "flowed from the front" in the early spring of 1915 "a torrent of complaints," to which Kitchener had to reply that every British factory "was working to its utmost power, that the orders already given were far in excess of the capacity to produce, and that deliveries even of the reduced amounts were enormously in arrear."[2] When the fact was disclosed that, after months of such representations from the general staff, only 7 per cent of the army's artillery supply was suited to

[1] London *Times*, May 12, 1915; Col. Repington, *The First World War*, p. 36.
[2] Winston S. Churchill, *The World Crisis*, 1915, p. 320.

the changing methods of the conflict,[1] public clamor compelled radical change of policy and reconstruction of the ministry. In May, Lloyd George became Minister of Munitions and a program of orders for high explosives, limited only by the capacity of accessible producers, was at once adopted. This meant unlimited requisition on American manufacturers.

In the confusion of ideas which prevailed during the first weeks of the war, there had been some popular doubt of our right, as a neutral state, either to float war loans for belligerent governments, or to sell war munitions to them. In the matter of loans to the governments at war, our State Department had itself published a memorandum, two weeks after the war began, which discountenanced such action. "There is no reason," Secretary Bryan then wrote in response to inquiries from bankers, "why loans should not be made to the governments of neutral nations, but, in the judgment of this government, loans by American bankers to any European nation which is at war are inconsistent with the true spirit of neutrality."[2] That this view of the question

[1] Repington, p. 35.
[2] Statement of Secretary W. J. Bryan, Aug. 14, 1914.

was at least wholly unsupported by accepted precedent, our market's large loans of 1904 and 1905 to Japan, then at war with Russia, proved sufficiently[1]; also the American market's subscription to more than $200,000,000 loans of Great Britain during that country's war with the Transvaal Republic in 1900, 1901 and 1903.[2] England had similarly taken Japanese loans during the Manchurian War; France had equipped Russia financially in that conflict. Whether the statement of August, 1914, was actually the Administration's judgment of the time or was merely expression of Mr. Bryan's personal ideas (which were frequently erratic) did not clearly appear. But at any rate, this hastily-assumed attitude was tacitly abandoned when Bryan left the cabinet in June, 1915. Eventually not only France and England, but Germany as well, placed war loans in New York.

But Bryan himself had to recognize the diplomatic propriety of selling munitions of war to the belligerents, even if Germany was cut off from such traffic by the war blockade. At the beginning of 1915, the Secretary of State officially declared that "there is no power in the Executive to pre-

[1] *Forty Years of American Finance*, pp. 320–322.
[2] *Ibid.*, p. 282.

vent the sale of ammunition to the belligerents."
Replying to Congressional protest against that
attitude, he pointed out that German manufacturers had equipped the belligerents with arms in
both the Russo-Japanese War of 1904 and the
Balkan wars of 1913. To the argument that
Germany herself was shut out from access to our
producing markets, making shipment of munitions
to her enemies discriminatory, he further stated
that the German Ambassador at Washington had
himself admitted in December to our State Department that, "under the general principles of international law, no exception can be taken to neutral
states letting war material go to Germany's enemies from or through neutral territory."[1]

Up to that time, the largest requisition on American producers of munitions had been an $83,000,-
000 Russian order placed with the Canadian Car
and Foundry Company, which in March had
sublet $23,000,000 of its contracts to twenty-
seven steel and powder manufacturers in the
United States. Beginning in May, however, with
a $100,000,000 British order on the Bethlehem
Steel Company for lyddite shells and shrapnel, the

---

[1] Letter of Secretary of State Bryan to W. J. Stone, Chairman
U. S. Senate Foreign Relations Committee, Jan. 24, 1915.

urgent European demand absolutely changed the American industrial position. The work was not restricted to munition manufacturers. Large establishments, previously engaged exclusively in electrical work or in production of locomotives, cars or machinery, altered their plant and took contracts for explosives running into the tens of millions for each establishment.[1] The Bethlehem Steel alone, which had on its books total unfilled orders of $24,865,000 at the end of 1913 and $46,513,000 at the end of 1914, reported $175,432,000 at the end of 1915.[2] Whereas the year 1915 had begun, in the words of an expert commercial reviewer, "with little prospect that the predictions of large business resulting from the war were anywhere near realization," the early summer proved that "the single factor of steel to be fired from the guns of European belligerents was amounting to tonnages sufficient, with the stimulation given to home demand, to create an actual scarcity."[3] The effect on the country's export trade was instantaneous. As against

[1] N. Y. Chamber of Commerce, Annual Report, 1915–16, Part II, p. 115.

[2] Annual Report of Bethlehem Steel Co. for 1915.

[3] Chamber of Commerce Report, p. 115.

February's shipments of only $6,700,000 in categories covering war munitions, that class of exports rose to $27,000,000 in August, 1915, and to $69,000,000 in December, when the value of the munitions exports was more than double that of the same month's export of all breadstuffs. For the calendar year 1916 the stated value of such exports was no less than $1,290,000,000, a sum which exceeded the similar shipments of 1914 by $1,250,000,000 and those even of 1915 by $960,000,000.[1]

The magnitude of these munitions shipments gave rise to very common belief, both during and after the war, that the entire war-time expansion in our export trade was based on materials for military destruction. But this was by no means true. Not to mention the already-cited increase of $428,000,000 in our export of all foodstuffs in 1915 as compared with the year before, our shipment of such commodities as cotton goods and men's shoes increased $68,000,000, mostly on orders for the European armies. Furthermore, as the year progressed and the normal processes of international trade recovered the equilibrium lost in

[1] Monthly summaries of Foreign Commerce; U. S. Department of Commerce, 1914, 1915, 1916.

the first shock of war, neutral countries which had previously bought manufactured goods from England found that, with British industry mobilized for war, their needs could no longer be filled by British manufacturers. Through force of necessity they turned to the United States. Our total exports to the six neutral countries of Europe, during the whole of 1915, were $178,000,000 greater than the year before. Part of that increase represented grain and part of it, also, goods which the Dutch and Scandinavian markets bought for the purpose of reshipping to Germany before England had made its blockade of the Central Powers effective. But this was not true of our exports to Asia, South America, and the North American markets outside our own boundaries, to which our shipments increased $77,000,000 in 1915 and $473,000,000 more in 1916.

Still another addition to our export trade came from transactions which brought an extremely curious reminder of long-forgotten commercial and political history, when it was found that exports to Europe from other countries in the Western hemisphere, hitherto carried in British vessels which were now commandeered for war transport work, had to be sent to the United States and thence reshipped to Europe. Until 1915, the largest total ever reached by such "foreign re-exports" from the United States was in 1806, when French and British frigates of the Napoleonic war were seizing enemy merchant ships and when, therefore, our neutral vessels were used to bring West Indian merchandise to both France and England. The value reached in that year by foreign merchandise reshipped was $60,283,000. Immediately prior to 1914 it averaged barely $35,000,000 annually, but in 1915 the high record of a century before was for the first time duplicated with a figure of $61,440,000. It had required another world war to make the thing possible.

The result of this many-sided combination of influences on our outward trade was bound to be something beyond all previous experience. Total export of merchandise from the United States, which had reached $2,364,000,000 in the fiscal year 1914 and $2,768,000,000 in the twelve months ending with June, 1915 (at the time a high record in our history), rose to $4,333,000,000 in the subsequent fiscal year and to $6,290,000,000 in the fiscal year 1917. Our largest surplus of exports over imports in any calendar year before the war had been $691,421,000, in 1913. The export surplus of 1915 was $1,776,074,000. In 1916 it was $3,089,769,000.

Whether judged by its magnitude or by the suddenness of its occurrence, it is perfectly safe to say that this achievement, in only two years of foreign trade, was something unparalleled in the world's commercial history. The expansion of our exports between 1897 and 1901 had itself been described at the time as beyond all precedent; we discovered how far-reaching an influence it could exert on our national prosperity and international prestige.[1] But whereas the increase of our annual export surplus during that four-year period was $356,000,000, or 112 per cent., the increase between 1913 and 1916 was $2,398,000,000, or 347 per cent. Its effect both on the country's relations with Europe and on its home position, financial and industrial, was bound to be proportionately great. First let us trace its consequences in the domestic situation.

I have shown with what uncertainty, at times with what despondency, the prospects of our internal trade were regarded during the last five months of 1914 and the first three or four months

[1] *Forty Years of American Finance*, pp. 282–284.

of 1915; but the change came now with great
rapidity. The American steel industry, and along
with it other manufacturing industries whose
plant had been diverted to the work of munitions
production, necessarily sprang almost at once
into unprecedented activity. Before the war, the
largest monthly output of iron in the United
States had been 2,782,000 tons, in December of
1912. It was barely 1,500,000 tons in December, 1914, and even in April, 1915, when it rose
a trifle over 2,000,000 tons, production was less
than the monthly average of 1913. Following the
foreign orders which began in May, however, the
output crossed the 3,000,000-ton mark in the
following December for the first time in the iron
trade's history. In October, 1916, it had reached
3,500,000.[1] Prior to 1914 the country's maximum
yearly output of steel was 31,300,000 tons, in
1913, and it had fallen to 23,513,000 in 1914.
The production of 1916 was 42,773,000, and it
passed 45,000,000 in 1917.[2] It has been officially
computed that all of our steel or iron producing
companies combined, whose net earnings on invested capital in 1915 had averaged 7⅜ per cent,

[1] *Iron Age* estimates.
[2] Annual reports, American Iron & Steel Institute.

earned 21⅛ per cent in 1916.[1]   Labor was fully employed, at wages 14 per cent above the pre-war rate.[2]

As had always happened on previous occasions of immensely stimulated production of finished steel, heavy requisitions were made on materials for plant extension.   During the four-and-a-half-years' period of the war, the United States Steel Corporation enlarged the producing capacity of its mills, already the greatest of any single company in the world, by no less than 41⅛ per cent;[3] it was estimated after the war that the period's expenditure, for that purpose alone and by all producers, exceeded $1,000,000,000.[4]   But that was only incidental; the sequel in other industries was still more remarkable.   The immediate large-scale demand for new tools and machinery to re-equip plants for munition manufacture created so great a volume of orders that, in the case of many companies producing the requisite material, profits of the single year 1915 equaled in amount

[1] "War-time Profits and Costs of the Steel Industry," Federal Trade Commission, 1925, p. 29.

[2] U. S. Steel Corporation, Annual Report for 1916.

[3] *Ibid.*, reports 1919, 1920.

[4] J. G. Butler, address to American Iron & Steel Institute, May 23, 1919.

their entire capital stock.[1]   Other products than iron and steel were affected.   Output of copper in the United States had been cut down nearly 7 per cent in 1914 and the beginning of the war had carried its price 25 per cent below the average of 1913; but total production in 1915 ran 32,000,-000 pounds beyond any previous annual record, with the price at the year-end nearly double that of November, 1914.[2]   As for the wheat-growers, whose earnings over and above all cost of production from the crop of 1913 had been estimated at $56,710,000, they were officially stated to have cleared $284,896,000 from the harvest of 1915 and $296,252,000 from that of 1916.[3]

In no industry were the later results of 1915 more unexpected than in the cotton trade.   I have described the seemingly desperate condition of the American cotton-producer when the war broke out.   In the conferences of September, 1914, between the Treasury and the business men, a "loan fund" had been hurriedly arranged to save the planters from ruin.   It was based on

[1] N. Y. Chamber of Commerce, Annual Report, 1915–16, Part II, p. 115.

[2] *Engineering and Mining Journal*, Jan. 8, 1918.

[3] U. S. Grain Corporation, report of May, 1925, on "The Stabilization of the Price of Wheat During the War," p. 85.

subscriptions by banks and bankers, in the amount of $100,000,000 (subsequently increased to $135,-000,000), to a central fund from which advances could be made to planters unable to sell their cotton; the cotton itself to be pledged as security at the rate of 6 cents a pound.[1] The opportunity for such borrowings was held open during the month of January, 1915, but with a curious result; for applications from cotton-producers actually footed up only $28,000, as against the $135,000,000 offered.[2] It was in fact already becoming plain that the acute misgiving entertained in August, 1914, had misjudged the cotton-producer's outlook almost as completely as it had misjudged the wheat market. Germany did, to be sure, disappear as a visible purchaser of our cotton, but Holland and Scandinavia increased their takings in the first year of war a million bales over the preceding twelvemonth[3]—mostly, no doubt, for reshipment into Germany. Although this still left total exports some 600,000 bales below the preceding season, the larger purchases by

[1] Treasury Report for 1914, pp. 14-17.

[2] Statement by Cotton Loan Committee, Feb. 8, 1915, N. Y. *Financial Chronicle*, Feb. 6, 1915, p. 435; Feb. 13, p. 519.

[3] N. Y. Chamber of Commerce, Annual Report, 1915-16, Part II, p. 48.

American mills nearly counterbalanced that decrease,[1] and in the season beginning with August, 1915, when a much smaller cotton crop had been planted and harvested, further increase of nearly a million bales in home consumption fairly swept away the unsold surplus of 1914. It was taken at prices above the pre-war average.

This quite unprecedented home consumption of cotton, during the late months of 1915 and afterward, was only one among many indications of the sudden trade revival. A considerable part of the increase in home purchases, of cotton as of other materials of manufacture, arose from the greatly enlarged production of finished goods for export. It was said that, on one day of 1916, a single American textile house made shipments to fourteen different foreign markets which had never imported American cloths before the war,[2] and it was estimated that not less than 600,000 bales of cotton were used in the fiscal year 1916 solely in connection with manufacture of explosives for export.[3] But the expanding demand of home

[1] "Cotton Movement and Crop of 1914-15," *Financial Chronicle*, Aug. 21, 1915, p. 581.
[2] N. Y. Chamber of Commerce, Annual Report, 1916-17, Part II, p. 104.
[3] *Ibid.*, p. 47.

consumers had also now become recognized as a paramount influence. It had suddenly grown evident that the West was immensely enriched by the enormous export of its food products, the East by the steel trade's spectacular activities and at length the South by a profitable cotton crop. Operations of the cotton mills, it was reported in 1916, were limited only by the ability to obtain sufficient labor.[1] Middlemen in the dry goods trade "never knew such a prosperous year." Manufacturers' profits were the largest that had ever been earned.[2]

There was hardly an American industry which by 1916 was not making similar reports, and the scope of trade expansion was vividly reflected in the amount of checks drawn on the banks. Before the war, the largest total of such checks ever exchanged in a single month by all American banking institutions was $17,146,000,000, in December of 1912. The monthly total fell to $9,900,000,000 in August, 1914, and even in March, 1915, it was only $13,800,000,000. But it rose to $20,000,000,000 in the last month of 1915 and to $27,000,000,000 in December of 1916.

[1] N. Y. Chamber of Commerce, Annual Report, 1916–17, Part II, p. 45.
[2] *Ibid.*, p. 99.

There were occasions when it began to appear as if every element of economic fortune was working for the United States. We have seen that the war had created a virtually unlimited demand for American foodstuffs. The only question of doubt as the growing season of 1915 progressed was whether, with the usual vicissitudes of agriculture, the country could raise enough grain to meet Europe's requirements. For 1915 our farmers, encouraged by the highly profitable export market, had planted a greatly increased acreage; as it happened, Nature provided a perfect growing season. The wheat yield overtopped a thousand million bushels, a figure never reached before or since and exceeding by 120,000,000 the largest previous harvest; the corn crop was greater by 127,000,000 bushels than any other year's production, the oats crop by 122,000,000. It was estimated by the Department of Agriculture that, although prices for the five important cereals did not average as high as in the preceding season, the total market value of the harvest was $162,000,000 beyond that of the same crops in 1914 and $541,-000,000 greater than the pre-war maximum.

This was the course and character of the "war boom" in our domestic trade, which surpassed in scope all previous episodes of the kind in the country's history (perhaps also in the history of any other country) and which, so to speak, laid overnight the foundations of the American national wealth that became proverbial throughout the world a very few years later. But the longer results of the episode which I have just described—especially in regard to the international position—were so far out of proportion with those of any other period of American prosperity and economic power that it will be advisable to examine more closely the manner in which they were attained. Experience with an abnormal "American export surplus," an exceptional American credit balance on the international market, was not new; we have seen what happened after 1899 and 1900. But the unusual aspect of the war-time change in our relations with the outside world was the extent to which it was emphasized as the years passed on.

The talk of 1901 about our country's "new rôle in world-finance" was forgotten by 1903 or 1907; the international position had been reversed again and we were once more borrowing from Europe. Whether, in the longer future of economic history, such a change will again become possible, is a question for the prophets; but there certainly was no sign of it in the decade after the war. The unaccustomed position of the United States as the world's money centre, the dispenser of credit to the rest of the nations and, in general, the arbiter of the world's financial fortunes, was not only never once shaken in the trying period of post-war readjustment, but was recognized with far greater unanimity ten years after 1915 than in the war period itself. Let us trace exactly the succession of events which had this remarkable result.

I have heretofore pointed out that, whereas a pre-war surplus of American exports over imports amounting to about $500,000,000 annually would be balanced by annual payments regularly due from the United States to foreign markets on other accounts, our export surplus rose in the calendar year 1915 to $1,776,000,000 and in 1916 to $3,091,-000,000. How was the outside world, belligerent Europe in particular, to meet this prodigious accruing indebtedness; coming as it did at an hour when the second largest item in our yearly debit to Europe, freight charges for American goods carried in European ships, had been heavily cut down by the pressing of European merchant vessels into military transport service? We have seen that it was partly met by Europe's selling back to us our own securities. The estimate of such sales in 1915, based in the case of railway stocks on transfer of share ownership on the books of the companies and in the case of bonds on federal income tax returns, I have already cited. A later and extended compilation, which included an estimate of industrial as well as railway company securities, indicated that the face value of all such sales, in the eighteen-month period from January 31, 1915, to July 31, 1916, was $1,500,000,000.[1]

That paid for part of the period's debt of the outside world to America on merchandise account, but, as the figures show, only for perhaps one-third of it. Export of gold from Europe to New York came next. Gold had been used in the past to settle a sudden and heavy balance against Europe, as when our wheat was bought, in quantities then unprecedented, during 1879 and 1897.[2] No one imagined that the account of 1915 and 1916 would or could be balanced in that way, but the gold shipments nevertheless reached figures

[1] Speech of L. F. Loree to N. Y. Merchants' Association, Oct. 20, 1916. Third estimate of L. F. Loree, Sept. 25, 1916.
[2] *Forty Years of American Finance*, pp. 58 and 271.

quite beyond any prediction. It will be remembered that export of gold from the United States to Canada on account of England slackened in November, 1914, and ceased in December. Presently the movement turned. By March, 1915, our monthly import of gold reached $25,600,000; in June it was $52,300,000 and in October we received $79,600,000, which passed the previous high monthly record of the country's history—the $63,500,000 imported during November, 1907, when London and Paris were sending gold in response to the 4 per cent premium of the New York panic days on any kind of money.[1] Prior to 1915, the largest import of gold by the United States in any full calendar year had been $158,-100,000, in 1898. In the single month of March, 1916, we imported $122,700,000. For the calendar year 1915 the total importation of gold was $451,900,000; in 1916 it was $685,900,000.

These sums were wholly unprecedented in the history of international gold movements; before 1915 they would have been incredible, yet in some respects they were typical phenomena of the period. Transfer to a single country of a thousan million dollars in gold within two years was

[1] *Forty Years of American Finance*, p. 375.

not logically out of touch with a situation in which single war loans, annual public revenues and, in the case of the United States, the yearly surplus of exports over imports, rose to multiples of that figure, whereas a hundred millions would have been considered a formidable sum for most of them, a year or two before. But that did not explain how the gold for this enormous movement to America was procured. Gold holdings of the European banks, as publicly reported prior to 1914, were of no such size that they could spare the amounts which were actually shipped to the United States. In American values, the Bank of England held $185,000,000 gold at the outbreak of the war, the Bank of France $800,000,000. The bulk of our $1,137,800,000 gold imports of 1915 and 1916 came on account of London and Paris. If the gold had merely been drawn from the British and French reserves of 1914, those reserves would have been entirely exhausted before the end of 1916. But in actual fact the gold held by the Bank of England was then nearly $80,000,000 more than in 1914, and the gold in the French Bank's vaults only $146,000,000 less.[1]

[1] Weekly statements Bank of England and Bank of France, July 30, 1914; Dec. 28, 1916.

For this there are several explanations. To begin with, whereas gold was in use before the war as circulating money in every important European country, the governments had now virtually taken possession of it, substituting war time paper currency. A subsequent official estimate reckoned that the gold coin in use as pocket money in Great Britain during June, 1914, or held in the reserves of other institutions than the Bank of England, amounted to £123,000,000, or slightly under $600,000,000.[1] Gold coin circulating in France outside the Bank of France had been estimated before the war at $1,200,000,000.[2]

Although free gold payments had been suspended in August, 1914, the French Government in the middle of 1915, imitating the action taken by Germany, appealed to the people's patriotism to surrender their hoarded gold at face value in exchange for notes of the Bank of France; it thereby obtained about $240,000,000.[3] Part of

[1] First interim report to the House of Commons of the Committee on Currency and Foreign Exchanges after the War, Oct. 29, 1918. London *Economist*, Nov. 2, 1918, p. 618; N. Y. *Financial Chronicle*, March 13, 1920, p. 1029.

[2] London *Economist*, Paris correspondence, Feb. 27, 1915, p. 437.

[3] Annual report of the Bank of France, January, 1916. London *Economist*, Paris correspondence, Dec. 18, 1915, p. 1016.

this was sent to London and New York. The British government, after suspending free gold payments, had arranged in August, 1914, for the issue through private banks of a new fiduciary paper currency known as "currency notes," based on the pledge of government securities by the issuing banks and amounting by the end of 1916 to £150,000,000, or $730,000,000. It had thereby dislodged from general circulation the gold sovereigns and half-sovereigns previously used as pocket-money—some of which were undoubtedly hoarded, but a very substantial part of which came into possession of the banks and was now sent to New York, directly or through Canada. In addition to this the Russian government, between 1914 and 1917, drew $340,000,000 from the Imperial Bank's pre-war gold reserve and shipped it to London, Canada or New York to finance the war.[1]

Finally, the British possessions in South and West Africa produced from their mines in 1915 and 1916 the largest amount of gold in their history—more than $200,000,000 per annum— and, under the conditions created by the war,

[1] "The Russian Gold Reserve: What Became of It?" London *Economist*, May 30, 1925, p. 1066.

there was no other way to market the gold except
by selling it to the Bank of England or shipping it
to New York for account of London.[1]   As a matter
of fact, the Transvaal did not send its new gold
product to London, as in days before the war,
because that would have meant the crossing of a
dangerous war-time ocean highway by the treasure-
ships.   The bulk of it was unquestionably shipped
to Canada by the Pacific route; which partly explains why, although Canada itself then produced
less than $19,000,000 gold annually, our custom
house reports showed that, of the $451,900,000
gold imported into the United States in 1915,
$218,900,000 had come from Canada, with a
similar origin for $579,300,000 out of the $685,-
900,000 total gold import of 1916.[2]

There is, then, no mystery about the source of
the thousand millions in gold shipped to the United
States in 1915 and 1916.   By far the greater part
of it represented, first, gold which had previously
been used in Europe's hand-to-hand circulation
and, second, gold which would have gone in normal
times to increase that circulation or else (as in the

[1] Report of British Gold Production Committee, January,
1919. London *Economist*, Jan. 4, 1919, pp. 3, 4.
[2] U. S. Department of Commerce, Monthly Summary for
December, 1916, p. 5.

first decade of the century) to pile up larger bank reserves in Europe. From the strict economic viewpoint this huge transfer of gold, from countries which had suspended gold redemption of their paper currency to the one country where the gold standard was maintained, may be considered an illustration of the old economic principle that recourse by governments to an inferior currency will automatically drive out gold from countries where such inferior currency had been introduced. But although the general principle undoubtedly holds good, the economic machinery did not this time work in exactly the way which "Gresham's law" had indicated. The gold that came to us in 1915 and 1916 was sent under the British government's own auspices; it was distinctly given up to pay for Europe's unprecedented purchase of goods in America, and those purchases had no relation to the international level of prices, but were made for the most part from sheer military necessity.

Such was the extraordinary effort made by belligerent Europe to pay for its American purchases in gold. Nevertheless, a little calculation will show that even this expedient failed to balance the international account. The $4,867,000,000 surplus of merchandise exports over imports in our foreign trade of the two years 1915 and 1916 had been met, first, by re-sale of $1,500,000,000 American securities between January, 1915, and the end of July, 1916; or, if $500,000,000 be added for the last half of 1916, $2,000,000,000. The $1,137,800,000 gold imports of the same two years, less the $187,000,000 gold exports of the period, paid for $950,800,000 more. The net sum of the shipments of securities and gold to the United States, thus calculated, was therefore $2,950,800,-000 and, if we add the "invisible items" of $500,-000,000 per annum whereby Europe met the export surplus of our pre-war trade in merchandise (probably they were less after 1914), the total offset accounted for was $3,950,000,000.

With the exception of the imports and exports of gold, which are reported at the Custom House and whose valuation does not vary, these figures cannot be taken as absolutely exact. The amount of securities transferred is partly estimated. Some of them, although owned abroad, had previously been held in trust by American institutions, so that their sale was prima facie a domestic transaction and, in the case of bonds, may have escaped identification. With all of them the proceeds must have varied with the fluctuating Stock

Exchange prices. Even the official valuation of merchandise exports is fixed by a more or less arbitrary average of prices at the date of shipment. It cannot allow for consignments on which the price had been arranged long in advance of delivery, and the same condition exists with import valuations. The resultant possible error, however, affects both sides of the account, and the figures which I have used are reasonably safe. But even so, it will be seen that the outside world's $3,950,000,000 miscellaneous credits, in trade with the United States during the two-year period, were still nearly a thousand million dollars short of its $4,867,000,000 debit on account of merchandise. If, indeed, any doubt existed as to whether Europe had as yet even approximately balanced the account, the course of foreign exchange rates would have disposed of it.

In January, 1915, sterling was quoted at $4.85; a rate within the normal pre-war range. Not until the middle of February did it fall below the normal "gold point" of $4.82, and it held around $4.78 until the immense war-orders were placed in America during June. After that month, however, a very swift and continuous decline ensued, which brought sight sterling bills at the opening of September, 1915, to $4.50. This was depreciation of 7½ per cent in the pound sterling; nothing like that had been witnessed since England's period of suspended gold payments in the Napoleonic wars. The tradition that sterling went at New York to the equivalent of less than $4 in the panic of 1857, when the London Bank Act was temporarily suspended, is perhaps correct;[1] but that was as brief and abnormal an incident as the rise of sterling to $4.90 in Wall Street during the panic of 1907.

The fall to $4.50 in September, 1915, caused something of consternation; first, because it gravely impaired Great Britain's international prestige, second, because it made vastly more expensive the British purchases in America, whose contract price was fixed in dollars. Furthermore, there was no assurance as to where the depreciation would end. Experienced bankers predicted $4.25 or even $4.00, as against the normal gold parity of $4.86⅝. That the break had resulted primarily from the accumulating and as yet not settled American trade balance against England, there could even then have been little doubt.

[1] Letter of Henry Hentz, *Financial Chronicle*, Feb. 27, 1915, p. 667.

Only one recourse was left; large-scale borrowing of money in the United States and use of the proceeds to pay for part of the purchases in America, so that sterling bills would not have to be drawn and "sold." Acting with France, whose own exchange had fallen 15 per cent below gold parity at New York, England now planned an American loan; the two governments making in the summer of 1915 joint application for $1,000,-000,000. This was a larger operation than American bankers were willing to undertake; but eventually, after long negotiation with the Anglo-French Debt Commission, the offering was fixed at $500,000,000 in five-year 5 per cent bonds, payable interest and principal in American gold coin, sold to the underwriting syndicate at 96 and to investors at 98, but bearing no special security beyond the pledge of the borrowing governments.

Even at the lower figure, the loan represented the largest sum ever asked from American investors in a single offering, the previous high mark having been the $200,000,000 Spanish War loan of the United States government during 1898. The Anglo-French loan was not placed altogether easily. Our investing community had yet to discover its own financial power; German-Ameri-

can financial influence was strongly exerted
against the operation; the public was doubtful
over the outcome of the war and puzzled at the
fall in sterling. Subscriptions were solicited on a
large scale, however, not only from banks and individuals but from manufacturing companies
handling European War orders,[1] and in the autumn
of 1915 the bonds were fully taken. Following
this, in 1916 France placed another loan of $100,-
000,000 in the United States and England two
more loans of $250,000,000 each; the state of the
market being indicated by the fact that the interest rate was raised to 5½ per cent notwithstanding the fact that, unlike the loan of 1915, all
of these 1916 loans were secured by pledging with
a New York trust company American and other
securities previously held abroad.

But it will be observed that these borrowings
of France and England at New York, in the aggregate exceeding $1,000,000,000 during the two years,
had at length balanced the international account
of 1915 and 1916. Sterling exchange rose to $4.75
when the Anglo-French loan was placed; it held
around that price until 1917. The depreciation
indicated even by that rate probably measured at

[1] N. Y. *Times*, Oct. 1, 1915; list of large subscribers.

the time only financial doubts of a currency irredeemable in gold. That sterling should sell at gold parity again, so long as resumption of gold payments could be only a matter of remote conjecture, was not to be expected. At the end of 1916, however, it may fairly be said that the wholly abnormal American export surplus, rolled up since the beginning of the war, had been paid for by the outside world. The extent to which and the means by which it was balanced in the next two years, covering the period between the entry of the United States into the conflict and the surrender of Germany, belong to another chapter.

It should now be clear how belligerent Europe and the rest of the outside world managed to arrange the extraordinary payments necessitated by our export trade in the days of American neutrality. But it remains to inquire how the American markets were affected by them. Contrary to all the apprehensions of 1914, the recovery of prices for investment securities which had begun with 1915 was not arrested, either by the sale of European holdings of our stocks and bonds or by the heavy demand on American capital for European loans. At the end of 1916, even prices

for existing investment bonds were higher than
at the beginning of 1915.[1] But Europe had paid
in gold as well as in securities, and the effect
of the gold imports on our financial markets must
also be considered.

Investigation of that question opens a very
singular episode of banking history. Between the
end of 1914 and the end of 1916, as a result of the
period's gold importation and a home production of
$193,600,000, offset by $88,800,000 used for commercial purposes in this country,[2] the total stock
of gold in the United States was estimated to
have risen from $1,815,976,000 to $2,864,841,000.[3]
An increase within so brief a time of 58 per cent
in the basis of credit and values might have been
expected to produce momentous results. That
expansion occurred, moreover, at the very moment
when the machinery of the new Federal Reserve
Law had enlarged facilities for a possible super-
structure of credit, through reducing percentage
requirements of private bank reserves and through
the counting, as part of those reserves, deposit

[1] N. Y. *Times*, Daily Bond Market Averages, Dec. 31, 1915,
and 1916.

[2] U. S. Mint Report, 1917, pp. 65 and 67.

[3] Monthly circulation statements U. S. Treasury, Jan. 1, 1915,
1916, 1917.

credits created by rediscount of the private banks'
commercial loans at the Federal banks.[1] When
the Federal Reserve opened for business in November, 1914, it held $203,415,000 gold,[2] obtained
through subscription of private banks in the
Federal Reserve system to the capital stock of the
new Reserve banks; payment of such subscription
being required by the law "to be in gold or gold
certificates."[3]

After the gold import movement had attained
large proportions in 1915, the private banks that
first received the gold turned over most of it to the
Federal Reserve, where it could be used by them
either as a basis for increased note circulation or
as an enlarged reserve of their own to support a
proportionately larger grant of credit to their customers. At the end of 1915 the Reserve System's
total gold holdings were $542,413,000; at the end
of 1916 they were $753,774,000. Aside from this
two-years' increase of something over $550,000,000
in gold held by the Federal Reserve banks, about

[1] Treasury Report, 1914, pp. 500, 501.

[2] Statement of Federal Reserve Board, Nov. 21, 1914; N. Y.
Financial Chronicle, Nov. 28, 1914, p. 1566.

[3] Federal Reserve Act, Section 2.

[4] Statements of Federal Reserve Board, Dec. 31, 1915, and
Dec. 29, 1916.

$150,000,000 was added by private banks in the national banking system to the reserve in their own vaults;[1] the war-time amendment requiring member banks in the Federal Reserve to keep their whole reserve with a Federal Bank had not then been adopted, and until 1917 any part of its reserve could be kept by a member bank in its own possession. If we allow, further, for gold which went into other than national banks or was used in circulation, also for about $187,000,000 exported during the two-year period (mostly to South America, the West Indies, and Japan), the distribution of the gold imports of 1915 and 1916 will be plain enough.

It evidently opened facilities for such expansion of American credit and American currency as had never been witnessed in our history. The $150,-000,000 gold which went into vaults of national banks would of itself, under the provisions of the Federal Reserve Law, support ten or twelve times as great an amount of loans as were outstanding at those institutions. But the Federal Reserve's own position was far more remarkable. When the rapid expansion of American trade occurred

[1] Annual report Comptroller of the Currency for 1916, Vol. II, p. 206.

in the summer and autumn months of 1915, there was naturally an equivalent expansion of credit and circulating medium at the Federal Reserve. Nevertheless, so rapid was the accumulation of new reserves as a result of the season's gold imports, that at the end of 1915 the Reserve Banks held $145,000,000 more gold than the percentage required against their increased note and deposit liabilities.

At the end of 1916, although by that time the Reserve system's outstanding notes and deposits were greater by $558,000,000 than at the beginning of 1915, its gold reserve was $415,900,000 larger than the law's percentages required. In other words, the increase in the system's credit operations and fiduciary currency had not been half as great as the increased gold reserve would legally have permitted. The loans of the country's national banks, which were largely supported by reserve credits in the Federal banks, had actually risen $2,000,000,000 in the two-year period, but an increase three or four times as great was at least conceivable and legally permissible.

It might be contended, then, that all the elements making for inflation in American trade and prices were at work. We have seen already that spectacular expansion of trade activity ensued; that the amount of business done, measured by bank checks exchanged at the clearing-houses, had run far beyond all precedent. Prices of commodities had risen also. The average of such prices hardly changed in the first half of 1915, before the British war orders were placed on the new scale of magnitude. The "index number" of the United States Labor Department, based on 100 as the average of 1913, worked out at 99 in January, 1915, and at 100 in September; but by the end of 1915 it had risen to 108, by the middle of 1916 to 124, and by the end of that year to 146.[1] Here was an advance in the two-year period of nearly 50 per cent in prices, which might plausibly enough have been ascribed to the influence of the mass of foreign gold poured into our currency and credit organism. The economic aspects of the matter were not, however, quite so simple.

Both the increase of the period in trade activity and the rise in prices were direct results of the abnormally large purchases of our products by other countries. Those purchases were a purely

[1] U. S. Department of Labor, Bulletin of Statistics No. 367, Feb., 1925; Wholesale Prices 1890–1923.

arbitrary result of the European war and, so far as concerned the European orders, were conducted practically regardless of cost; a process which necessarily tended to force up American prices irrespective of the currency conditions. If Europe had not been able to send us gold it is possible that high money rates in the United States, caused by the conducting of an immensely increased trade on insufficient banking reserves, might have arrested the rise of prices. But that is one of those puzzling economic episodes in which cause and effect are so inextricably mixed that a plain inference is not easily drawn. All that we can say with absolute certainty is that the immensely increased activity of trade in the United States during 1915 and 1916 required an equivalent expansion of American bank credit, and that for this legitimate expansion the gold importations provided the necessary base.

But it was distinctly a result of the huge gold importation that a spectacular trade revival should have been financed without a ripple of disturbance on the American money market. The Reserve banks began by fixing their own official discount rates at $5\frac{1}{2}$ to $6\frac{1}{2}$ per cent, but reduced them as low as $4\frac{1}{2}$ within a month and to 4 per cent later on; the last-named rate being maintained with little change during 1915 and 1916.[1] At the end of 1916, our own official "bank rate" was the lowest of any country in the world.[2] Of rates on the open money market, measured by the charge for discount of good commercial paper, the Reserve Board officially declared that in 1915 they had "never approached so uniform a level."[3]

In the two most notable earlier years of American trade expansion, 1879 and 1898, the Wall Street rates for all kinds of loans had repeatedly, in response to the urgent demand for new credit, risen to 7 per cent or higher; "money stringency" was constantly reported by merchants. But on the New York market of 1915, commercial paper rates never went above $4\frac{1}{2}$ per cent and frequently commanded only $3\frac{1}{2}$; time loans on Stock Exchange security ranged between $2\frac{1}{2}$ and 3; demand loans in May commanded only 1 per cent and the year's highest rate was $2\frac{1}{2}$. No rates as low as these had been quoted at any time during the twenty years before the war, except for a few weeks in 1914, 1909 and 1908. Never since 1894, when trade activity and use of credit were at the

---

[1] Annual reports Federal Reserve Board for 1915, p. 27; for 1916, p. 6.

[2] *Ibid.* for 1916, p. 6.   [3] *Ibid.* for 1915, p. 5.

low ebb of the generation, had a full year's average rate for money been as cheap as in 1915. Similar conditions continued to prevail during 1916, and even when call-money rates went momentarily to 15 per cent in a violent year-end stock market reaction, hereafter to be described, time loans and merchants' paper never rose above 4½ and the weekly surplus reserve of the New York Associated Banks ranged from $41,000,000 to $100,000,000.

With credit thus abundant and with profits of trade and industry rising to exceptional heights, the Stock Exchange was bound to reflect the situation. The advance which occurred after the tentative reopening of Stock Exchange business in November, 1914, I have already described. Prices grew more irregular during the first two months of 1915; then, in March, an upward movement of unusual scope and rapidity began. One record of daily average prices of typical shares on the New York Stock Exchange shows that in February, 1915, the year's low level of 58.99 was reached, that the ensuing rise carried up the average to 94.13 in October and that, after falling back to 80.91 in April, 1916, it reached 101.51 in the following November.[1] Since 1906 a "million-share

[1] N. Y. *Times*, daily Stock Market Averages, 1915 and 1916.

day" on the New York Stock Exchange had been
an abnormally large business; in the early months
of 1914, the daily sales had averaged barely
300,000 shares. In the autumn of 1915, they
ran repeatedly above a million shares; in the
two final months of 1916 came a long succession of days in which upward of two million
shares changed hands, for the first time in ten
years.

The course of Stock Exchange prices was naturally governed primarily by the immense and increasing prosperity of American industry; in
particular cases, shares of industrial companies
handling war orders scored such advances as the
rise of Baldwin Locomotive stock from 40 to 154½
during 1915 and of Bethlehem Steel from 46¼
in January, 1915, to 700 in November, 1916.
But, although the general upward trend of prices
was continuous, the movement of investment
shares was influenced also by the course of the
European war, and in a singularly confusing way.
The sympathy of the American community, taken
as a whole, was strongly on the side of the Entente
Allies; the first tendency, therefore, was for the
stock market to advance on news of Allied successes
and to decline on news of German victories. It

soon became evident, however, that the matter was not so simple as this would seem to indicate.

On the one hand there was the question, very insistent from the start, whether the United States would not ultimately be drawn into the war, with all of the possible economic consequences to itself. When the Cunard liner *Lusitania* was sunk by a German submarine on May 7, 1915, with 188 American citizens on its passenger list, of whom 114 were lost, intervention by our government seemed for a time inevitable. The already considerable number of Americans who had insisted, ever since the German invasion of Belgium, that our place was in the war on the side of France and England, found themselves heavily reinforced by previously hesitant citizens, and for a week it was believed to be possible that the Lusitania episode would necessitate breaking off of diplomatic relations with Germany. That particular crisis was averted, notwithstanding the highly unsatisfactory reply of the government at Berlin to our State Department's demand that responsibility for the attack on the *Lusitania* be disavowed. But in the meantime an almost panicky break on the Stock Exchange carried down prices of numerous industrial company shares 20 or 30 per cent.

Since Germany's submarine attacks on merchant ships with American passengers on board were not relinquished, shocks of that kind recurred at intervals, nor was that the only disturbing influence. Financial confidence was on several occasions shaken by another and curiously contrasting influence; arising, it might be said, not from fear of war but from fear of peace. It had grown evident, early in 1915, that the war would not soon be ended by the decisive military victory of either side. But in 1916 there came to public knowledge, first, the suggestion in neutral Europe of possible mediation in behalf of peace and next, in March and again in October, rumors that the German government itself was about to request the United States to mediate. Under ordinary circumstances, the prospect of terminating so destructive a conflict would have been received with relief and hopefulness in financial markets. All Stock Exchanges had made precisely that response to rumors of peace negotiations in the Russo-Japanese war of 1904, the Boer War of 1899, the American Civil War and the wars of Napoleon, a century ago. But the position of the United States in 1915 and 1916 was unlike that of any country, neutral or belligerent, in those older conflicts.

Over against the return to normal economic conditions which peace would indicate stood the unmistakable fact that the immense governmental requisitions on our produce and manufactures would cease with termination of the war, leaving the greatly expanded plant, the very high values of commodities and of industrial company shares, to confront the process which afterward came to be popularly described as "deflation." The markets knew that every great war of the century past had been followed by a period of sweeping economic reaction; partly a consequence of the prodigious waste of capital, no longer disguised by wholesale use of credit raised through war loans, but also resulting largely from the totally altered position of producers of grain and war materials when orders from the fighting governments were suddenly canceled. The stock market's action in 1916 showed which aspect of a sudden peace was weightier in the financial mind.

On one day of unfounded "peace negotiation rumors" during March, declines of 2 to 7 points occurred on the Stock Exchange. In

October, similar and better-substantiated rumors of a German request for mediation were followed by a break of 10 to 20 per cent. Finally in December, when Germany actually appealed to the neutral powers and when it became known that President Wilson had asked the several belligerent governments to state their purposes, so that "some common ground" might be discovered on which to "get together and arrange the settlement,"[1] something like panic occurred in the speculative markets—not only on the Stock Exchange, where the decline in prices was the most violent of the whole war period, but in the grain market also, where wheat fell 28 cents a bushel in four days. Yet such was the prevalent spirit of the day, that most of these downward reactions in the speculative markets appeared in retrospect only as incidents in a continuous upward sweep of trade prosperity, industrial earnings and investment values.

The Stock Exchange commotion in response to the recurrent "peace rumors" of 1916 was recalled with peculiar interest four years later, when all

[1] U. S. State Department's identical note of December 18, 1916, to Great Britain, France, Italy, Japan, Russia, Belgium, Montenegro, Portugal, Rumania and Servia; also to Germany, Austria-Hungary, Turkey and Bulgaria.

American markets were actually under the influence of the post-war industrial readjustment. During the earlier war years, however, it was quickly forgotten, being completely superseded by the evidence of uninterrupted and seemingly limitless prosperity. Gold pouring into the country was traditional proof of it; labor was fully employed at rising wages; the agricultural West and South were earning almost unprecedented profits. It was only momentarily that the resultant enthusiasm would be chilled by warnings of how the windfall of good times might perhaps disappear in a twinkling if the war were suddenly to end or the United States itself to be dragged into it. From this attitude there arose in a very great body of the American people a feeling, not of angry impatience with the war itself (as in 1914), but of gratification that we were not entangled in the conflict and had prospered because of our neutrality. That was the time when, rightly or wrongly, the indifference of the Western communities to the larger issues of the war became proverbial.

Into that situation was projected the Presidential election of 1916. Mr. Wilson's renomination by his party was a matter of course; Justice

Charles E. Hughes left the United States Supreme
Bench to accept the Republican party's candidacy.
The resultant electoral campaign was governed
by a very unusual series of conflicting influences,
which made its outcome doubtful up to the counting of the votes.   Mr. Wilson had in his favor the
advantage which national prosperity always con-
fers on the party in power.   Because of that
prosperity and because of the apparent indifference
of the Middle West to the issues of the war, he also
benefited by the widespread spirit of satisfaction
that the United States had been kept out of the
conflict.   He had against him, on the other hand,
the reputed hostility of large masses of German-
American voters who, the politicians thought, re-
sented what they chose to consider the discrimina-
tion of the State Department against Germany
and in favor of England.

By way of contrast he had incurred the opposition of Eastern men of influence, who believed
that the Administration had favored Germany
by not taking issue peremptorily with its government after the *Lusitania* was sunk.   This very
diversity, however, in the influences making for
or against Mr. Wilson's re-election rendered it
difficult for his opponent to frame a consistent

campaign program.   Had Mr. Hughes denounced
the administration's policy towards Germany as
too lenient, he would have risked antagonizing the
contented West and the German-American vote.
Had he denounded it as too harsh, he would have
antagonized the East.   For the same reason
prudence forbade his declaring, even conditionally,
either for or against declaration of war on Germany
by the United States.   His personal campaign,
therefore, inevitably became colorless, culminating
in an effort to revive the protective tariff issue—
an effort which was so strangely out of touch with
the foreign-trade situation of the moment as to
excite only wondering surprise.

What it would have meant in the German-
American relations of the next five months if Mr.
Wilson had been defeated and Mr. Hughes
elected, it is not altogether easy to imagine.   We
know now, as the voters could not have known
in November, 1916, that Germany was even then
preparing the policy of submarine ruthlessness
which was to make the entry of America into the
war inevitable.   Whether recourse to that policy
by Germany would have been deferred if Mr.
Wilson had been defeated, and with what results,
it is impossible to say.   But in any case a virtual

interregnum of four months between November 7,
1916, when the victory of the opposition party
would have been announced, and March 4, 1917,
when the new administration would have taken
office, must necessarily have created a difficult
situation, a legislative and perhaps a diplomatic
deadlock.

That was not destined to happen. The vote by
states was astonishingly close; even the morning
newspapers of Wednesday, November 8, mostly
conceded the victory to Mr. Hughes, and only the
full count of a very close vote in California, not
completed until three days after the election, made
Mr. Wilson's victory certain. His majority in the
Electoral College was only 23, whereas in 1912 his
plurality had been 347 over Roosevelt and 339
over Roosevelt and Taft combined. But this vote
by states did not fairly measure the poll of the
people. Wilson's popular vote in the whole United
States in 1916 was greater by 2,836,250 than in
1912, an increase of more than one-third. In 1912
he had polled less votes by 1,311,444 than were cast
for the two Republicans combined; in 1916 he ran
581,941 ahead of the single Republican candidate.
The choice of the people was expressed with sufficient emphasis.

Events thereafter moved with great rapidity. I have already spoken of Germany's overture for peace on December 12, 1916, and of Mr. Wilson's application on December 18 to the various belligerents for a statement of their ultimate purpose in the war, with a view to possible terms of peace. On December 30 the Entente Powers jointly and unanimously answered President Wilson, rejecting Germany's suggestion of a compromise peace and stating terms which, two weeks later, the German government tacitly rejected, while at the same time refusing to state its own terms of peace. At last, on January 31, the German Foreign Office notified the United States that Germany would adopt the submarine policy of "forcibly preventing, after February 1, 1917, in a zone around Great Britain, France, Italy and in the Eastern Mediterranean, all navigation, that of neutrals included," and that "all ships met within the zone will be sunk." With singular misconception of the American attitude and the American temperament, the German government added that, by way of special favor to the United States, one weekly steamer from America to England would be allowed and one from England to America, provided the course and port prescribed by Germany were adopted, a flag specially designated by Germany carried at each masthead, and the ship itself marked in vertical stripes of red and white.

To this particularly insolent declaration, the response of the United States government was prompt and unmistakable. Nearly a year before, in April, 1916, our State Department had warned Germany that if its government intended "to prosecute relentless and indiscriminate warfare against vessels of commerce by the use of submarines," regardless of "international law and the universally recognized dictates of humanity," then the United States government could have "no choice but to sever diplomatic relations with the German Empire altogether." The German government had thereupon pledged itself that merchant ships "shall not be sunk without warning" and that the government would "do its utmost" to confine war operations "to the fighting forces of the belligerents." The Berlin declaration of January 31, 1917, was therefore necessarily followed on February 3 by the formal breaking-off of relations with Germany and the handling of his passports to Count Bernstorff.

This was not war, but with Germany in her

mood of desperation, it pointed to war as inevitable. Public utterances of the day and data
published since the peace have shown that Germany's policy of submarine "ruthlessness," although strongly opposed in many important
German quarters, was adopted chiefly because of
the prevalent conviction that England would be
starved into surrender before any possible assistance from America could be available, but partly
also because of widespread official skepticism as to
any serious military consequences from America's
entry into the war.[1] The program of submarine
ruthlessness was not even momentarily suspended
because of the attitude of Washington. American
as well as other ships were sunk and then, by way
of hastening the inevitable decision, it was discovered that on January 19, before either the
publication of Germany's submarine note or the
severance of diplomatic relations, the Government
at Berlin had instructed its Minister at Mexico to
propose a German alliance with that government,
whereby the United States in case of war should
be attacked and Mexico should "reconquer the
lost territory in New Mexico, Texas and Arizona."

[1] Chancellor Michaelis, Speech to German Reichstag, July 19,
1917; Admiral Von Tirpitz, *My Memoirs*, chapter xix.

This fantastic performance, which also contemplated Japan as deserting her European allies to join in attacking the United States and which the German Foreign Office publicly acknowledged and defended, caused only amazement or ridicule in diplomatic circles, but its effect upon public sentiment in our own non-belligerent West was precisely what any one but the authors of the overture to Mexico would have anticipated. On April 2, 1917, when the President made his war speech to Congress, it was evident that he had the whole country behind him. By vote of 82 to 6 in the Senate and of 373 to 50 in the House, it was at once declared that war already existed by the act of Germany.

CHAPTER IV

THE UNITED STATES ENTERS THE WAR

THE President's message to Congress on April 2 had outlined the war program of the United States. Our participation in the war, he declared, would mean the "organization and mobilization of all the material resources of the country, to supply the materials of war and serve the incidental needs of the nation in the most abundant and yet the most economic and efficient way possible." It would render necessary not only "the utmost practicable co-operation in counsel and action with the governments now at war with Germany," but "the extension to those governments of the most liberal financial credits, in order that our resources may, so far as possible, be added to theirs." In addition to the full equipment of the navy, the President asked for "immediate addition to the armed forces of the United States . . . of at least 500,000 men" and "au-

thorization of subsequent additional increments of
equal force as soon as they may be needed."

These statements of the government's purposes
were necessarily framed in general terms. It is
not easy to say exactly what interpretation the
American public placed upon them when it heard
them first, or what practical sequel it expected.
Mr. Wilson's declaration was greeted with nation-
wide enthusiasm, also and very generally with
relief; for a not wholly unreasonable doubt had
existed as to whether an administration which
so long and under so great provocation had avoided
committing the United States to war would conduct the war, when once committed to it, with
unrelenting energy. The curious precedent of
1812, when our country went to war with the
particular European belligerent against whom
it had a grievance but otherwise took no part in
the European conflict, was familiar to every
American from his school-days. Probably few
people imagined repetition of such a policy in
1917; indeed, it was impracticable, from both the
political and the military viewpoint. But the
public mind had certainly not grasped beforehand
the full scope of the undertaking in which the
country had now engaged.

The task before the navy was abundantly recognized, but there was little expectation of an American expeditionary force on the European battlefront, unless for the presence of a division or two from our small but already mobilized regular army.[1] Ex-President Roosevelt's declaration of his plan to raise two volunteer divisions for service in France, followed by his announcement, six weeks after the war message, that 285,000 men had been enrolled for that service,[2] was based apparently on belief that the sending of a new American army for active service in Europe was not anticipated. Even in its Army Bill of May, Congress inserted a paragraph authorizing the President "to raise and maintain by voluntary enlistment" such an independent force up to four infantry divisions and, although the President disapproved the plan, its proposal in an act of Congress reflected Washington's doubts regarding the larger probabilities.

Appropriations for public expenditure had been substantially increased in the Congressional session which ended just before the United States

[1] Clarkson, *Industrial America in the World War*, p. 35. *Financial Chronicle*, April 14, 1917, p. 1443; April 21, p. 1534; May 26, p. 2050.

[2] Order of Theodore Roosevelt to enrolled volunteers, May 20; Clarkson, p. 35.

entered the war and those appropriations were believed, in the words of a member of the Senate Finance Committee, to be "of such magnitude that they would take care of all the expenditures incident to any war in which we might engage."[1] At the start, the majority of the people probably imagined that, if our government were to make loans to the Entente Allies while reserving all private capital for its own borrowings, such advances would at most involve no greater outlay in a year than what had been borrowed by those governments in our general investment market of 1916—about $850,000,000.[2] In regard to the "organization and mobilization" of the country's material resources, the public at large had in April only vague ideas of what was to be expected; the government itself was certainly far from foreseeing the actual scope of control which was destined to be applied to American productive industry. The most that the majority of the American people probably pictured in April, 1917, from the President's reference to "organization and mobilization of all the country's material resources," was such co-operation of our industrial

[1] Senate speech, Reed Smoot, July 24, 1917.
[2] *Financial Chronicle*, Jan. 6, 1917, p. 12.

leaders with the government as had been system-
matically achieved in August, 1914; supplemented
in 1917 by the fixing of maximum prices for such
essential commodities as steel or wheat, with a
view to preventing extravagant rise in values
through purely speculative operations.

All such ideas of restricted participation in the
war were promptly and decisively dispelled.
Nothing is more remarkable in the entire episode
than the largeness of vision with which the government outlined its general plan and stated its
financial requirements at the very outset. In the
nature of the case, the complete program for
what afterward became the Expeditionary Force
could not have been set forth at once on our declaration of war. Questions of preliminary training of
recruits, of shipping capacity for transportation, of
protection from submarines, had to be settled first
with the British and French Commissions, which
did not arrive in this country until near the end
of April; yet two weeks before their arrival a
finance program had been presented by the Administration and enacted by Congress, fully adapted
to the requirements which subsequently developed.

Secret estimates submitted in March by the
various branches of the service, as to the cost of

establishing an army of a million men, named $1,250,000,000;[1] but the estimates were not made with confidence and the Secretary of the Treasury asked Congress, three days after declaration of hostilities, to provide nearly three times that amount.[2] Largely on the basis of thorough examination of the question with the statesmen sent by our European allies to confer with the government at Washington, the Treasury also applied to Congress for $3,000,000,000 "to supply credit to the governments making common cause with us,"[3] and by April 17 a law to that effect had passed both houses of Congress. Those credits, based on equivalent internal borrowings by the United States, were destined during the subsequent nineteen months of war to reach the prodigious sum of $8,171,976,000, which was actually six or seven times as large as the country's entire interest-bearing public debt outstanding in April, 1917. Congress was asked at once to authorize an army of a million men, based on the principle of universal liability to service and recruited through a selective draft; such a law, providing for the immediate

[1] Clarkson, p. 33.
[2] Secretary McAdoo, statement to Congress, April 5, 1917.
[3] Secretary McAdoo, statement of April 9, 1917.

equipment of 500,000 men, with 500,000 more at such times as the president should determine, was enacted on May 18. On the same day a full division of the regular army and a regiment of marines were ordered to Europe under General Pershing. By November, large bodies of the new recruits were arriving in Europe and being distributed to the training camps;[1] by the middle of 1918, not only were our expeditionary troops engaged in important military operations, but the Secretary of War was able to report that 1,019,115 American soldiers had been despatched to France.[2] The number had reached 2,086,000 when the war ended, with 1,671,624 more training in America.[3]

Considering what had been the previous views in a great part of the country regarding our participation in the war, it might have been imagined that these prodigious and immediate requisitions would have met with criticism in Congress, if not with outright opposition. The draft, it is true, encountered spirited resistance, yet the law ordaining it was passed by a vote of 65 to 8 in the Senate and of 199 to 178 in the House. While de-

[1] War Department, Annual Report for 1917, p. 51; for 1918, p. 7.
[2] Secretary Baker, letter to President Wilson, July 1, 1918.
[3] War Department, Annual Report for 1919, p. 4.

bating the $3,000,000,000 appropriation for loans to our European Allies—in many respects the most startling and portentous innovation of all the government's proposals—the contention was occasionally made that Congress had no constitutional authority for such action.[1] But the prevalent attitude was altogether favorable to the grant.

The leader of the House Opposition declared his conviction that "when we take the responsibility of engaging in war, we ought not to expect that it will be a mere paper war or a mere academic discussion," and expressed the belief that the amount appropriated "will be more than doubled in a year."[2] Another Opposition legislator, who unreservedly approved the naming of so great a sum, merely described it as "a most magnanimous proposal."[3] Still others rested their decision wholly on the ground that "the Administration, which is in possession of all the facts, thinks that this is a proper amount,"[4] or that "we must trust the President; it is the only way now."[5] The magnitude of the loans suggested to the mind of

[1] W. H. Stafford, H. R. speech, Apr. 13, 1917.
[2] J. R. Mann, H. R. speech, Apr. 13.
[3] J. W. Fordney, H. R. speech, Apr. 13.
[4] Claude Kitchin, H. R. speech, Apr. 13.
[5] J. H. Moore, H. R. speech, Apr. 13.

the legislators, not that we might be exhausting our own resources but that this use of them "brings to our nation definitely and finally the control of the finances of the world." [1]   One senator of long public service expressed dislike at making our government a creditor of foreign governments, and warned the Senate that such action would create for the longer future "an embarrassment from which the men of those times will find it difficult to escape"—a highly interesting prophecy. [2]

But even he coupled his objection with the statement that he was "perfectly willing to give any of the Allied nations the money which they need to carry on our war," and voted for the bill. Even Senator La Follette, after denouncing the plan and suggesting the alternative that the United States give England the money in exchange for her North American possessions, [3] waived his objections because he did not wish "to hamper our own effort," and cast his vote accordingly.   The vote for the bill was in fact unanimous both in House and Senate. This attitude of the congressmen appeared fully and faithfully to reflect

[1] W. P. Borland, H. R. speech, Apr. 13, 1917.
[2] A. B. Cummins, Senate speech, Apr. 17.
[3] R. M. La Follette, Senate speech, Apr. 13.

the attitude of their constituents, once the proposals had been made. Contemporary newspaper discussion of the Administration's program of loans to the foreign governments contained practically no criticism or objection regarding its scope and magnitude. It was evident that the country was ready, in the President's words, to pledge its entire resources to a successful issue of the war.

The first question to which the government had to address itself was the raising of the financial resources to conduct the war. This made it necessary to determine what the war would cost, and that in turn necessitated clearly foreseeing the scope of our military undertakings and of the needs of the foreign governments for credit. In the last preceding fiscal year, ending with June, 1916, the government's actual ordinary expenditure had been $724,492,000, of which $319,664,000 was spent by war and navy departments. But the growing probability that the United States would be forced into war had already caused an increase. The original estimate for the fiscal year 1917, submitted to Congress in December, 1916, had been $1,058,126,000;[1] in March, 1917, when the govern-

[1] Treasury Report 1916, pp. 44, 46.

ment had broken with Germany and when war was increasingly predicted, the appropriation carried, if the post-office item is deducted, $1,629,-426,000.[1] It was recognized that, in the period of mobilization, expenses would not reach the sum which European nations were disbursing; nevertheless, the estimates were already larger than any European belligerent had fixed for itself at the outset. They were rapidly increased by the Treasury.

Its first "war budget," submitted by the Secretary to Congress on April 5, 1917, placed the probable expenditure up to the middle of 1918, for our war purposes alone, at $3,502,558,629, to which sum was added the $3,000,000,000 asked for advances during the same period to the European governments at war with Germany.[2] This, added to the appropriations made in March, meant a total outlay for the year of $8,400,000,000. Three months afterward, and before Congress had completed its war-revenue bill, the Treasury announced that, on the basis of actual expenditure in the intervening period, it had increased its estimate of

[1] Speech of Senator Reed Smoot, July 24, 1917.
[2] Secretary McAdoo, statements to Congress, Apr. 5 and 9, 1917.

our necessary expenditure for the fiscal year ending with June, 1918, to $15,000,000,000.[1]   When
the Treasury's annual report was submitted to
Congress in December, the estimates were again
revised.   Whereas in April $8,400,000,000 had
been fixed as our own necessary expenditure, it was
now stated that total disbursements in the fiscal
year ending June 30, 1918, exclusive of loans to
foreign governments, would be $12,316,295,223,
of which "it is estimated that $11,527,709,023 will
be for war purposes."[2]   Since the estimate of the
fiscal year's advances to foreign governments was
at the same time raised to $6,115,000,000,[3] this
meant that more than $18,000,000,000 total ex-
penditure in the period was expected.[4]   The
December estimate, however, turned out to be
almost as much too high as the April estimate was
too low; actual public expenditure during the
fiscal year 1918 was $13,771,000,000 including,
$4,739,000,000 advances made to foreign govern-
ments.[5]

It was recognized at the outset, then, that in

[1] Statement of McAdoo to Senate Finance Committee, July
24, 1917.
[2] Treasury Report 1917, p. 56.
[3] *Ibid.*, p. 72.   [4] *Ibid.*, p. 80.
[5] Treasury Report 1918, p. 129.

addition to the amount voted by Congress in the pre-war session, new resources ranging from seven thousand millions to twelve thousand millions would be required to meet the government's expenditure in the first full year of war. For a substantial part of that huge sum, Congress had to make immediate provision. Legislation for increased taxes would necessarily require careful committee discussion and full Congressional debate and, when the law should have been passed, actual collection of the taxes would be possible only after much delay. But public expenditure had already increased portentously. Even in April, the government's disbursements rose to $297,574,000 against $60,534,000 in April, 1916.

During the three months ending with June, 1917, they ran $1,657,000,000 beyond the disbursements of the corresponding period of the preceding year. Revenue collected in those months of 1916 exceeded expenditure by $93,000,000 and in the same months of 1917 the revenue was twice as large; nevertheless, so great was public expenditure in the first three months of war that it exceeded the actual tax receipts by $1,268,000,000.[1] To

[1] Monthly statements of the Treasury. *Financial Chronicle*, May 26, 1917, p. 2090; July 7, p. 46; July 28, p. 363.

meet these imperative requirements, Congress acted quickly.

Its "war finance bill" of April, 1917, authorized, first, the sale of $2,000,000,000 interest-bearing notes, running not more than one year and designed merely to anticipate either subsequent revenue collections or a subsequent long-term bond issue; second, the sale of $5,000,000,000 long-term bonds. In conformity with the practice of our government, during and since the Civil War, it was stipulated in the law that these new obligations should be offered at not less than par. They were to carry an interest rate "not exceeding 3½ per centum per annum," and the "principal and interest thereof . . . shall be exempt, both as to principal and interest, from all taxation, except estate or inheritance taxes, imposed by authority of the United States or its possessions, or by any state or local taxing authority." The terms compared with a 3½ per cent bond sold at par in the British government's first war financing of 1914, and a 5 per cent bond at 97½ in Germany's initial offer. The proceeds of the American loan were to be used either "to meet expenditures authorized for the national security and defense" or, up to $3,000,000,000, "to purchase at par from foreign governments engaged in war with the enemies of the United States their obligations hereafter issued."

That second proviso was the origin of the celebrated "war debt of Europe to the United States government." The statute of 1917 prescribed that the foreign obligations were to bear the same rate of interest as the United States bonds issued to procure the money, and that "payments made by foreign governments on account of their said obligations" were to be used in redemption or purchase "of any bonds of the United States issued under authority of this act." The last stipulation was re-enacted in subsequent War Loan Acts; it had a special interest, then and afterward, as giving conclusive evidence that our government's advances to the European governments at war with Germany were in no respect regarded, like Great Britain's loans to her Continental Allies between 1793 and 1805, as "subsidies" which would presumably never be repaid, but as lawfully contracted debts.

The Treasury used its new authority in the issue, for subscription by the banks, first of one-month notes or "certificates of indebtedness" bearing 3 per cent interest, then of notes with slightly longer maturity and a 3½ per cent rate. These sales covered the immediate public deficit until, in June, 1917, $2,000,000,000 thirty-year bonds were offered with a 3½ per cent interest rate and with the immunity from taxation which the law prescribed. The experiment was interesting in more than one respect; because, although the rediscount rates at the Federal Reserve banks had been fixed at 3 or 3½ per cent for short maturities, the open money market at New York was asking 4¾ to 5¼ per cent for merchants' paper. It is true that even 2 per cent United States bonds of pre-war issues were selling on the Stock Exchange at 98. But those bonds were available as a basis for bank circulation under the old National Bank Act and the privilege of such issues had not been wholly withdrawn by the Federal Reserve law; whereas the war loan act of April, 1917, prescribed that the new 3½ per cents "shall not bear the circulation privilege."

The immunity from virtually all federal, state and city taxation, which the War Loan authorized and the Treasury granted, was in line with the uniform practice of our government in its previous war loans. That practice had been defended by economists, sometimes on the ground that for the government to contract to pay a given rate of interest, and then indirectly to cut the rate by an income tax on holders, was theoretical violation of the understanding, but more often on the ground that the uncertainty created by the power to tax the interest would cause the investment market to demand a higher interest rate.[1]   Nevertheless, the success of the first war loan of 1917, under circumstances which I shall presently review, led to the dropping of the full immunity from federal taxation in all subsequent war loans, thereby reversing, except as regarded state and city taxes, the long-term practice of the government.   The market's view of the bearing of that change on intrinsic values is illustrated by the prices at the end of the war, when the 3½ per cents sold on the Stock Exchange at par but the 4¼ per cents, with only limited freedom from taxation, at 98.   On September 24, 1917, Congress passed a second war loan act, authorizing issue of $7,538,945,000 bonds in addition to those already sold, this loan to bear 4 per cent interest, and in November a second loan of $3,800,000,000 was offered, in which immunity from the basic income tax was still allowed but not immunity from the graduated

[1] H. C. Adams, "Public Debts"; pp. 232, 233.

surtax or from war profits or excess profits taxes. In the following month of May, 1918, the Treasury offered a third public loan of $4,200,000,000, bearing interest of 4¼ per cent.

Thus the government asked for no less than $10,000,000,000, in subscription to loans offered at less than the market price of money and with a net interest yield 1 to 2 per cent below that of outstanding high-grade company securities. The war loans no longer had the "circulation privilege" which had floated most of the Civil War loans; even the old-time immunity from Federal taxes was curtailed. It was evident that our own previous experience would throw little light on the probable success or probable financial consequences of a single public subscription for $2,000,000,000, followed within six months by another of $3,800,-000,000. The largest increase in the American public debt during any single twelvemonth had been $941,902,000, in 1865,[1] made up of sales spread over the whole period; the largest loan ever floated by our government in a single operation was $200,000,000, in the Spanish War of 1898. A considerable body of experienced financiers held that it would not be prudent to begin

[1] Treasury Report 1865, p. 18.

in 1917 with a single offering of more than $500,-
000,000 or $1,000,000,000, and they so advised
the Treasury.[1]

Belligerent Europe had, however, tried between
1914 and 1917 the experiment of war loans in
wholly unprecedented amounts, and the results
had made new financial history. The largest
single loan of the British government placed before
1914 was the £60,000,000 Boer War loan of 1901,
and that was partly placed abroad; the total pre-
war British public debt was £651,000,000. Yet
individual British borrowings of the existing war
had ranged in amount from £350,000,000 in the
first loan of November, 1914, to £947,000,000 in
the third loan of January, 1917, and all of them
had been quickly and sometimes heavily over-
subscribed. The same result accompanied the
French 5 per cent loan of November, 1917,
which produced 15,130,000,000 francs, and the
six German 5 per cent war loans placed up to the
time the United States declared war, subscriptions to which ran from four billion to thirteen
billion marks.

These extraordinary achievements in the Euro-

[1] Treasury Report 1917, p. 6.   Harding, "Formative Period
of the Federal Reserve System," p. 89.

pean investment market were ascribed by every
one, in 1917, to the discovery by the borrowing
governments that wholly unsuspected sums could
be obtained through direct and urgent appeal to
small as well as large investors. That plan had
been pursued by the United States in the Civil
War, when Jay Cooke, in the words of the Treasury report of that day, "distributed throughout the whole country and among all classes of
our countrymen, . . . chiefly through the inde-
fatigable efforts of the general agent and his
sub-agents, bonds to the amount of nearly $400,-
000,000 in denominations of $50, $100, $500 and
$1,000."[1] The experiment of individual solici-
tation through an army of canvassers had not,
however, been repeated in subsequent years and,
since the loans of the European War had to be
offered and subscribed immediately, there was
evidently necessitated a canvass for individual
subscriptions far more intensive than Jay Cooke's,
which was indefinitely continuous. England's
first war loan of 1914 made no special appeal to
the small investor,[2] but Germany began at once
with an organized nation-wide campaign. Mass

[1] Treasury Report 1863, p. 14.
[2] London *Economist*, June 12, 1915, pp. 1201, 1202.

meetings were addressed by eminent public men; committees of citizens were organized for the canvass; newspaper and bill-board advertising, even parades and public demonstrations, were invoked.

Names of large subscribers were ostentatiously published in German newspapers; the loan of 1916 was floated through a "drive" in which personal solicitation of every citizen was attempted, with advertisements whereby the public's eye was confronted at every turn with assurances to the effect that "the new loan stands under the sign of Hindenburg."[1] The upshot was that individual subscriptions even to the first German war loan of September, 1914, numbered 1,150,000, of which 200,000 applied for 100 to 200 marks apiece and 700,000 for 200 to 2,000,[2] and that to the second war loan there were 2,691,060 subscribers. The British Treasury spoke contemptuously of "the expedients to which Germany has had to resort"[3] and the German Treasury itself retorted, with reference to some expedients used in the later British loans, that "to employ the methods of the circus for the serious business

[1] London *Economist*, Sept. 16, 1916, p. 488.

[2] Speech of President Havenstein of the Reichsbank, Sept. 29, 1914.   London *Economist*, Oct. 17, 1914, p. 645.

[3] Lloyd George, speech in British Parliament, Dec. 3, 1914.

of war is offensive to German taste."[1]   But the
urgency of the public need was sufficient to sweep
aside all objection based on traditions of governmental dignity, to a program that produced such
results, and the success of the German war loans
led to the prompt and general adoption of these
methods by all other Treasuries.

They were instantly utilized when the United
States government, in May, 1917, offered its first
war loan.   As might have been expected from the
American temperament and the American habits
of company promotion, they were applied with
even more spectacular emphasis than in Europe.
The Treasury announced its decision "to call this
issue 'the first Liberty loan'" because the proceeds "were to be used for the purpose of waging
war against autocracy,"[2] and as "Liberty loans"
our war-time obligations are classified at the present day.   Each of the twelve Federal Reserve
Banks created "Liberty loan committees" in
every city of its district; the work of solicitation
was then distributed to sub-committees, which
enlisted the personal co-operation of bankers,

---

[1] Finance Minister Helfferich, speech in German Reichstag,
Aug. 20, 1915.   *Frankfurter Zeitung*, Aug. 21.

[2] Treasury Report 1917, p. 5.

business men, bond houses, newspapers, press associations, even of fraternal organizations and the Boy and Girl Scouts. The Secretary of the Treasury personally visited twenty or more cities during the period allotted for subscriptions, making speeches for the loan in each.[1] In the campaign for the Fourth War loan of 1918, twenty-four railway trains traveled over the country with exhibits of captured war material, ordnance and ammunition, accompanied by veteran soldiers and sailors.[2] The designing, distributing, displaying of "Liberty loan posters" became in its way a new art and industry of the day.

It was in the unremitting personal appeal to large audiences, however, that the movement surpassed every previous demonstration of the kind. All-day "Liberty loan rallies" in public squares, where crowds of citizens were addressed by a series of well-known speakers, became a familiar incident of each successive canvass. An equally familiar incident was the calling for subscriptions from theatre audiences between the acts, after an impassioned appeal by a well-known actor or

[1] Treasury Report, 1917, p. 6.
[2] Treasury Report 1918, p. 63.

actress, a wounded soldier, or a Red Cross nurse.
In the closing week of the Fourth "Liberty loan
drive" of October, 1918, $4,800,000 was raised
from a single audience at Carnegie Hall when
Caruso, McCormack and Galli-Curci had sung
under the auspices of the Liberty Loan committee.   At an open-air meeting in Times Square,
New York, on the last day of the drive, $3,000,000
was subscribed after speeches by the Governor
and Mayor.   During that same week, whole pages
of advertising space were bought up in the city
newspapers and used for signed appeals from the
various trades and professions; one of them con-
taining an address to the people by the best-
known moving-picture stars.   The Treasury itself reported that, in the "Victory loan campaign"
of May, 1919, speeches were made by 5,000 well-
known men and women and "Liberty loan ser-
mons" delivered by 100,000 clergymen.[1]   In
each of the three last loan campaigns, President
Wilson proclaimed a special "Liberty Day" at
the climax of the "drive," and it was generally
observed as a holiday devoted to the final effort.[2]

In the longer retrospect, some of these expedi-

---

[1] Treasury Report 1919, p. 71.
[2] Treasury Report 1918, pp. 63–65.

ents seem curiously emotional, but of their practical effectiveness no doubt was ever entertained. The result was such as could not have been imagined in pre-war days. When the later war loans were offered, the plan was introduced of fixing the "quota" or share in the subscription expected from each state and Federal Reserve district, based on its estimated wealth and subscribing power, and rivalry as to which should most largely exceed its quota became a matter of high popular interest. In the third Liberty Loan campaign of April and May, 1918, every state exceeded its quota allotment, the excess ranging from 14 to 196 per cent and the oversubscription from \$2,148,000 in Nevada to \$165,638,000 in New York.[1] Even the first war loan of 1917, which the Treasury had fixed at \$2,000,000,000, elicited applications for \$3,035,226,850 in four million separate subscriptions.[2] The second loan asked for \$3,000,000,000, and \$4,617,532,300 was applied for by 9,400,000 subscribers.[3] For the third loan, in May, 1918, the offering was \$3,000,-000,000 and the applications \$4,158,599,100.[4]

[1] Treasury Report 1918, p. 8.
[2] Treasury Report 1917, p. 6.
[3] Treasury Report 1917, pp. 10 and 11.
[4] Treasury Report 1918, p. 7.

For the fourth loan of October, 1918, the Treasury announced a $6,000,000,000 issue and $6,992,-927,100 was taken;[1] the number of individual subscriptions to the third loan being 18,376,815 and to the fourth loan 22,777,680.[2]

Including the $4,500,000,000 "Victory loan" of April, 1919, which was floated five months after the armistice and oversubscribed by $749,-000,000,[3] and excluding short-time certificates of indebtedness put out in anticipation of loans or taxes, the five war-time bond issues of the United States aggregated $21,326,777,000.[4] The total public debt, which had stood at $1,282,000,000 on April 5, 1917,[5] reached its maximum of $26,596,-000,000 on August 31, 1919.[6] This increase of $25,314,000,000 in two years and four months compares with an increase of Great Britain's public debt, in the four years and eight months between August 1, 1914, and March 31, 1919, amounting to £6,871,700,000,[7] or $33,400,000,000 with sterling reckoned at par value. The war-time addition to our own public debt averaged

---

[1] Treasury Report 1919, p. 31.   [2] *Ibid.*

[3] *Ibid.*, p. 52.

[4] *Ibid.*, p. 30.   [5] *Ibid.*, p. 31.

[6] Treasury Report 1920, p. 23.

[7] London *Economist*, April 5, 1919, p. 555.

$11,000,000,000 per annum, against Great Britain's average annual increase of $8,000,000,000.

Such an achievement raises the double inquiry, how it was possible for the community to obtain the prodigious sums of capital involved in the subscription, and how the drawing of that capital out of the general fund affected the country's economic condition. It was quite true that Europe's economic resources did not appear to have been paralyzed or exhausted by the unprecedented subscriptions to the war loans of 1915 and 1916; it was also true that the wealth which had accrued to America in its period of neutrality should have created exceptionally abundant sources for obtaining capital. But it was equally evident that our own country's industrial expansion in every conceivable direction, contrasting with Europe's relinquishment of all activities for other than war purposes, had made necessary proportionately larger requisitions on both credit and capital. The familiar explanation for the obtaining of the subscription money was that the nation-wide campaign had gained access to surplus earnings and accumulated savings of a population of 100,000,000, by far the greater number of whom had never invested in a government bond before.

Undoubtedly this was the main key to what might otherwise have appeared an economic mystery. There were other although less plainly visible explanations, however; of which one, and not the least important, was subscription by powerful incorporated companies from their surplus funds. The United States Steel Corporation, for instance, took $127,950,000 of the four Liberty loans,[1] and the total of company subscriptions ran to many times that amount. One interesting result of that process was the subsequent payment of dividends to shareholders by numerous companies in the shape of Liberty bonds.[2] As early as February, 1918, the Treasury requested all banks and trust companies to reserve out of their gross resources about 1 per cent to lend against short-term United States loans,[3] and the institutions not only complied very generally with that request, but became immensely large purchasers of long-term bonds. In 1916 the national banks of the United

---

[1] U. S. Steel Corporation, Annual Report for 1918, p. 34.

[2] American Woolen Co., Annual reports for 1918 and 1919; extra dividend announcements, 1918 and 1919, of American Hide & Leather Co., American Shipbuilding Co., American Steel Foundries Co., Mexican Petroleum Co., Pan-American Petroleum Co., Underwood Typewriter Co., Union Bag & Paper Co.

[3] Letter of Secretary McAdoo, Feb. 6, 1918.

States owned $729,777,000 United States bonds, mostly as security for national bank note circulation.[1]   In the Autumn of 1919 they reported holdings of $1,186,392,000 Liberty bonds and Victory notes, in addition to $1,147,920,000 short-term certificates.[2]   With banks outside the national system, holdings of United States bonds rose from $7,462,325 in 1916 to $985,945,000 in 1919.[3]

But bank credit was invoked in yet another way to increase subscriptions to the war loans.   From the outset, a great number of individual subscribers had not only drawn on their accumulated savings but had borrowed in anticipation of prospective income and had subscribed the proceeds.   In the loan campaigns of 1918, when doubt arose as to whether the remaining reservoir of free capital was adequate to cover the subscription, concerted efforts were made by the "Liberty Loan committees" to extend such use of credit.   Before the $6,000,000,000 loan of October, 1918, was offered, Congress by special act enlarged the authorized powers of national banks to lend on

[1] Treasury Report, 1916, p. 479.
[2] Treasury Report, 1919, pp. 939 and 954.
[3] *Ibid.*, p. 1044.

3

Liberty bond collateral,[1] and practically all large national banks, as a result of pressure by the loan committees and of special facilities granted by the Federal Reserve,[2] announced through public advertisements to subscribers that "we will lend you money secured by the Fourth Liberty Loan at 4¼ per cent [the interest rate on the loan itself] for 90 days, with renewals at the same rate covering the entire period of one year." The extent to which subscribers used this privilege was shown by the increase in the amount of war bonds held as collateral for loans at all the national banks, from $340,757,000 in March, 1918, to $1,213,030,000 in September, 1919.[3]

This expedient was wholly justifiable in so far as it concerned the assigning in advance of an assured future income. It had the precedent of the Bank of England, which announced in the British war loan canvass of 1914 that it would lend on the new bonds at the issue price "at a rate not exceeding 1 per cent below the current bank rate" (which was then 5 per cent) and that "repayment will not be demanded by the bank

---

[1] Treasury Report, 1918, pp. 74 and 175.
[2] Annual Report Federal Reserve Board for 1919, p. 68.
[3] Treasury Report, 1918, p. 905; 1919, p. 955.

before March 1, 1918, provided interest is punctually paid."[1] But in the case of the American subscriptions on the basis of bank borrowings the longer results, as we shall presently see, were by no means fortunate. Many subscribers on that basis overlooked the time limit of October, 1919, fixed in the offer of banks to carry individual subscriptions to the Fourth War Loan of 1918, or else neglected to save their subsequent income; with the result that, when the year had expired in which they paid on their bank loans only the rate of interest carried by the war bonds, they found themselves confronted simultaneously with a rising money market and a fall in the price of Liberty bonds. There were other and even more troublesome ultimate results of the huge credits, created by bank loans on Liberty bond collateral, and they were not unforeseen by experienced bankers. But in 1918, rightly or wrongly, the policy was defended as a necessity in a critical situation.[2]

Through these expedients, supplemented by immense enthusiasm on the part of the general

---

[1] *Stock Exchange Weekly Official Intelligence*, London, Dec. 26, 1914. *Financial Chronicle*, Jan. 23, 1915, p. 269.
[2] Annual Report Federal Reserve Board for 1919, pp. 1 and 2.

public, $10,000,000,000 was raised from the invest-
ment market in the first twelve months of our participation in the war. The sum was greater than
any American would have deemed possible a year
before; yet it still would not have covered the estimated or actual expenditure of the period, especially as two-thirds of the subscription to the
War Loan of May, 1918, was not payable until
after the close of the fiscal year, and the difference
had to be bridged by the war-taxation act. All
responsible public men recognized that the bulk
of the additional revenue required, which ran into
the thousands of millions, would have to be provided from a tax on incomes and business profits.

The last important requisition of the kind, that
of the Spanish War of 1898, had been financed,
so far as revenue was concerned, by addition of
excise taxes of various descriptions; but that brief
and localized conflict increased total public expenditure in the year by only $161,700,000,[1]
and the income tax was not then a feasible expedient. Such a tax had been imposed in the Civil
War and for a short period thereafter, but it was
clumsily assessed, in order to conform with the
fundamental law, and it never produced more than

[1] Treasury Report, 1899; pp. xx., cxl.

$72,900,000 in any single year.[1] A generation later, the law which attempted to revive the income tax in 1894 was pronounced unconstitutional by the Supreme Court.[2] In February, 1913, however, ratification of the Sixteenth Amendment to the Constitution, declaring that "Congress shall have power to lay and collect taxes on incomes, from whatever source derived," opened the way for this form of revenue. It was in October of the same year that the first effective Federal income tax law since Civil War days was enacted.

It fixed the moderate rate of 1 per cent, with a graduated surtax rising from 1 per cent on incomes between $20,000 and $50,000 to 6 per cent on incomes over $500,000. This tax had produced $60,710,000 revenue.[3] In September, 1916, when Congress was moving to fortify the public revenue on the eve of war, the basic income-tax rate was raised to 2 per cent and the highest surtax to 13 per cent; that tax produced $359,681,000."[4]

The War Revenue Act, which after prolonged discussion became law on October 3, 1917, fixed

[1] Treasury Report, 1866.
[2] *Forty Years of American Finance*, p. 228.
[3] Treasury Report, 1917, p. 56.
[4] *Ibid.*, p. 63.

4 per cent as the basic income tax and graduated the surtax rate from a minimum of 1 per cent
to a maximum of 50 per cent; it increased the tax
on corporation incomes to 6 per cent and it imposed an "excess profits tax" on the business
earnings of individuals and corporations, ranging
from 20 per cent of a defined net income not exceeding 15 per cent of invested capital to 60 per
cent on income exceeding 33 per cent of such
investment.   This new and very heavy taxation, supplemented by increased excise taxes
imposed on every kind of luxury—club dues,
railway tickets, admissions to amusements, Pull-
man berths, chewing-gum, phonograph records,
telephone and telegraph messages—was expected
to produce $3,400,000,000 annual revenue, of
which $2,427,000,000 was assigned to the income
and excess profits division.[1]   In the result, the
forecast was much more than realized.   Receipts
from those two kinds of taxes in the fiscal year
ending with June, 1918, were $2,938,000,000.
Including other taxes such as customs duties,
carried over from the legislation of preceding year,
the period's total revenue was $4,174,000,000,[2]

[1] Treasury Report, 1917, p. 71.
[2] Treasury Report, 1918, p. 126.

and total receipts from government loans were
$9,268,000,000.[1]

From these sources the Treasury obtained
$13,442,000,000 during the fiscal year, to meet
an actual public expenditure (if the $4,739,000,-
000 advanced to foreign governments is included)
of $13,700,000,000.[1]   Annual public expenditure
by our government, prior to the European war,
had never exceeded the $1,297,555,000 of the
twelvemonth ending with June, 1865, when the
War of Secession was in its culminating stage; it
had ranged from $525,000,000 to $700,000,000
during the decade before 1914.   The war was
destined to carry both public expenditure and
revenue from taxation far above even the figures
of the fiscal year beginning in the middle of 1917.

In the subsequent fiscal year, half of which
elapsed before the armistice, total public expenditure rose to $18,952,000,000, or five billions
more than in the first year of our participation in
the European conflict.   With these immensely
increased requisitions in sight, the income tax
rate was raised by the Act of September, 1918,
to 12 per cent on all incomes exceeding $4,000,
as against the 4 per cent rate of the 1917 stat-

[1] Treasury Report, 1918, p. 128.   [1] *Ibid.*, p. 129.

ute, the highest surtax rate being advanced to 65
per cent and the range of excess profits tax rates
being fixed at 35 to 70 per cent, as against the
20 to 60 per cent of the year before. The total
cost of the war to the United States, in the two
and a half years between April 7, 1917, and completion of demobilization in October, 1919, has
been calculated by the Treasury at $32,830,000,-
000;[1] which was not only nearly ten times as great
as the $3,344,000,000 expenditure of the United
States government in the four years of the Civil
War,[2] but exactly twice as large as the sum total
of our entire federal expenditure from 1789 to
the end of the nineteenth century.[3]

One highly important precedent was fixed by
the program of war finance in 1917. When the
United States entered the conflict, animated controversy arose at once over the extent to which
the war should be paid for by the tax-payers of
that day or by future generations which would
have to provide for interest and principal on the
long-term loans. Concerning that question the
President had merely said, in his war message of

---

[1] Treasury Report, 1919, p. 25.
[2] Treasury Report, 1865, p. 257.
[3] Treasury Report, 1900, p. cxxx.

April 2, that "it would be most unwise to base
the credits" for the war "entirely on money borrowed"; but he had rested his argument on the
evils "which would be likely to arise out of the
inflation which would be produced by vast loans."
The experience of our own War of Secession had
in that regard been unfortunate; in the first
twelve months of that conflict, more than nine-
tenths of the public expenditure was defrayed by
borrowings. Even in the fiscal year 1865, after
repeated increase in the federal taxes, only $335,-
000,000 was drawn from ordinary revenue, while
$1,475,000,000 was raised by loans.[1] When war
began in 1914, European governments had not
done much better. Great Britain, in the first
full fiscal year of the World War (covering the
twelve months beginning April 1, 1915), enlarged
the public revenue by £110,000,000 over the preceding fiscal year, but total government expenditure
increased during the same period nearly £1,000,-
000,000.[2] Germany had relied almost entirely
on loans, assuming openly that the public debt
incurred would be paid off by a war indemnity

[1] Treasury Report, 1865, page 93.
[2] Accounts of British Exchequer for year ending March 31,
1916; London *Economist*, April 8, 1916, p. 674.

imposed on Germany's antagonists after their
defeat.[1]

Since $4,174,000,000 of the $13,442,000,000
raised by our government in the first fiscal year
of its participation in the war was obtained from
public revenue, it followed that approximately
one-third of the cost was met by tax-payers and
two-thirds from the loan market. At the end of
that first year, the Treasury publicly announced
that this policy would be continuous,[2] and in the
long run the purpose was achieved. A post-war
official estimate calculated that 32 per cent of
the expenditure for the entire period of war and
demobilization had been met from ordinary revenue.[3] Even this percentage, which was much
higher than any known precedent of history, was
pronounced too low by critics who insisted that the
larger part of the war costs ought to be placed
on the shoulders of contemporary tax-payers;
the argument being, not only that danger of
inflated credit through the piling-up of government loans would thereby be diminished, but that

[1] Speech of Finance Minister Helfferich to Reichstag, August
20, 1915; London *Economist*, Sept. 4, 1915, p. 358.
[2] Secretary McAdoo to Chairman Kitchin of H. R. Ways &
Means Committee, June 5, 1918; Treasury Report, 1918, p. 46.
[3] Treasury Report, 1919, p. 25.

the people who elected to engage in war ought not to be allowed to shift so great a part of the burden to posterity.

But to this contention the reasonable answer was made, first, that at some point mounting war taxation would become so far confiscatory as to cripple the operations of legitimate war-time industry and, second, that the 32 per cent calculation included in war costs the $4,739,000,000 advanced to foreign governments in the fiscal year 1918 and the grand total of $9,406,000,000 thus disbursed between April, 1917, and November, 1919. Expenditure for that purpose resulted in a valid indebtedness of foreign governments which was eventually payable, interest and principal, to the United States government, the proceeds of such payment being by law allotted to redemption of the war debt.[1] To raise by taxation the money to make such loans would, it was forcibly argued, be a palpable injustice. But if advances to foreign governments are eliminated from the calculation, it will be found that the remaining war expenditure was actually covered up to 49⅝ per cent by ordinary revenue in the

[1] War Loan Act of April 24, 1917, Section 3; War Loan Act of September 24, 1917, Section 3.

fiscal year 1918, and up to 43 per cent in the whole war period.[1]

What, then, was the effect on the financial and economic organism of these utterly unprecedented drafts on private capital and credit? In the light of past experience, there were some unpleasant possibilities. Diversion of private capital on such a scale from its ordinary uses might cause extreme scarcity of money; withdrawal of capital from other investments for subscription to the war loans might completely demoralize the Stock Exchanges. Financial tradition taught that such immensely heavy borrowings might result in very high money rates and a great decline in outstanding stocks and bonds. Yet neither result accompanied the war borrowings of 1917 and 1918. Even at the climax of war activities in the Autumn of 1918, the rate on ordinary demand or time loans never rose in Wall Street above 6 per cent.[2] Although private corporations were at times compelled to put an interest rate of 7 or 7½ per cent on new issues of their own securities,[3] the average price of a selected list of high-grade outstanding

---

[1] Treasury Report, 1918, p. 4; 1919, p. 26.
[2] Treasury Report, 1918, p. 855.
[3] *Financial Chronicle*, "Annual Review of 1918," p. xviii.

bonds ranged on the New York Stock Exchange even in 1918 between 75⅝ and 82⅜, whereas the same bonds had at one time averaged 81½ in 1915 and 85½ in the pre-war year 1913.[1]

The first explanation of this seeming paradox,—relatively easy money and relatively firm security markets in the face of the prodigious drain of capital into war uses,—was the low interest rate borne by the Liberty bonds and the maintenance of their price on the open markets. The fact that those 3½, 4, and 4¼ per cent bonds held during 1917 between par and 97 and during 1918 between par and 92¼, naturally sustained the price of other securities with a higher interest rate. But the low rate for money on the open market was the larger cause, and for that the attitude of the Federal Reserve was of paramount importance. The official rediscount rate of the Reserve banks was kept at 4½ per cent and a still lower rate was granted on rediscounts secured by war loan collateral. Discount rates were fixed with the primary object of assisting the Treasury operations; the policy of the Reserve banks was "necessarily co-ordinated . . . with Treasury require-

[1] N. Y. *Times*, "Bond Averages," Jan. 1, 1919.

ments and policies."[1] This statement tacitly
accepted the banking community's judgment that
the government's loans were placed at a rate below
what would normally have been warranted, under
all the circumstances, by the investment market.

Banking opinion of the day was that, without the
artificial measures adopted to keep down money
rates, the war loans would have paid 5 to 6 per
cent interest to investors, instead of the 3½ or
4¼ per cent at which they were allotted. But
the actual placing of the loans at those higher
rates would have necessitated additional annual
public expenditure for interest of about $350,-
000,000 and the higher rates would have caused
such depreciation in other outstanding investment securities as possibly to impede subscription
to the war loans; therefore the policy of low rates
was established in the War Loan Act and pursued to the full extent that circumstances admitted. But the quite inevitable penalty was
paid, as we shall see, in the money market and
the government bond market of the two years
after return of peace.

In order to render its co-operation effective, it
was necessary for the Federal Reserve to hold

[1] Annual Report Federal Reserve Board for 1918.

itself ready for an immense and immediate expansion of its credit facilities. In undertaking to keep the rate for money at what was in reality an artificially low figure, the Reserve banks had to be prepared to take over commercial loans of private banks at the rate prescribed. They were also confronted with the certainty that these private banks, called upon simultaneously to purchase the Treasury's short-term obligations and to provide for the heavily increased war-time requirements of their clients, would be compelled to enlarge very rapidly their own reserve credits at the Federal banks, against which the Federal institutions had to maintain on their own account a stipulated percentage of cash reserve.

When the United States went to war, the Reserve system's cash holdings, mostly built up with gold transferred by member institutions to the Federal banks, or pledged against circulating notes, amounted to 84¾ per cent of circulation and net deposits, but the gold pledged against note circulation was then carried as a special fund, so that technically the reserve ratio was only 51 ⅜ per cent. Since the law required only 40 per cent gold against the notes and 35 per cent cash against deposits, even this was suf-

ficient margin for the moment. But a very
rapid increase in such liabilities was clearly foreshadowed by the war finance plans. In actual
fact, subsequent war-time necessities caused expansion of the system's discounts from $100,-
663,000 in April, 1917, to $956,072,000 at the
end of 1917 and $2,006,611,000 at the end of
1918.[1] If, as a result of the period's increased
rediscounts, deposits credited to member banks
by the Federal Reserve had only doubled (which
would have meant an increase of $758,000,000
over April, 1917) and if the other items, including
the system's cash reserve, had remained unchanged, the ratio of reserve would have fallen far
below the minimum fixed by the Reserve Law. As
it turned out, the increase of such deposit liabilities
during war-time was twice as large as that figure.

The Bank of England had been confronted with
a similar dilemma when war began in 1914;
indeed, its case was worse than that of our Federal Reserve, because it had to guarantee and
assume at once something like $600,000,000 of
pre-war foreign bills due to British merchants,
which had become non-collectible because of

[1] Reserve Board's weekly statements; Apr. 6, 1917; Dec. 28,
1917; Dec. 27, 1918.

the outbreak of hostilities. The London bank met the situation, first by allowing its ratio of reserve to deposits to fall to 15 per cent, against a traditional pre-war minimum of 40, but second by suspension of redemption of Bank of England notes in gold. Neither recourse was considered by the Federal Reserve in 1917; the question of maintaining gold payments was regarded as having been settled by the United States in 1914, and the immense accumulation of gold in this country during 1915 and 1916 pointed distinctly away from a policy of suspension.

Between November, 1914, when the Federal Reserve was established, and the week when the United States declared war in 1917, the total gold supply of the country was estimated to have increased $1,253,500,000;[1] yet on April 6, 1917, the Reserve banks reported a gold reserve of only $565,102,000. There was no probability of immediate and automatic increase, first because all legal requirements for the deposit with the Federal institutions of the reserves of existing member banks had already been observed;[2] second,

[1] Treasury's Money Circulation statements, Nov. 1, 1914; April 1, 1917.
[2] Annual Report Federal Reserve Board for 1916; Feb. 3, 1917.

because, for reasons which I shall presently point out, import of foreign gold had ceased with our entry into the war. We have seen that in 1914 certain European belligerents, notably France and Germany, had acquired for the central banking reserve very large amounts of such outside gold holdings by appealing to the people's patriotism to exchange their gold for notes of the national bank. The United States government used a different method. In 1917, a great part of the gold outside the Federal Reserve was held or controlled by private American banking institutions; $715,000,000 being reported as in the vaults of such institutions,[1] and $390,765,000 being deposited by member banks with the Federal Reserve as a special fund to secure Reserve notes issued to them.

The government now undertook to obtain all this gold for the central reserve through the operation of the banking law itself. That purpose was effected through two amendments to the Federal Reserve Act, discussed and voted by Congress eleven weeks after the declaration of war and destined, then and afterward, to become

[1] Comptroller of Currency's statement as of June 20, 1917; Treasury Report, 1917, p. 690.

a focus of animated economic controversy. When the Reserve Law was originally passed in December, 1913, it provided that member banks might hold in their own vaults or in other banking depositories a stipulated percentage of their cash reserve, the remainder to be placed with the Federal Reserve. Under this provision, more than one-half of the reserve thus required for member banks was carried elsewhere than in the Federal banks.[1] The first Congressional amendment of June 22, 1917, reduced the percentage of reserve required for such private banks but directed that the whole of the cash reserve prescribed should be kept with a Federal Reserve bank. Thus transferred, the gold or lawful money would be added to the cash reserve carried against their own liabilities by the Federal banks, and it amounted in all to something over $250,000,000.[2]

The second amendment altered the status of reserve against circulating notes. The original act had provided that member banks when taking out note circulation should deposit, as security for such notes, an equivalent amount in ap-

[1] Reserve Board Annual Report, 1916.
[2] Annual Report Federal Reserve Board for 1917.

proved commercial obligations, and that a 40 per cent gold reserve should be maintained by the Federal Bank against outstanding notes "not offset by gold or lawful money deposited with the Federal Reserve agent." During the large gold import movement of 1915 and 1916, note circulation taken out was mostly offset, up to its full face value, by gold thus deposited. The notes were practically on the footing of the government's gold certificates and the gold held for that account amounted at the date when the law was amended, as we have seen, to $390,765,000.[1]

Being considered in the light of special collateral for the notes, it had not been counted as part of the system's active cash reserve. The amendment of June 22, 1917, however, provided that thereafter, "when the Reserve agent holds gold or gold certificates as collateral for Federal Reserve notes," such gold "shall be counted as part of the gold reserve which such bank is required to maintain against its Federal Reserve notes in actual circulation." The effect of this new provision was to carry this $390,765,000 gold into the system's general cash reserve, so that only 40 per cent in gold need be pledged against 100 per cent of

[1] Reserve Board statement, June 15, 1917.

notes. In the fortnight following the passage of these amendments, and as a result of the two changes in the law, the active gold reserve of the Federal Banks was officially stated to have increased from \$590,948,000 to \$1,294,512,000.[1] Whereas the system's total ratio of cash reserve to note and deposit liabilities had been reckoned at 51⅜ per cent on April 5 and at only 40⅞ per cent on June 15, it worked out at 75⅜ per cent on June 29.

This sweeping extension of the system's power to increase its discounts and circulating notes inevitably became subject of much hostile criticism, based on the possibilities of inflation both of credit and currency.[2] The action was taken, however, with a clear view to all its implications. It was defended as an absolutely essential measure, if the country's financial structure were to be properly strengthened for the unprecedented impending demands on credit.[3] The Treasury described the amendments as a matter of urgent and critical necessity;[4] the Congressional com-

---

[1] Reserve Board statements, June 15 and June 29, 1917.

[2] *Financial Chronicle*, June 23, 1917, p. 2480.

[3] Senate speech of J. D. Phelan, Apr. 30, 1917; H. R. speech of Carter Glass, Apr. 30, 1917.

[4] Letter of Secretary McAdoo to Senator Owen, May 5, 1917.

mittee reported the bill unanimously. Its provisions had been approved by the Advisory Council of eminent private bankers created by the Federal Reserve law, and had not been opposed by any private bank.[1] In retrospect, indeed, it is not easy to see how the services which the Reserve system performed in the financing of the war would have been possible without such extension of its credit facilities.

Whether all the changes of 1917 in the basis of reserves would have been adopted without the war emergency, may possibly be doubted. It should be observed, however, that the gradual gathering into the Federal Reserve of the gold held in private bank vaults as part of the member banks' reserve had been contemplated before the war. Even the original Reserve Act had fixed a date at which part of those reserve holdings should be thus transferred, and the amendment of 1917 merely anticipated the date prescribed. The Reserve Board had advocated that change of date as early as the preceding November. On the ground that the country's reserves of gold were "not used most effectively when they are in the vaults of a large number of banks scattered

[1] H. R. speech of Carter Glass, Apr. 30, 1917.

all over the country " and that "the United States should be in a position to face conditions which may call for an outflow of gold, without disturbances of our own or the world's business," the Board's annual report for 1916 had strongly urged that member banks be required to maintain with the Federal Reserve itself "amounts adequate to supply the necessary reserve basis."[1]

As far back as February, 1916, after pointing out that when note issues were secured up to face value by gold pledged by a member bank, the gold was not controlled by the Federal Reserve, the Board had formally pressed for a change in the law whereby gold thus deposited as collateral for note circulation should "count as part of the reserve required by the notes."[2]   Both proposals, therefore, antedated the period of war finance, and neither can be described as wholly a response to war-time necessities. It was, indeed, not altogether unreasonable to argue that even the transfer of gold, from a segregated account as collateral for notes to a place in the system's general reserve, did not depart from the spirit of the original act; whose main proviso for the note

[1] Annual Report Federal Reserve Board for 1916; p. 26.
[2] *Ibid.* for 1915, p. 22.

issues, requiring deposit of approved commercial obligations "in amount equal to the sum of the Federal Reserve notes thus applied for," sustained by "reserves in gold of not less than 40 per cent," was recognized in the Amendment of 1917.

It will now be evident, however, in what manner the Federal Reserve was able to provide the basis for increase of nearly $2,000,000,000 in the system's rediscounts during war-time, without an advance in money rates and without a fall in the ratio of reserve to liabilities below the lawful minimum. Along with the resultant expansion of credit facilities by the central banking organism, total loans of the national banks increased from $8,751,000,000 in May, 1917, to $9,918,-200,000 in November, 1918, the armistice month. Loans of all private banking institutions of the United States were larger in the middle of 1918 by $4,702,000,000 than they had been two years before.[1]   As a result the country's war-time trade, reflected in checks drawn on the banks during 1918 greater in amount by $70,400,000,000, or 26 per cent, than in 1916 and by $159,200,000,000, or 90 per cent, than in 1915,[2] was conducted with

[1] Treasury Report, 1917, p. 566; 1919, pp. 926 and 1070.
[2] *Financial Chronicle*, Jan. 18, 1919, p. 208.

no evidence of strain on credit. The comparatively easy money market did not help the Stock Exchange, on which a decline of 30 per cent. or more occurred during 1917 in the shares both of railway and industrial properties. The particular cause for that phenomenon I shall presently examine; but nowhere else in the field of finance and industry did the country's activities seem at the start to be checked or crippled by the war. Whether such immunity could continue was presently to be tested, with results which were certainly unforeseen in the spring of 1917.

CHAPTER V

MOBILIZATION OF AMERICAN INDUSTRY

THE American people entered the war in a mood of energy and purpose which reflected the government's grasp of the situation, and contrasted impressively with the apathy towards the European conflict that had seemed to characterize a great part of the country in our period of neutrality. Acquiescence in the government's program was unanimous; even the German-American sentiment of 1915 and 1916 on the side of Germany had entirely disappeared. The "almost bewildering stream" of applicants to the War Department, offering service of every kind, was described by the Department itself as "a superb and inspiring spectacle."[1] Into the emergency public service at Washington there was instantly drawn a volunteer body of "dollar-a-year men," recruited from experienced business

[1] Annual Report War Department for 1917, p. 11.

executives in all parts of the country;[1] these men were destined to play an extremely important rôle in the subsequent conduct of the war. Under the supervision of 4,557 Selective Boards, organized through the voluntary service of private citizens in every town, the draft proceeded with the utmost smoothness and expedition, and with no resistance.[2] Before the end of 1917, the new recruits in service numbered 516,000;[3] for their training, 16 army cantonments, each with 1,000 to 2,000 buildings, had been constructed with almost unimaginable rapidity.[4] Whereas the old army had numbered 190,000 in March, 1917, the new army reached 3,665,000 in November, 1918.[5] Its growth in sixteen months, the War Department pointed out, had been twice as rapid as that of the British army in the three-year period between the summer of 1914 and the summer of 1917.[6] The country appeared to have been transformed overnight, both in spirit and action, into an efficient war machine.

This nation-wide attitude was no doubt attributable primarily to the impulse of patriotism;

---

[1] Clarkson, *Industrial America in the World War*, pp. 76, 77.
[2] Annual Report War Department for 1917, pp. 16–18.
[3] Report for 1918, p. 16.   [4] Report for 1917, p. 29.
[5] Report for 1918, p. 13.   [6] *Ibid.*, p. 12.

it was reassertion, half a century afterward, of
the instinct which had so suddenly, and to many
people so unexpectedly, displayed itself in the
North during 1861 after the fall of Sumter. Possibly it resulted also, in the West especially, from
a spirit of individual and political adventure. In
the East it represented to a very considerable
extent the taking-up of a duty, from the performance of which the people had for two years been
unwillingly restrained by circumstance. But in
all parts of the country, there was manifest belief that the time had arrived for powerful intervention in the European conflict in order to put
an end to it, and that the United States possessed
both the opportunity and the capacity to carry
out that purpose. This conviction led to general
belief in speedy termination of the war, now that
America was engaged in it.

The American people had, to be sure, already
seen the confident prediction of experienced financiers, that the war could not last two years from
August, 1914, without being ended by economic
exhaustion of all the belligerents, disproved by
actual extension of the scale of military and financial operations long after the date assigned. But
for that very reason the idea was now positively

entertained that Germany must be near the end of her financial tether and that, with the immense American resources of capital and man-power thrown into the scale, her early surrender would be inevitable. Events proved that in the main this belief was right. But it led to the overlooking of the forces which could be called into play by a desperate belligerent for a final effort and it was therefore undoubtedly responsible, in the earlier months of 1917, for the underrating of the strain that was about to be imposed on America's economic organism. Under other circumstances, this prevalent belief might have led to ill-judged public policies or inadequate governmental preparation after our declaration of war, and the country was fortunate that the Administration had not misconceived the scope of its own necessary effort. But the general public's idea of the situation did not altogether prepare its mind for the later experiences of 1917 and 1918.

Failure to grasp the realities in that respect was evident in the expectations widely entertained, early in 1917, regarding the financial and industrial situation. On the face of things it was not difficult to argue that the prosperity of the United States would be enhanced, not impaired, by the country's entry into the conflict. The spectacular trade revival of 1915 and 1916 had been based on the inpour of war orders for products of American agriculture and manufacture. Demand for war purposes would now be immensely increased because our producers, with their enlarged plant and acreage, had still to provide for the needs of our allies while also executing the new and prodigiously large war orders for the American government. This double requisition was made certain by the well-understood fact that the $3,000,000,000 advances of capital, granted in April by the Treasury to the European governments, were to be spent in the United States for American food and war material. The draft, to be sure, was removing from productive occupation five out of every hundred male citizens of the United States, and the requisition on capital for the war loans was recognized as encroaching upon the fund which would otherwise have been applied to industrial uses. Yet the thousands of millions of dollars borrowed by the government were themselves poured back in the form of orders for material, and no sign whatever appeared of the cramping of productive capacity.

All visible indications, indeed, pointed to production, manufacture and trade on a scale not approximated in magnitude even in 1916. Every branch of industry was affected. The mere construction of cantonments and training camps called for an expenditure within sixteen weeks, for building materials and other supplies, half as great as the largest outlay of any single twelvemonth during the original construction of the Panama Canal and seven times as great as the total costs of building in the City of Washington during the fiscal year 1917, which had surpassed all precedent for such activities.[1] Writing in November, 1917, less than eight months after our government had entered the struggle, the Secretary of War reported that "of shoes more than two million pairs have already been purchased or are in process of delivery, of blankets 17 million, of flannel shirting more than 33 million yards, of melton cloth more than 50 million yards, of various kinds of duck, for shelter tents and other necessary uses, more than 125 million yards."[2]

This was all additional to the sources of the trade of 1916. During our nineteen months of hostil-

[1] Chairman Emergency Construction Committee to Quartermaster-General, May 25, 1917.
[2] War Department, Annual Report 1917, p. 44.

ities the War Department bought 82,500 trucks, 16,000 motor cars, 27,000 motor-cycles and 2,137,025 rifles, and its total purchases of clothing and footwear for army purposes involved payments of $514,000,000.[1] Orders placed for construction material and rolling stock, solely for use at European ports in preparing landing facilities for our Expeditionary Force, reached a sum "five times as great as all the purchases of material, equipment and supplies made for the Panama Canal."[2] These are only incidental particulars of the new orders which our manufacturers were instantly called upon to turn out.

So sudden and so immense an increase in home requirements made it impossible to keep the export trade in war materials wholly up to the magnitude of 1916; shipments of such materials during the twelve months beginning with June, 1917, decreased something like $750,000,000 from the preceding fiscal year.[3] But even this reduction cut down the period's total export of domestic products only $388,500,000 and left it $1,566,-000,000 in excess of 1915. In fact, as the Com-

---

[1] War Department, Annual Report 1918, pp. 41, 45, 59.
[2] *Ibid.*, p. 36.
[3] Annual Report Department of Commerce for 1918, p. 160.

merce Department pointed out in 1918, the fiscal year's $400,000,000 decrease in trade with Russia, due to the Bolshevist revolution in that country, would of itself account for all of the falling-off in total exports as compared with the year before.[1] Exports summarized in these comparisons, it should be observed, did not include the large supplies sent abroad on army and navy transports for the Expeditionary Force.[2]

The magnitude of this requisition on the country's productive capacity was very soon tangibly apparent. Steel production, in which the highest pre-war annual achievement was 31,300,000 tons and which had reached 42,773,000 in 1916, rose in 1917 to 45,000,000.[3] During the period from August 1, 1914, to April 1, 1917, the United States Steel Corporation had turned out for military purposes, practically all in behalf of the European belligerents, 6,067,640 tons; in the much shorter period from April 1, 1917, to December 31, 1918, it delivered 10,339,750 tons, exclusive of 2,042,070 manufactured in 1918 for the Railway Administration.[4] Consumption of

[1] Annual Report Department of Commerce for 1918, p. 156.
[2] *Ibid.*, pp. 156, 160.
[3] Annual Reports, American Iron & Steel Institute.
[4] Annual Report U. S. Steel Corporation for 1918, p. 30.

cotton by the home textile trade in the cotton year ending with July, 1918, although slightly less than in the preceding season, was a million bales beyond the highest pre-war record.[1]

The largest traffic carried on American railways in any year before the war was 2,058,035,487 tons, in the calendar year 1913; from which it had risen to 2,225,943,388 in 1916. It reached 2,270,035,053 in our own first war year and 2,305,-824,940 in 1918.[2] The farmers shared to the full in this enormous business. Actual yield of wheat in each of those two years was less by nearly 400,000,000 bushels than in the great harvest of 1915; but the higher prices brought the estimated value of the 1917 crop $335,800,000 above that of 1915 and $258,000,000 over that of 1916, and the crop of 1918 was valued at $596,000,000 more than the 1917 harvest.[3] No cotton crops in the history of the United States had ever commanded such an aggregate purchase price as those of 1917 and 1918.[4] Before the European war, the highest selling value ever placed on all the

[1] Census Estimates, Aug., 1918.
[2] Interstate Commerce Commission, Annual Reports 1913, 1916, 1917, 1918.
[3] Year Book, U. S. Department of Agriculture for 1918, p. 461.
[4] *Ibid.* p. 531.

American agricultural crops combined, in any single year, was the $6,138,000,000 of 1913. The Agricultural Department's estimate for the harvests of 1916 had been $9,054,000,000. In 1917, notwithstanding the decreased yield of wheat, its estimate was $13,479,000,000, and in 1918 $14,222,000,000.[1]

Judged by the criterion of all previous years, so extraordinary an increase of productive activities, in a market of almost unlimited purchasing and consuming capacity and with average prices rising, should have guaranteed a period of quite unprecedented American prosperity. In the light of the same financial precedent, the mere prospect of such trade achievement ought to have found reflection in a steady movement of foreign exchange in favor of New York and in a rapidly advancing stock market. We have seen with what vigor both of these movements proceeded when the European war orders were placed in 1915. Yet an exactly contrary movement occurred in 1917. Foreign exchange rates on every important neutral market moved with great rapidity against New York after our declaration of war. Prices on the Stock Exchange, when the

[1] Year Book, U. S. Department of Agriculture for 1918, p. 671.

sweeping decline of December, 1916, had spent itself, fluctuated uncertainly in the following month, but in February, 1917, on news of rupture of diplomatic relations with the German government, industrial shares fell 10 to 20 points.

In April, following the war message, they broke 5 to 10 points further. Instead of recovery on signs of vigorous prosecution of the war, an exceedingly rapid decline in the autumn months brought prices of nearly all active stocks 30 to 40 per cent below those with which the war year had begun. Prices for fifty active railway and industrial shares actually stood in the last week of 1917 at almost exactly the average reached by them on July 30, 1914, when Europe was desperately selling its American investments and just before the Stock Exchange closed its doors.[1] Easy money, and industrial activity wholly unparalleled in the country's history, were accompanied by financial markets such as in other days would have indicated financial panic.

The reasons for this paradox are written in the history of the first eight or nine months after our entry into war. The fall on the Stock Exchange could hardly have been caused by misgiving as to

[1] New York *Times*, Jan. 2, 1918; "Stock Market Averages."

the issue of the conflict; we have seen that no such doubt existed. In part, it must have resulted from diversion of capital to the war loans. But it very soon became evident, first that the heavy hand of government restriction under its war powers would prevent conversion of the increasing orders for industrial products into equivalent producers' profits; second, that the surplus profits of producers and manufacturers would be sweepingly curtailed by the war tax on such surplus earnings and, along with those new influences, largely foreseen by experienced financiers, there also appeared unexpected evidence of disorganization in our international exchange market through the operations of the government.

The movement of the neutral foreign exchanges against New York came first; it was a movement whose scope and violence caused great financial bewilderment. Within a month after our declaration of war, exchange on practically every neutral country sold in the New York markets up to 7 per cent above the maximum rate of normal times. Before the middle of 1918, exchange on Holland, Spain, Switzerland and the Scandinavian markets had moved so heavily against New York that at one time the price of the Dutch florin in American currency stood at a premium of 29⅜ per cent over parity, the Spanish peseta at a premium of 54 per cent, and the Swedish crown at a premium of 69¾.[1] The same thing happened with New York exchange on India, Japan and the South American republics, for which American merchants had to pay in 1918 a premium ranging from 7⅞ per cent in the case of Japan to 78¼ in the case of Chile.[2]

This occurrence was the more striking from the fact that, even in 1917 and 1918, our excess of merchandise exports over imports in trade with neutral Europe continued very large. With South America—notably Chile, which supplied the very essential nitrites—the visible balance against us in those years was large. But the export surplus was $52,098,000 in our trade with Sweden, for instance, during those two years, $37,341,000 in trade with Holland, $104,403,000 in trade with Spain.[3] Since the violent movement of exchange against New York could not be explained by reversal of the foreign trade balance, it was not at all unnatural that it should have been ascribed to inflation of the currency.

[1] Annual Treasury Report, 1918, p. 39.   [2] *Ibid.*
[3] Monthly Summary of Foreign Commerce, Dec., 1918, p. 6.

One result of the sudden and large additions of Reserve Bank facilities in June, 1917, was rapid increase of the note issues. During 1916, notwithstanding that year's great expansion of financial and industrial activities, the system's outstanding note issues increased only $86,327,000;[1] the additional currency required for hand-to-hand use in the larger trade was obtained through addition to the general circulation of $378,880,000 in gold certificates, issued by the Treasury, dollar for dollar, against gold produced or imported.[2] When the United States went to war in April, 1917, the outstanding Reserve notes amounted to $376,510,000, but they rose to $1,246,488,000 at the end of 1917 and to $2,685,244,000 at the end of 1918.[3]   Such an increase at once called forth assertions that the paper currency of the United States, like that of the European belligerents, was being inflated at a rate which had occasioned immediate depreciation; that this and the similarly rapid expansion of credit were the sole causes for the fall in value of the dollar, measured in neutral currencies;[4]

[1] Reserve Board, weekly statements Dec. 30, 1915; Dec. 29, 1916.
[2] U. S. Treasury, money circulation statement, Jan. 1, 1917.
[3] Reserve Board weekly statements, Apr. 6, 1917; Dec. 28, 1917; Dec. 27, 1918.
[4] Federal Reserve Board, Annual Report for 1917, p. 17.

in short, that what was happening to the American currency was exactly what had happened to the currencies of the European belligerents after 1914.

But the case was by no means so simple. In the first place, the increase of $2,300,000,000 in the Federal Reserve note issues, during our participation in the war, was offset and in large measure explained by the decrease, during the same period, of $1,300,000,000 gold certificates in general circulation.[1] With hand-to-hand use of money at its maximum these gold certificates, when drawn from outside circulation into the reserve of the Federal banks, had to be replaced by other forms of currency, for requirements of actual circulating medium increased with exceptional rapidity during our period of war. Not only were trade activities in the United States, as measured by exchange of checks at the country's banks, enlarged by 17¼ per cent in 1917 and by 8⅓ per cent more in 1918,[2] but average prices of commodities rose in the two years respectively 39 and 10 per cent;[3] which meant neces-

---

[1] Reserve Board weekly statements.

[2] *Financial Chronicle*, Jan. 18, 1919, p. 208.

[3] "Wholesale prices, 1890 to 1923," Bureau of Labor Statistics, 1925; p. 9.

sity for proportionately larger use of cash in every-day purchases.

The average rate of wages in the United States during 1916 had been 6 per cent above 1913. In 1917 it stood 12 per cent above the pre-war average, in 1918 it was 30 per cent above it,[1] and this rapidly rising scale of earnings occurred when the total number of workingmen actively and steadily employed was so great that official estimates in 1918 declared the supply even of unskilled labor to be short a million men of potential demand.[2] But increase in aggregate payrolls of manufacturing establishments traditionally requires immediate addition, on a corresponding scale, to the available supply of currency. Even adherents of the theory of a currency depreciated through excessive paper-money issues admitted the importance of these several considerations.[3] It also had to be recognized that, since Reserve notes could not be issued except on application of private banks, their increase in 1917 and 1918

[1] Bureau of Labor Statistics; "Union Scale of Wages and Hours of Labor," 1925, p. 17.

[2] Department of Labor, statement of Aug. 22, 1918; *Financial Chronicle*, Aug. 31, 1918, p. 860.

[3] A. C. Miller, director Federal Reserve Board, address to American Academy of Political and Social Science, Dec. 21, 1918.

bore no resemblance in character to the war-time
paper inflation of Europe.   In all the belligerent
continental countries, the state banks issued paper
money to the governments against pledge of
Treasury obligations, the governments then paying out the new paper-money to meet the public
deficit, regardless of actual requirements of trade.
But even in the matter of credit, the Treasury was
not permitted to lean directly on the Federal
Reserve.

At the very beginning of our participation in
the war, this rule was momentarily broken; the
Treasury borrowed $50,000,000 of the Reserve
Banks' resources, on a short loan placed pro-rata
with the twelve Reserve banks.[1]   But the action
was not allowed to become a precedent; on no
other subsequent occasion—excepting only when
the Reserve Banks, after the usual practice of state
institutions, opened immediate credits to the
Treasury against deposited checks for tax payments or loan subscriptions—did the government
borrow directly from those banks.   In marked
contrast to the war-time practice of European
state banks, all Federal Reserve credit used during
the war was represented by notes endorsed by

[1] Annual Report Federal Reserve Board for 1917, p. 3.

member banks and secured either by commercial paper or by government obligations in the possession of those private banks. Instead of continental Europe's virtually unlimited recourse by the Treasury to the central bank, which resulted in the issue of currency to the government quite as lavishly as if the state itself had put out fiat money, all of the borrowings from Reserve Banks carried two or more endorsements, with a bank obligation on every piece of paper.

The explanation for the adverse movement of the foreign exchanges during 1917 must be sought, therefore, somewhere else. To begin with, it must be observed that the premium on neutral currencies in terms of New York exchange, and with it the discount on the dollar in terms of such currencies, began before our entry into the European war, and therefore before the large increase of our Reserve note issues. In the middle of 1916, when Reserve note circulation hardly exceeded $150,-000,000, New York exchange on Sweden already stood at a premium of 16 per cent; one or two other neutral exchanges were running heavily against the United States during the same year. For that movement, at all events, inflation of our paper currency could not have been the cause.

To what, then, is the war-time movement of exchange against the United States to be ascribed? Primarily, to the facts that the rate for sterling exchange at New York was kept at a level far above that to which it fell in the other neutral markets; that, after we went to war, our own government's resources were employed to sustain this artificial value; that those other neutral markets sold their own sterling bills, the evidence of London's current indebtedness to them, to the market which paid the highest price for sterling; that our own market thereby assumed a great part of London's heavy indebtedness to the other neutral markets, and that the United States became consequently a debtor on balance to those markets, notwithstanding a balance of merchandise trade with them continuously in our favor.

This is the economic aspect of the matter; it cannot easily be disputed. An economic movement of the kind does not always proceed visibly and directly; in this case, its course of operation was obscured by a multitude of confusing phenomena. In the main, however, the series of incidents was reasonably clear. Even in 1916, the British government's large borrowings in America (upwards of $500,000,000), although mostly used to pay for war material, were also partly used for support of the sterling rate—a matter of obvious importance to England because, the further sterling depreciated at New York or on other markets, the greater proportionately would be the cost of products brought by the British government from those markets and paid for through drafts on London.[1] This support was effected sometimes by direct purchase of sterling bills at New York, sometimes by purchase at New York of exchange on neutral markets, through remittance of which the trade indebtedness of England to those markets could be partly met without drawing bills on London. The last-named operation necessarily caused great increase in the demand for New York exchange on neutral countries, not occasioned by any transaction of the United States itself with them. In the six months after the War Loan Act of April, 1917, when the United States Treasury granted credits of $1,425,-000,000 to Great Britain and of $1,075,000,000 to France and Italy,[2] the loans were designed primarily to finance purchases of food and war

[1] W. G. P. Harding, ex-Governor Federal Reserve Board; "The Formative Period of the Federal Reserve System," p. 101.
[2] Annual Treasury Report for 1917, p. 17.

material in the United States.   But the Treasury, expressly in order "to preserve the credit of the governments of the Allies and to maintain their purchasing power in foreign markets," had "permitted the support of the exchanges of Great Britain, France and Italy upon the United States exchange markets" with the proceeds of these loans,[1] and that was done through large extension of the operations already described.   It is stated that for a time, in 1918, the British government's direct purchase of sterling bills at New York (which might be re-sold at a more advantageous moment) averaged $40,000,000 per week.[2]

Even with England's use of drafts on its new American credits to pay for part of its purchases in neutral markets, however, the balance of current indebtedness against London in those markets remained very large; in the case of neutrals producing necessary war supplies, such as Spain, Sweden and Chile, it had doubled or trebled.[3] Therefore, even with England's draft on its New York credits to meet part of these trade obligations, sterling had depreciated more rapidly on

[1] Annual Treasury Report for 1918, p. 38.
[2] Harding, p. 101.
[3] British Board of Trade, report on overseas trade in 1917; London *Economist*, March 2, 1918, p. 380.

those markets than at New York, where the full force of the American war credits was utilized to support exchange. By April, 1917, this trade indebtedness, combined with England's abandonment of gold payments, had brought the pound sterling 12 to 13 per cent below parity on such markets as Madrid and Stockholm, whereas the New York sterling rate, being "pegged" by use of Great Britain's American credits, held virtually unchanged around $4.75½, or only about 2½ per cent under parity.

The result of this artificial situation was, first, increasing purchase of American remittances to the neutral markets by the belligerent European governments, with a view to preventing further demoralization of sterling in such markets; second, a very considerable amount of selling, in New York's relatively higher sterling market, of drafts on London drawn by the neutral markets. Since any sale of that nature was apt to be followed by remittance of the proceeds, from New York to the neutral market, the pressure of bids for neutral exchange at New York was necessarily increased by it still further.[1] What was actually happening was that the burden of meeting

[1] Harding, pp. 101 and 102.

London's payments to the outside neutral countries was in great measure thrown on the American market's shoulders.[1]

So far the case is clear enough. But the actual
scope of the movement is not explained by the
mere fact of foreign payments, made directly
or indirectly in behalf of our allies. All precedent
of the international market had shown that, whenever New York exchange on any foreign country
had risen to a rate at which gold could be shipped
to that country without loss, such shipments would
automatically prevent further advance in the
exchange rate. This "gold-export point," as commonly fixed in pre-war days for transactions with
Spain, for instance, was something near 19¾
cents per Spanish peseta, as against 19⅛ cents
for par of exchange. But New York exchange on
Madrid went to 20 cents even in 1916 and to 24 in
the following year.

The high rate of 1916 was quoted while the
United States was shipping gold to Spain; during
that year such shipments amounted to $17,000,000.
For this seeming anomaly the main explanation
was that cost of insuring and shipping gold, under

[1] Annual Report Federal Reserve Board for 1918, pp. 53, 54,
55.

the war-time hazards of ocean transportation, had widened the margin in exchange necessary to make such exports possible and had therefore fixed a higher "gold point" than in time of peace. In the case of Sweden, another influence predominated. Because of Sweden's position as a heavy seller of goods to both Germany and the Entente Allies, gold had accumulated rapidly in the national bank, and fear that prices would consequently be unsettled led the Swedish parliament in 1916 to authorize the national bank to refuse, during a year from date, further acceptance of foreign gold.[1] Application of this very unusual decree made it impossible for New York to settle in gold an adverse balance on exchange with Sweden; therefore exchange on Stockholm, which could not now be met in gold, rose as far above the gold-export point as the bids of England's agents for remittances or the purchases of Swedish bankers, bringing home from New York the proceeds of their sales of sterling, would carry it.

But for the much higher premium on all the neutral exchanges after our declaration of war, the action of our own government was responsible.

[1] Riksdag law of Feb. 8, 1916; London *Economist*, Feb. 26, 1916, p. 407.

The movement of foreign gold to the United States (mostly for account of England), which had caused a very large excess of gold imports even in the first four months of 1917, came to a halt when the Treasury's program of war finance was put into effect. Its "complete cessation," the Federal Reserve Board stated, was "a result of the entry of the country into the war and of the large credits given to the Allied governments."[1] During the first four months of 1917 our export of gold was $77,700,000; but our import was $334,-500,000, leaving $256,800,000 surplus of importations. In the next five months, however, our gold exports, because of the above-stated movement of the neutral exchanges, had risen to $271,200,000, while our gold imports, chiefly because of absence of the former necessity to send us gold on behalf of England, had fallen to $193,700,000.[2] In three months of the summer of 1917, the net loss of gold by the United States on foreign account reached $100,000,000.[3] This outflow did not immediately impair the gold fund of the Federal Reserve, because the transfer of reserves from

[1] Annual Report Federal Reserve Board for 1917, p. 20.

[2] Monthly Summary of Foreign Commerce for September, 1917, p. 4.

[3] Federal Reserve Board, Annual Report for 1917, p. 20.

member banks was still in progress. In July, however, even the Federal Reserve banks began to report a decreased gold reserve; it had fallen $26,000,000 before the end of August, and the decrease bade fair to be continuous.[1]

The Treasury then acted to control the movement. A statute adopted by Congress in October of 1917 provided that the president might "investigate, regulate or prohibit . . . any transactions in foreign exchange, export or earmarkings of gold or silver," and might apply such restriction to transactions "between the United States and any foreign country, whether enemy, ally, or otherwise."[2] These powers were now, by Presidential orders of September 7 and October 12, invoked to authorize such discretionary regulation by the Federal Reserve,[3] and to declare that, unless on the express approval of the Reserve Board, coin or bullion "shall not be exported from or shipped from or taken out of the United States or its territorial possessions."[4] In pursuance of this order, the Board presently reported that

[1] Weekly statements of the Reserve Board, 1917.
[2] Trading with the Enemy Act, Oct. 6, 1917; *Financial Chronicle*, Oct. 13, 1917, p. 1479.
[3] Treasury Report, 1918, p. 41.
[4] Annual Report Federal Reserve Board for 1917, p. 21.

"applications for permission to ship gold to European neutral countries have been invariably declined."[1] The interdiction was destined to continue, with gold released only for other countries whose requirements arising from our own war-time trade were urgent, until June 9, 1919.[2]

From the economic viewpoint, this action completely changed the situation. The government at Washington had not, it is true, formally suspended gold payments. Unnecessary use of gold coin in private circulation had been officially discountenanced,[3] but the Reserve banks still professed to redeem in gold Federal Reserve notes actually tendered for redemption. The course of European war finance had already shown, however, and was destined to show even more clearly after the war that, inasmuch as the principal occasion for asking redemption of paper currency in gold was to obtain the gold for export, an embargo

---

[1] Annual Report Federal Reserve Board for 1917, p. 21.

[2] Federal Reserve Board, Annual Reports for 1917 and 1919. Harding, p. 93.

[3] N. Y. Assay Office, orders of Aug. 30 and Sept. 9, 1918. War Department, order of July 30, 1918, against officers taking gold abroad; Treasury Department, ruling of 1918 against use of gold coins for holiday gifts. *Financial Chronicle*, Aug. 3, 1917, pp. 443, 444; Nov. 10, 1917, p. 1845; Sept. 7, 1918, p. 939; Sept. 14, 1918, p. 1047.

on gold exports was equivalent to such suspension. Even Great Britain, when the war began, officially described not only Bank of England notes but the war-time "currency notes" as redeemable on demand in gold;[1] but when free gold exports were prevented—indirectly at first and afterwards directly, through introduction of a system of official licenses—the resultant actual depreciation of the British currency was never seriously questioned. When gold payments on that currency were formally resumed in April, 1925, the resumption statute made no pretense of merely restoring gold convertibility of the notes; indeed, the power to redeem them in gold for possible purposes of hoarding was carefully circumscribed. The Act of 1925, in its language and intent, simply removed the embargo on "free gold exports," and all the markets recognized that action as return to the gold standard.[2] This being so, it is difficult to deny that our own embargo on gold exports from October, 1917, to June, 1919, was equivalent to suspension of gold payments during that period.

The question, whether the action was or was

[1] Currency and Bank Notes Act, Aug. 6, 1914.
[2] Winston Churchill, Chancellor British Exchequer, speech to Parliament, April 28, 1925.

not actually necessary, must remain indefinitely a matter of dispute; there is high authority for either conclusion. Even those responsible public officials, however, who today consider the embargo of 1917 to have been unnecessary, admit that continuance of unrestricted gold exports might have resulted during war-time in the shipment of some $400,000,000 gold which, as we shall presently see, actually occurred in 1919 when the embargo was removed. The real question, therefore, concerns the probable effect on public confidence if gold withdrawals of such magnitude had been made from the Federal Reserve in war-time, and, therefore, the possible effect on the public attitude towards the government's war finance. The two conclusions which appear to be incontrovertible, in the light of all the circumstances, are, first, that the war-time depreciation of the dollar was occasioned, not at all by our own domestic exigencies but by our government's shouldering of the fiscal burden of its European Allies; second, that the large increase of Reserve note circulation during 1917 was itself in no respect a cause.

If the Reserve Act had not been amended when we entered the war, and if the system's gold reserve had been left at the much smaller sum which was held before June, 1917, the inducement to obstruct gold exports of such possible magnitude would obviously have been far greater. The depreciation of the dollar lasted only until the artificial "pegging" of sterling at New York was abandoned in March, 1919, shortly followed by removal of the embargo on gold exports. Nevertheless, even in the later months of 1918 the premium on neutral currencies had been greatly reduced by skilful use of government funds to "stabilize" the market.[1] It is important to observe, as the Reserve Board pointed out at the time, that throughout the episode the single standard of prices was maintained in the United States and "not a double standard, one based upon the gold dollar and the other upon the paper dollar, as was the case during and after the Civil War."[2]

We have seen, then, what were the causes for the war-time movement of foreign exchange against the United States. It remains to examine the causes for the apprehensive action of other

[1] Treasury Report, 1918, p. 39.
[2] Federal Reserve Board, Annual Report for 1918, pp. 86 and 87.

financial markets, in face of easy money and of unprecedented buying of every kind of merchandise. Three urgent problems came instantly into sight as the country prepared for war—the impending congestion and blockade of the railway system, under the double strain of military and commercial orders; the violent rise in the price of food, whether bought for the army or for other uses, and, last of all but soon assuming a place of paramount importance, doubt over the possibility of instantaneous production of munitions in the quantity necessary to carry on the war, without shutting off essential home consumption, or clogging the ports and channels of distribution, or driving prices to unconscionable heights.

Trouble on the railways began at once. From the beginning of our participation in the war, it had become a critical question how the companies, in an investment market whose entire resources were being absorbed into the war loans, could finance the unprecedented strain on their facilities through selling of new securities. But that was only one phase of the problem, and to the public a minor phase. Demand for immediate transportation to the Eastern seaboard, of the urgently-needed grain from the Middle West and the war material from Pittsburg or Chicago, soon exceeded the capacity of the half-dozen trunk line railways connecting the necessary points. In the phrase of the day this freight, delivered to such connecting roads from scores of other Western and Southern railways, was now "poured through the neck of the bottle." The trunk lines were blockaded with side-tracked freight, to move which there were neither sufficient main-line track facilities nor sufficient motive power. One obvious recourse was that railways whose location subjected them to no such abnormal strain should be called on to help out with their own locomotives and rolling stock, and in fact the Railroads War Board, organized by the railway executives from their own membership five days after declaration of war, pledged in behalf of 631 separate railways with 262,000 total miles of track that "during the present war they will co-ordinate their operations in a continental railway system; merging, during such period, all their merely individual competitive activities in the effort to produce a maximum of national productive efficiency."[1]

But this was more easily said than done. Although the board's powers were only advisory,

[1] Clarkson, *Industrial America in the World War*, p. 81.

not mandatory, the railways honestly strove to comply with its requests. At one time, in response to a call for spare equipment to break a serious Eastern blockade, it was immediately announced that "one hundred powerful locomotives will start within the next 24 hours to assist in moving the congested traffic East of the Mississippi and north of the Ohio," the locomotives being provided by Western lines in proportion to the number owned by each.[1] Nevertheless, the larger the active facilities, the more bewildering grew the confusion caused by the blocking of east-bound loaded cars by west-bound "empties," the simultaneous pressure to get foodstuffs and munitions, the conflicting orders of different government departments for delivery of their consignments in advance of other freight. The railways finally declared that, in order to prevent an utterly paralyzing blockade, "action not within their power is essential"; that there must be "co-operation of important military and industrial agencies of the government to avoid unnecessary congestion"; that "a traffic officer with whom the railways can deal" ought to be at once

[1] Fairfax Harrison, President Southern R. R., statement of Dec. 12, 1917.

appointed "to represent all important government departments in transportation matters."[1]

But the congestion grew worse instead of better; in December it was approaching a condition of chaos.[2] When the traffic blockade threatened to become complete, the Chairman of the Interstate Commerce Commission reported to Congress that a decision as to government operation must be made at once; that, if the railways were to continue under private operation, they must be ready, whenever economy of necessary movement so required, for "surrender of exclusive use of terminal facilities, surrender at times of profitable traffic to other carriers, and acceptance of less profitable traffic with resultant loss of revenue."[3] Dissenting from this suggestion that private management could under any circumstances cope with the situation, another Interstate commissioner asserted that private operation was wholly unable to accomplish such results; because, as the experiment from April to December had in his opinion proved, "the element of self-interest, the traffic influence, is a persistent

[1] Fairfax Harrison to Chairman Senate Interstate Commerce Committee, Dec. 9, 1917.
[2] Interstate Commerce Commissioner McChord, Dec. 5, 1917.
[3] Commissioner H. C. Hall, report to Congress, Dec. 5, 1917.

factor in postponing and resisting measures that
seek to disregard individual rights in the effort
to secure transportation results as a whole."
Therefore he urged that the President "exercise
the power . . . to take possession and assume
control of the transportation systems."[1] All the
commissioners agreed that, if this were to be done,
there ought to be "suitable guarantee to each
carrier of an adequate annual return for use of
its property, as well as of its upkeep and maintenance."[2]

When the decision could no longer be deferred,
President Wilson accepted the view that government operation was inevitable and, on December
26, 1917, announced that all the railways would be
immediately taken over by the government. At
the same time he suggested, as the basis of compensation to the railways by the government,
"the average net railway operation income of
the three years ending June 30, 1917."[3] This
proposal Congress incorporated into law, providing also for operation by the government not only
during the war but "for a reasonable time there-

[1] Commissioner C. C. McChord, report of Dec. 5.
[2] Commissioner H. C. Hall, report of Dec. 5.
[3] President Wilson's address to Congress, Jan. 4, 1918.

after, not exceeding twenty-one months after the Treaty of Peace."[1] The public received this news with something of consternation; the railways, unquestionably with relief.[2] Unprecedented as was the magnitude of freight pressing for transportation, they had seen themselves menaced with disastrously reduced net earnings; partly as a result of the always costly traffic blockade, partly because of the swiftly mounting cost of wages and supplies, partly because of the difficulty of raising money in a market monopolized by the war loans. During the first nine months of 1917, gross receipts of the railway that carried most of the war munitions had increased 11⅝ per cent over 1916, yet its net income from operation actually decreased 17 per cent,[3] and this was typical of all the trunk line railways. The compensation clause as framed in the Act of Congress, on whose terms it had been impossible to reckon beforehand, meant at least that a living income would be guaranteed to them.

[1] Federal Control Act, March 21, 1918.

[2] S. D. Warfield, report to National Association of Owners of R. R. Securities, Jan. 15, 1918.

[3] Samuel Rea, President Pennsylvania R. R., testimony before Interstate Commerce Commission, Nov. 5, 1917.

Under the government's Director-general, whose orders were thenceforth to supersede all existing statutes and regulatory bodies, the transfer of authority was made. The immediate result was sweeping reduction of non-essential passenger train service, which amounted in all to 2,200,000 miles per month;[1] redistribution, to roads which had not enough of cars and locomotives to move their freight from inland producing points to the Atlantic seaboard, of surplus equipment reported by other railways; diversion to the least congested lines of empty cars returning westward; transfer of traffic, wherever possible, to railways whose grades were most favorable to rapid and economical transportation; finally, common use by all railways of the terminal facilities of any company at the large commercial centres.[2] This radical readjustment was mandatory, not advisory; all railways in the country were operated as if they constituted a unified system with a single ownership. The unified operation broke the traffic blockade, although with very great incidental change in the traffic affiliations of many railways

---

[1] Report of A. H. Smith, regional director for the East, to Director-General of railways, May 29, 1918.

[2] *Ibid.*

and with sweeping upward revision both of transportation rates and wages of labor; all of which colored deeply the railway situation after the war.

Some of the roads, whose location was especially favorable for rapid Eastward shipment of grain and war munitions, enlarged immensely their hold on highly remunerative traffic. The facilities of others were restricted to one class of freight; some of the less-advantageously located lines lost what had previously been their most profitable business, or were used for hauling back westward the empty cars which had brought freight to the coast over other lines. A strong effort was made to reduce incidental "overhead expenses" through unified control. Individual ticket offices, except in the railway stations, were replaced in the cities by "consolidated offices"; the Director General reported saving of $25,566,633 on that account in the first seven months, and of $7,000,000 in advertising.[1] These savings, however, counted little against the rising tide of increasing costs in other directions. The same report admitted a rise of 50 to 70 per cent in cost of materials and in wages for the 1,700,000 railway employees.

[1] Report of Director-General McAdoo to President Wilson, Sept. 3, 1918.

Demands for higher wages were in fact conceded with little or no hesitation; but the advance in freight rates, granted to offset this mounting cost of operation, was only 25 per cent.[1] A little later, control of the telegraph lines and cables was taken over by the government[2] but with less important consequences to the condition and earning power of those industries, whose private operation was already highly centralized. What the new dispensation would mean in the longer future, especially in regard to the much-discussed government-ownership propaganda, it was left for circumstances to determine. The Congressional statute set forth (with scrupulous care not to commit itself) that "nothing herein is construed as expressing or prejudicing the future policy of the Federal government concerning ownership, control or regulation of the carriers."[3] We shall presently see how that policy was determined, and why, in the legislation of 1920.

At the very moment in which this new chapter of railway history was unfolding, the government was forced to immediate action on the price of

[1] Report of Director-General

[2] Proclamations of President Wilson; July 23, Nov. 2, 1918.

[3] Act to Provide for Operation of Transportation Systems while under Federal Control, March 21, 1918.

food.   The American wheat crop of 1916 had run short; it was barely half the harvest of 1915, and wheat had touched $2 per bushel at Chicago in November.   After falling back in January, 1917, it rose to $2.15 on our government's declaration of war in April, and on May 11 reached the high point of $3.45.   This was a much higher price even than the maximum reached in our own depreciated-money period of the Civil War, when the Chicago market never got above the price of $2.85, paid in May, 1867.   Such an advance made it evident that speculation could not be left to run an unobstructed course, especially as another equally short crop was foreshadowed for 1917.

On May 12, 1917, the Chicago Board of Trade itself officially suspended transactions in wheat for delivery during that month, fixing at $3.18 the "settlement price" for trades already made.   On August 8, Congress passed a measure which it had been debating for three months; it authorized the President, "as far in advance of seeding time as practicable, to determine and fix . . . a reasonable guaranteed price for wheat."   To make such a price effective, he was authorized also "to purchase any wheat for which a guaranteed price shall be fixed . . . and to hold, transport or store it, or to sell, dispose of, and deliver the same to any citizen of the United States or to any government engaged in war with any country with which the government of the United States is or may be at war."[1] The statute coupled this discretionary authority with the stipulation that the price for standard grades of wheat raised in 1918 should be fixed "at not less than $2 per bushel at the principal interior markets," this minimum to be "binding until May 1, 1919." It should be observed that the price thus designated by statute, although much below the market's price of $3.45 on May 11, had never but once been reached between 1869 and 1916 on the Chicago Board of Trade, that single exception occurring in the famous "Hutchinson corner" of 1888, when the normal price ranged around 75 cents shortly before and after the speculative operation.

The President's first action was to appoint a Food Administrator; he selected Herbert Hoover, who had already achieved world-wide celebrity for his extraordinarily successful administration of food relief in Belgium. The Administrator was

[1] Food Control Act. Aug. 8, 1917.

to conduct his operations through a so-styled Grain Corporation of seven members, with a capital stock of $50,000,000; subscribed by the United States government[1] and afterwards increased to $500,000,000. The "fair price" of wheat was next fixed for the crop of 1917, by an independent committee named by the President, at $2.20 per bushel,—lower than the $2.50 price which the farmers asked, but higher than the $1.50 price for which the purchasing foreign governments argued or the $1.84 price urged by the representatives of labor.[2] The decision for this relatively high price was based, first on the shortage of the American wheat crops of 1916 and 1917, —for the harvest of our first war year, 636,000,000 bushels, was no larger than the short crop of 1916 —second, on the wish to stimulate increased planting for the next year's crop, third, on the desirability of restricting home consumption without excessively burdening the consumer.[3] At the beginning of the 1918 crop year, the guaranteed

[1] President Wilson, executive orders of Aug. 10 and Aug. 14, 1917.

[2] Report of the President's Committee on Wheat Prices, Aug. 30, 1917. "The Stabilization of the Price of Wheat during the War," U. S. Grain Corporation, 1925; p. 43, 44, 45.

[3] *Ibid.*

price was by proclamation raised to $2.26, Chicago, in order to compensate for a 25 per cent rise in railway rates.[1]

The minimum price having thus been established on August 30, 1917, the government's Grain Corporation undertook nothing less than to purchase at the $2.20 price all of the American wheat crop that should be offered to it.   Produce thus purchased was re-sold, either at cost or at a very moderate profit, to home and foreign buyers. Any private grower of wheat was at liberty to sell to private purchasers for more than the guaranteed price, if he could get it.   In point of fact, as much as $3.50 per bushel was paid at Chicago, on private sale, during the period of the Food Administration's activities, for exceptionally good wheat.   But a lower price than $2.20 per bushel, so long as the quality of the wheat came up to the grade prescribed, was not possible while the Grain Corporation's bid held good.   Speculation in wheat had been prohibited by the grain exchanges themselves at the request of the Food Administration,[2] and whereas the speculator, through the

[1] "Stabilization of the Price of Wheat," p. 17.
[2] Herbert Hoover, letter to Chicago Board of Trade, Aug. 11, 1917; Statement by President Chicago Board of Trade, Aug. 21; by Minneapolis Chamber of Commerce, Aug. 22.

"carrying charge" involved in his operation, had in the past paid most of the cost of holding wheat for deliberate sale and distribution when sale of all at once at harvest-time would have swamped the market, that cost was now assumed by the government's agency.

The actual situation of the wheat trade, during the thirty-three months of the Corporation's existence from September 1, 1917, to May 31, 1920 (for its work extended over the year and a half after the armistice), was that the so-called "financing of the wheat crop," always one of the largest autumn burdens on the grain markets and the banks, had been wholly assumed by the United States government.[1] How great a requisition was thereby lifted from private industry may be judged from the fact that the Grain Corporation, during that period, actually bought and marketed 492,000,000 bushels of wheat and 57,600,000 barrels of flour; the cost of all the foodstuffs thus purchased with the corporation's capital, and its war-time bank borrowings of $385,000,000, exceeding $3,735,000,000.[2] We shall find this fact— the government's assumption of the responsibil-

[1] "Stabilization of the Price of Wheat," pp. 13, 17, 58.
[2] *Ibid.*, pp. 17 and 58.

ities usually undertaken by the banks and the money market—to have been very singularly overlooked by the grain trade during 1920. Yet after all these immense transactions, the Grain Corporation was able in the end to repay to the Treasury the $500,000,000 which by that time the government had invested in its capital stock, plus $59,000,000 interest and surplus;[1] a most unusual achievement in war-time finance.

The result of the Food Administration's handling of the wheat crop was that, whereas normal home consumption would ordinarily have left practically no surplus for export from so small an American yield as that of 1917, in actual fact 138,000,000 bushels were shipped to the Allied countries, whose own harvests of 1917 had fallen 231,000,000 bushels short of their pre-war average.[2] From the wheat harvest of 1915, American home consumption was 590,000,000 bushels; from that of 1916 it was 493,000,000; from that of 1917 (marketed mostly in 1918), it was only 452,000,000. As against an average per capita consumption of 5.74 bushels from the 1915 crop and an average of 5.30 bushels from the ten crops preceding that of 1918, the figure fell to 4.30 for

[1] " Stabilization of the Price of Wheat," p. 59.

[2] *Ibid.*, pp. 12 and 16.

the crop consumed in 1918.[1] This remarkable result was achieved partly through the Food Administration's method of distributing the wheat which it purchased, but much more directly through the government's appeal to the people for economy in use of food and the people's voluntary response to that appeal. At the end of 1917 Mr. Hoover publicly announced that "all exports of wheat from now onward are limited entirely to saving made by the American people in their consumption,"[2] and the response was immediate. The decision of city hotels, restaurants and railway dining cars to observe "wheatless Wednesdays" and "beefless Tuesdays" resulted in a single week, the Food Administrator stated, in the saving of 116 tons of meat and 620 barrels of flour.[3]

When the crisis grew more urgent, the Food Administration urged the observance of two "wheatless days" each week instead of one and the sale of wheat flour by retailers only along with

---

[1] Chicago *Daily Trade Bulletin* estimates; Year Book U. S. Agricultural Dept. for 1918, p. 681.

[2] Statement for Food Administration, Dec. 10, 1917.

[3] N. Y. City Hotel Association, Oct. 2, 1917. Statement of Food Administration, Nov. 22. *Financial Chronicle*, Oct. 6, 1917, p. 1366; Dec. 1, p. 2145.

sale of an equal weight of other cereals,[1] and at
the beginning of 1918 the President called for
further reduction of 30 per cent in home consumption of wheat.[2]   The British Food Commissioner had cabled the Food Administration in
January that, unless our wheat exports to the
Allies were to be 75,000,000 bushels in the next
six months, he could not "take the responsibility of assuring our people that there will be food
enough to win the war."[3]   We had already exported all the surplus which normal home consumption would have left from a wheat crop as
small as that of 1917;[4] yet, between that date
and the end of the grain season, we exported
73,000,000 bushels more.[5]   The wheat used for
home consumption from the 1917 crop was less
by 112,000,000 bushels than in the season after the
harvest of 1915.[6]   Nevertheless, such was the
pressure to provide for the urgent needs of Europe
that in July, when the new crop of 1918 began

[1] Food Administration, notice of regulations, Jan. 26, 1918.

[2] Proclamation of Jan. 18, 1918.

[3] Message of Lord Rhondda to Food Administration; statement
of Food Administration, Jan. 25, 1918.

[4] *Ibid.*

[5] U. S. Agricultural Department reports. "Stabilization of
the Price of Wheat," p. 39.

[6] *Ibid.*

to come upon the market, there was less than ten-days' supply of the old crop left.[1]

As to what, immediately or in the long run, was the effect of the government's operations on the price of wheat and the farmer's profits, compared with probable results in a free and open war-time grain market, on that point there has been some dispute. The fixed-price policy was certainly adopted with the primary view of stopping the extravagant speculation which had carried the price above $3; hence the very general belief that the market was kept down by government intervention. On the other hand, the Allied governments had pointed out that, at the moment when the American price was being fixed at $2.20 in August, 1917, wheat was selling in Australia at $1.14 and in India at $1.07, and had been officially placed by the European consignees at $1.80.[2] Mr. Hoover's judgment, stated after the wheat-control experiment had ended, was that, but for the action of our government, "the farmer would have realized far less for his wheat."[3] The Grain Corporation's statistician calculated that in

---

[1] Food Administration, statement of Dec., 1918.
[2] " Stabilization of the Price of Wheat," pp. 13, 21, 43, 76.
[3] *Ibid.*, p. 7.

1917 actual profits of American wheat farmers over all expenses were more than double the maximum profits of any year since the war began and that the profits of 1918 were larger still—$815,545,-000, as against $642,837,000 in 1917 and $296,-252,000 in 1916; also that wheat had held further above the pre-war price during those two years than the general run of non-agricultural products.[1]

That the farmer was a direct beneficiary, and on a very substantial scale, from war-time conditions, was therefore reasonably evident; the farmer's own view of the case was indicated by the increase of 4 per cent in the area sown to winter wheat in the autumn of 1917 and the further increase of 16 per cent in the next autumn's plantings.[2] But the question of manufacturing production presented a different aspect. Even before the United States entered the war, the demand of the belligerents for war material exceeded the capacity of the American industrial plant; in March, 1917, the price of metals and metal products averaged 40 per cent above the

[1] " Stabilization of the Price of Wheat," pp. 8 and 85.
[2] Department of Agriculture, December estimates, 1917 and 1918.

same month in 1916 and 160 per cent above July, 1914.[1] All indications pointed to a further and much more rapid advance if the market was left to its own devices, with the war orders of the United States government superimposed on the steadily increasing requisitions from the European belligerents.

As a natural consequence, prices of manufactured products, especially of materials for war munitions, rose violently when the United States declared war. Iron, for instance, advanced between March and July, 1917, from $32¼ per ton to $52½, steel plates from $4⅓ to $9; the average price of metals being then 3½ times the average of 1913. Copper, of which the army and navy needed 45,000,000 pounds at once and whose average price at the end of 1915 had been 22½ cents a pound and 29½ at the end of 1916, had risen to 37 cents; chemicals, which in 1916 had averaged 81 per cent above 1913, went in September, 1917, to a figure 123 per cent above the pre-war average.[2] Along with these exorbitant prices, all industries were in confusion because of

[1] "Wholesale Prices, 1890 to 1923," U. S. Bureau of Labor, Statistics, 1925, p. 16.

[2] Clarkson, *Industrial America in the World War*, pp. 162 and 164; "Wholesale Prices, 1890 to 1923," pp. 9 and 17.

the sudden overstrain on labor and transportation.

The situation plainly demanded regulation, yet it was not practicable for the government to take over manufacture as it had taken over the wheat trade. The only official body in the field was the War Industries Board, organized on July 8, 1917, by the Council of National Defense. That council had been established by law in 1916 to investigate the industrial situation,[1] and its own statement of purpose in organizing the War Industries Board was merely that the new board, which as a separate organization was unknown to the statute law, should "act as a clearing-house for the war-industry needs of the government," determine "the best means of increasing production," report on "the relative urgency of the needs" of the different services, and "consider price factors."[2]

The program was purely advisory; it was based on absolutely no mandatory powers. The advisory powers were exercised at the start only in the way of argument and persuasion addressed to

---

[1] B. M. Baruch, *American Industry in the War; a report of the War Industries Board*, 1921, pp. 21, 22; Clarkson, p. 22.

[2] Baruch, p. 22; Clarkson, pp. 36, 37.

industrial producers. Even this, however, accomplished such considerable results in the spring of 1917 as agreement on a price of 16⅔ cents a pound for copper, in an army order placed when the open market stood at 37.[1] That arrangement was made even before our actual declaration of war; shortly afterward, contracts for steel, lead and lumber were made at prices running to a cut of one-third below the market.[2] But divergence of opinion was very great, resistance frequent, and meantime the chaos of conflicting "priority orders" from different government bureaus was reducing deliveries by railway to such complete confusion and uncertainty that the blockade of inland yards actually necessitated at times the lifting-out of hopelessly side-tracked cars with cranes, while the congestion of ocean terminals compelled the unloading of freight in open fields twenty or thirty miles back.[3]

In this paralyzing situation, when the American army was at last moving in force to Europe, when the European campaign was itself approaching the crisis of the war and when, therefore, demand for instantaneous shipment of the block-

[1] Clarkson, p. 162.   [2] *Ibid.*, p. 164.
[3] *Ibid.*, 138, 139.

aded war munitions to the coast became extremely urgent, President Wilson formally extended the functions and powers of the War Industries Board with a view to "creation of new facilities," "conservation of resources," advice to the government's purchasing agencies "with regard to prices to be paid" and "determination of priorities of production and delivery;"[1] the last-mentioned function referring to the guarantee of right-of-way for speedy shipment over the congested railways or the refusal of any such privilege. The board's authority, thus cautiously described in order not to exceed the letter of the law, was in reality supported and was known by industry to be supported with the almost unlimited executive war powers, formulated or implied.[2] The Chairmanship of this important commission was entrusted to Bernard M. Baruch, a man of great personal energy, independence of business affiliations and knowledge of industrial conditions, who in due course surrounded himself with a group of equally energetic and experienced men of affairs. These administrators severally assumed control of

[1] President Wilson, letter of instructions to B. M. Baruch, March 14, 1918.

[2] Clarkson, p. 95.

such tasks as granting priority of transportation, allocating materials and manufacturing resources, determining prices, applying commercial economy and conservation, directing conversion of industrial plants from "non-essential" to "essential" production; the criterion for judgment as between the two qualities being, first the imperative needs of war and second, the irreducible minimum of home requirements.

Although lacking statutory authority in any of these directions, the Board indirectly possessed wide powers. It was known to be able, by virtue of the President's co-operation, to act through the Railway Administration in granting or withholding "priorities" of shipment; through the war power of the army, navy, food, fuel and shipping boards in the matter of outright commandeering, and through its own ability to control distribution of material for manufacture. Acting on the advice of the War Industries Board, the Director of Railways could relegate to the "non-essential category" the transportation of raw material consigned to an obstinate manufacturer, which would mean indefinite delay. The War or Navy Department could in the same way appropriate to its own uses the manufacturer's raw material, and the War Industries Board could exert its own pressure on the producer of raw material to send the consignments elsewhere. It is to the credit of American manufacturers that this direct coercion rarely had to be applied. The instinct of patriotism in the walks of industry itself, when appealed to by visibly efficient and responsible public officials, rendered application of the compulsory powers usually unnecessary.[1]

Exercising these legally vague but practically very effective powers, and purely by negotiation with the manufacturers, the War Industries Board brought down the price of steel billets for war purposes to $45 per ton as against a ruling market price above $100, of lead from 11 cents to 8, of aluminum from 60 cents to 32, and so through a long list of other essential materials.[2] This achievement called a halt in the traditional "war profiteering," but it was only a part of the Board's task. Industries "non-essential" for the needs of war were not, as had at first been suggested in public discussion, put out of commission,[3] but thousands of plants were made to convert their productive facilities from non-essential to

[1] Clarkson, pp. 94–99, 177, 188–190.
[2] *Ibid.*, pp. 318, 356, 359, 399.   [3] *Ibid.*, pp. 184, 185.

essential products, and some were asked to close their doors to release the labor needed elsewhere.[1] In the matter of passenger automobiles, after prolonged negotiation, preference in allotment of materials was granted by the Board to manufacturers who should agree not to exceed 25 per cent of the 1917 output.[2] At the same time, the work of enlarging capacity of war production was extended by every conceivable device.

The process of "converting" machinery from commercial to military output was not confined to turning locomotive and kindred plants to production of shells, as in 1915. In the war production of 1918, automobile plants were diverted to production of air-planes, toy-plants to packing-boxes, manufactories of stoves to grenades and mortar-bombs, of carpets to army blankets and duck, of furniture to ammunition boxes, of horse-shoes to trench picks.[3] In the close economizing of material under the scrutiny of the Board's "conservation division," pressure was successfully applied to reduce the sizes and types of ploughs, wheels and wagon bodies, to shorten the "uppers"

[1] Clarkson, pp. 244, 245.
[2] Baruch, p. 271; Clarkson, pp. 336–343.
[3] Baruch, p. 42; Clarkson, p. 248.

of shoes for civilian use, to adopt the simplest
standards of clocks and pocket-knives, to limit
the length of coats and overcoats, to restrict the
use of wool in shawls, of steel in corsets, even of
brass and copper in funeral apparatus.[1] The
conservation policy touched the civilian even more
closely when, in addition to the "meatless Tuesdays" and "wheatless Wednesdays," the Fuel
Administration added "heatless Mondays" for
fuel conservation,[2] in observance of which order
department stores, factories not working on war
material, even the Stock and Produce Exchanges,
suspended business on that day,[3] and when rigid
restriction of superfluous street lighting transformed even New York City's "White Way" into
a sombre evening thoroughfare.[4]

The result of this energetic program, to which
the country submitted willingly and even enthu-
siastically, was soon strikingly visible in the wholly
unimagined stream of war material which poured
out from the United States to the European
army storage centres and which, through concentration of labor and material on the new ship-

[1] Baruch, pp. 63–67; Clarkson, pp. 221 and 224.
[2] Order of N. Y. State Fuel Administration, Jan. 17, 1918.
[3] *Financial Chronicle*, Feb. 2, 1918, p. 448.
[4] Order of Fuel Administration, Dec. 31, 1917.

construction industry, made possible that industry's extraordinary achievement—production of a transport fleet that grew from practically nothing in April, 1917, to nearly 500 ships before the armistice, with a tonnage of 3,800,000, or twice the entire American ocean marine of 1917.[1] It was largely the work of the War Industries Board in regulation of industry, combined with its close watching of "priorities" of freight on the unified railway system and supplemented by the amazingly effective work of the instantly-constructed shipbuilding plants, which made possible the arrival in 1918 of 2,000,000 American soldiers at or near the battle-front with an inexhaustible supply of ammunition, followed by Château-Thierry, the breaking of the Mihiel Salient, and the retreat of the German army.

But the Board's achievements had a different result in another direction. The program of regulation laid a heavy hand on the "war profits" of 1916 and 1915. While prices for essential materials were, as we have seen, held down in a manner never attempted before our own government's entry into the war, wages were rising on the average more than 20 per cent over 1916 and all costs

[1] Clarkson, p. 134.

of production were similarly advancing. On top of this handicap to expansion of profits in proportion to the increased orders, the "excess profits tax" on corporations, for which $2,045,000,000 was assessed in the budget for the fiscal year 1918,[1] drew heavily on surplus earnings of the companies.

Gross receipts from its sale of manufactured goods by the United States Steel Corporation in 1918 were $1,744,312,000, against $1,683,962,000 in 1917 and $1,231,473,000 in 1916; but manufacturing costs increased $235,875,000 in 1917 and $131,656,000 more in 1918. When the Federal war tax was deducted—$233,465,000 in 1917 and $274,277,000 in 1918—total net profits in 1918 were smaller by $120,071,000 than in 1916, although gross earnings had risen $512,839,000. Net earnings of the General Motors corporation were $6,472,000 larger in the calendar year 1918 than in the twelve months ending with July, 1917, but payment of war taxes had increased $16,060,000. Sales by the Baldwin Locomotive Company, whose plant was largely converted to manufacture of war material, were greater by

[1] Commissioner of Internal Revenue; Treasury Report, 1918, p. 943.

$63,960,000 in 1918 than in 1916, but its net profits after deducting war tax increased only $3,133,-000. The du Pont de Nemours powder plant made $10,276,000 larger sales in 1918 than in 1916, but its final net earnings were $34,792,000 smaller.

This was the story of practically every war-time industry. It answers somewhat conclusively the sweeping allegations which are still repeated regarding the abuse of "profiteering" during our participation in the war, and it also explains what seemed at the time the paradoxical decline in shares of such companies on the Stock Exchange, in face of the unprecedentedly large war contracts. Railway shares had recovered when the worst apprehensions of the companies were relieved by the terms of government control, and the basing of the guaranteed compensation on the actual results of the three years prior to 1917 fixed for the criterion a period in which net annual income of the railways, as reported by the Interstate Commerce Commission, averaged larger than in preceding years.[1] But the duration of the government's guarantee was strictly limited. Back

[1] Interstate Commerce Commission Annual Reports; 1917, p. 91; 1914, p. 93.

of all these considerations, in the markets of 1917 and 1918, stood the doubt which had repeatedly overclouded the financial horizon in the earlier war years—what would happen to trade in general and to the expanded industrial organization in particular, if the war were suddenly to end.

Nevertheless, in spite of adverse foreign exchanges, immensely increased taxes and reduced industrial profits, the economic position of the United States in the last stages of the war was in all essential respects extraordinarily strong. The export surplus in our foreign trade ran well beyond $3,000,000,000 during both of the calendar years 1917 and 1918, as against $1,776,000,000 even in 1915. The gold-import movement of 1916 had ceased, yet the country's stock of gold at the end of 1918 was 40 per cent of the whole world's reported gold reserves,[1] whereas in 1914 the proportion could not greatly have exceeded 25 per cent. Notwithstanding the very great increase in note and deposit liabilities of the Federal Reserve between April, 1917, and November, 1918, the twelve reserve banks reported in armistice week cash holdings larger by $496,000,000 than was required for the stipulated legal percentage of

[1] U. S. Mint, Annual Report 1919, pp. 278–283.

liabilities.[1] With the advances of our government to its European Allies, after April, 1917, the
United States had become indisputably the creditor nation of the world, and it was certain to
retain that position on return of peace. Calculations of economic experts, it is true, subsequently
reached the conclusion that on international
account the total payments made by the United
States to other nations, between July, 1914, and
the end of 1918, had been $437,000,000 greater
than the payments made by the outside world to
the United States.[2] But that was a manifest
consequence of the prodigious loans to Europe
by our market and our government; actually,
therefore, the estimate provided further testimony to the country's economic resources.

The attention of the American people was
directed far more closely to the progress of the
war itself, during the eighteen months after April
6, 1917, than to economic vicissitudes at home.
Even the financial markets, despite their general
downward trend, responded by rapid movements
in one direction or the other to the series of epoch-

[1] Federal Reserve Board, weekly statement of Nov. 8, 1918;
Annual Report for 1918.

[2] Harvard University *Review of Economic Statistics*, July, 1919;
"The Balance of Trade of the United States."

making events on the European battlefront—the futile attack on the "Hindenburg line" in the summer of 1917; the collapse of the Russian campaign in July, followed by the Bolshevik revolution in November; the rout of the Italian army in October; the breaking of the British line by Ludendorff's offensive of March, 1918; the forward movement of Foch in the following July with his American reinforcements, which marked the beginning of the end. It might have been imagined that the Stock Exchange would have responded with a greatly accelerated fall of prices to the ominous news of March, when consternation seized on our people, when the newspapers published Sunday afternoon "extras" to cover the latest battle news, when the talk was sometimes of the British army "driven to its ships" and sometimes of continuance of the war through 1919, and when even Marshal Foch was quoted as sententiously expressing his doubt as to whether the Americans might not "miss the 1918 train."[1]

But the Stock Exchange displayed at that moment its traditional power of insight; the stock market held absolutely firm in the face of the alarming news, began to advance when Foch

[1] Clarkson, p. 133.

launched his counter-offensive on July 18, then rose vigorously when Germany, disastrously defeated along the entire battle-front, at last made its appeal to the President for terms of peace on October 6. On the false report of November 7, that the armistice had already been signed, the markets reflected by a violent upward movement the outburst of popular jubilation which accompanied that curious incident. Just as the people at large, the force of whose enthusiasm had been largely spent in the premature celebration of the 7th, received in something like a spirit of calmness the authentic news, on November 11, that the war was actually over, so the financial markets paused uncertainly, more disposed to discuss the probabilities of the unknown future than to express exultation over what had already happened. No one professed to foresee with any clearness what would be the next chapter of our financial and industrial history.

CHAPTER VI

THE FIRST YEAR AFTER THE WAR

IT is not easy to discover exactly what immediate movement of events was expected, even by statesmen and financiers, to follow termination of the war. Politically the belief had been entertained, long before the armistice, that the Austro-Hungarian Empire would disintegrate, that important changes in form of government would occur in the rest of Central Europe as they had already occurred in Russia, and that probably the German Kaiser's abdication would be inevitable. But those expectations scarcely prepared the world for the events and incidents which crowded on one another's heels at the news of peace, in such rapid succession as to leave the reader of the news almost as bewildered mentally, and quite as unable to know what to look for next, as he had been in the first week of August, 1914. The instantaneous downfall, not only of the Kaiser but of the Austrian Emperor and of all the hereditary provincial potentates of Germany, the reversion of the old and the new states of Central Europe to republican government, came in a simultaneous rush of news which left the imagination ready for anything.

It had been predicted by public men and intimated by labor leaders, while the war was still in progress, that labor would not submit to a policy whereby the wage-earner, as had happened in the sequel to certain other wars, might have to bear the brunt of hardship in the readjustment period. But not even Russia's Bolshevist coup-d'état had seemed to prepare the scene for the seizure of political dictatorship by Communist-Labor factions in several of the European succession states, or for the open attempt of the German communists to overthrow the provisional government and prevent a popular election. The menacing attitude of European labor; its demand for admission into the management of British manufactories; its actual seizure of the industrial plant of Italy; the submission to our own Congress, under the menacing pressure of organized labor, of a demand that the government should own the railways and grant to railway working-

men a direct share in the management and profits
of the transportation industry—this seemed at
times in 1919 to foreshadow formidable and world-
wide change in the social order.

Along with it came the utterly confusing series
of incidents in the arranging of the terms of
peace—President Wilson's departure in December, 1918, to attend the peace conference, that
being the first occasion of our history when a chief
executive in office had left the United States for
an absence in foreign parts; the memorable outburst of enthusiasm with which his presence, as
embodying militant America and its aspirations
for peace, was received by the European people;
then the prolonged friction and deadlock which
beset the conference itself, and the disappointment over its compromises. The resistance of
our Senate to the Peace Treaty with that docu-
ment's provision for American participation in
the League of Nations followed quickly; the bit-
ter controversy between the White House and
the Capitol; the withholding of the necessary sen-
atorial ratifying votes unless with important res-
ervations in the treaty; the President's refusal
to concur, and eventually, although not until
more than a year after the armistice, the sign-

ing of the Peace Treaty by all of the recent belligerents except the United States and the inaug-
uration of the League of Nations with the same
omission, leaving the United States to negotiate
as an isolated power a separate and individual
peace with Germany.

In all this series of spectacular episodes there
was sufficient material to warrant doubt and uncertainty as to the course of post-war political reconstruction. The question of industrial readjustment to the changed conditions seemed even more
obscure. Very seldom in our history has judgment regarding the immediate financial and industrial future been so confused as it was at the
beginning of 1919, and never has the result been
more extraordinary. History threw uncertain
light on the question, what kind of industrial situation would follow return of peace, and such
information as it gave was not reassuring. The
first abdication of Napoleon in 1814 and the
consequent temporary suspension of hostilities
were immediately followed on the London markets by a movement in which, it was testified at
the time, "prices got up to an enormous height
and came down as fast."[1]   But on the definite

[1] Thomas Tooke, *History of Prices*, Vol. II, p. 6.

ending of the Napoleonic wars, in 1815, British trade fell into what contemporary economic writers described as "a period of the greatest depression in almost all branches of industry," of "the most extensive suffering and distress";[1] prices, after averaging in 1814 more than 50 per cent above the pre-war level, went down in the first full year of peace to an average only 9 per cent above that level.[2]   Return of peace in 1865, after our own War of Secession, had been presently followed by financial and commercial depression; immediately ascribed to the London panic of May, 1866, but greatly emphasized by reaction in home trade when the war orders terminated and when American commodity prices, which in 1865 had averaged $216^7/_8$ on the basis of 100 for 1860, fell in 1866 to 191 and in 1868 to $160\frac{1}{2}$.[3]

There was also, it is true, a tradition of sudden and urgent demand for goods for ordinary consumption on the ending of other wars.   That had been the nature of the commercial and industrial movement which followed the Franco-Prussian War of 1871 and our own Spanish War

[1] Tooke, Vol. II, p. 12.
[2] Stanley Jevons, *Investigations in Currency and Finance*, 1884.
[3] "Report on Prices, Wages and Transportation," U. S. Senate, March 3, 1893.

of 1898, and it was occasionally argued at the
beginning of 1919 that absolute requirements to
offset the prodigious waste of war, to make good
the world's exhausted stocks of private merchandise, to provide for the long-suspended building
construction program and to rebuild the towns and
cities devastated by the German invaders, would
amply replace the canceled military orders.[1] We
shall presently see how much or how little of ac-
curacy subsequent events proved this judgment
to have possessed. But the gloomier view unquestionably prevailed as the nations emerged
from war; even the cheerful prognosticators predicted a prolonged decline of prices.[2]

It was recognized that belligerent Europe was
now confronted with financial exhaustion and
national poverty; that the hardship of war-time
and the enormous taxes had probably crippled
buying power. It could not be ignored that even
American production had been keyed up to a
wholly artificial prosperity by Europe's war purchases and, in the case of wheat, by the Government's high guaranteed price. The manufacturing industry faced the predicted shrinkage in for-

[1] N. Y. *Evening Post*, Dec. 31, 1918, "Forecasts of the Future."
[2] *Ibid.*

eign demand with its producing plant enlarged
on a scale indicated by the United States Steel
Corporation's war-time increase of 41⅓ per cent
in active mill capacity;[1] the farmers approached
it with an acreage already sown, for the American
winter-wheat crop of 1919, larger by 60 per cent
than the record-breaking pre-war acreage of the
great crop of 1914.[2]

These aspects of the situation were further
complicated by what seemed to be the problem
of labor. Disbanding of the citizen army and
suspension of war production, the secretary of
the American Federation of Labor stated to Congress in January, 1919, had created so menacing
a condition that, without government relief, there
would possibly be "bread lines in every industrial
centre before May 1."[3] Citing his district reports
of increased unemployment since the armistice,
the Director-general of the United States Employment Service declared in January that, if tendencies then visible were to proceed unchecked, the
country would reach "before the winter is over a

[1] Annual report 1918, U. S. Steel Corporation.
[2] U. S. Agricultural Department, December estimates, 1913
and 1918.
[3] Testimony of Frank Morrison before H. R. Immigration
Committee, Jan. 21, 1919.

situation fraught with grave peril."[1] No great surprise was occasioned when the head of the Bethlehem Steel Company, who in December had declared that the problem of industrial readjustment would be "easily met," predicted in January, in an interview cabled from Europe, that "America will not obtain much business from reconstruction work in the devastated regions" and that "an era of industrial depression in the United States" was to be expected, with "little business expansion for a long time to come."[2]

The actual course of events in trade and industry at the beginning of 1919 seemed, in fact, fully to bear out these misgivings. In the first month of that year the price of cotton declined 21 per cent, of cotton cloths nearly 19 per cent, of copper 13 per cent, and nearly all other products followed. The steel mills, which had been working at full capacity up to November, 1918, were down to 60 or 65 per cent of capacity the next January. Production of iron fell from the 3,354,000 tons of November, 1918, to 2,108,000 in May, 1919. Advance orders on the books of the United

[1] N. A. Smyth, address to the American Academy of Political and Social Science, Philadelphia, Jan. 24, 1919.

[2] Cincinnati *Enquirer*, Jan. 21, cabled interview with Charles M. Schwab.

States Steel Corporation decreased in the same period 42 per cent; a shrinkage never matched for sweeping rapidity in the company's history, except for the six months following the panic of 1907.[1] Very naturally, these manifest signs of industrial reaction caused uneasiness at Washington, where the Secretary of Commerce in February proposed the official "formulation of a scale of prices at which the government departments and other buyers would be justified in buying freely, and at which the manufacturers would be willing to sell with a view to maintaining or restoring business activities."[2] His plan, however, was not tried. It was opposed in Congress and coldly received by industry. The price-fixing committee of the War Industries Board, in announcing that all war-time agreements of the sort would terminate by the first of March, 1919, had itself already reported to the President that "no new price regulations seem to be called for," and had accordingly tendered its resignation.[3] But more than this, as we shall see, a turn

[1] Monthly statements of unfilled tonnage, U. S. Steel Corporation.

[2] Statement of Secretary William A. Redfield, Feb. 6, 1919.

[3] Letter of B. M. Baruch to President Wilson, Dec. 17, 1918.

in the trade situation itself, in some respects the most extraordinary of our economic history, was destined to terminate all discussion of relief.

The turn came first in the very direction where the general public had seemed at the time of the armistice to expect it least—in the export trade. Many manufacturers in close touch with the home market were convinced, at the beginning of 1919, that the sudden disappearance of ordinary domestic orders resulted only from fear on general principles of a precipitous fall of prices. Merchants and middlemen could not be expected to buy freely so long as the possibility was thought to exist that, by waiting two or three months, they would get the benefit of prices lower by 25 or 50 per cent, and for a time this precautionary abstention of buyers had naturally gone far towards causing the very condition which the merchants apprehended. The case of the world outside the United States, however, was different; for Europe, virtually deprived of ordinary necessities during four successive years, and in a less degree South America and Asia, with their stocks of merchandise for peace-time uses reduced to the exhaustion point by diversion of shipping to the war, were unable to wait. All of such foreign buyers had somehow acquired the purchasing power, and even in January, 1919, the value of our export trade was $118,000,000 greater than in the same month of 1918.

In June, when it reached $928,000,000, it was actually larger by $315,000,000 than in any previous month of our history and, although prices during the intervening twelvemonth had risen on the average only 6 per cent, it was more than double the export of June, 1918. During the seven first months of 1919, when our total exports were $1,092,000,000 greater than in the same months of 1918 and when $871,000,000 of the increase occurred in shipments to Europe, the composition of the post-war export trade was as significant as its destination. As against decrease in that seven-month period of $83,000,000 in our total export of steel, which in 1918 had been destined almost entirely for war purposes, of $73,-000,000 in copper and brass, the material for ammunition, and of $137,000,000 in explosives, the export of cotton increased $254,000,000, of cotton manufactures $52,000,000, of boots and shoes $20,000,000, of wearing apparel $13,000,000, of paper $29,000,000, of agricultural implements and ordinary hardware $12,000,000. Shipments of structural steel, of paint, of steel rails, of cutlery, even of type-writing machines, were increased by tens of millions. In two such staples of peace-time export as cotton cloth and rails for the foreign railways, our shipments during the whole of 1919 were actually larger by 40 per cent or upward than in the pre-war year 1913.[1] The total yearly exportation, which had been $6,233,-000,000 in 1918, rose to $7,920,000,000 in 1919; it was destined to each $8,228,000,000 in 1920.

On the face of things it was evident that Europe, and with her to a less extent the rest of the outside world, were hurriedly laying in fresh stocks of the goods of which they had been deprived for civilian uses during war-time. The admittedly urgent need of these other countries for our merchandise on this immensely expanded scale did not explain how they were to pay for it. During the whole of 1919 our surplus of exports over imports, in trade with the recent European belligerents alone, was no less than $4,700,000,000.[2] But part of the payment for these huge consignments was made by our Allies, through drawing

[1] Department of Commerce, "Monthly Summary of Foreign Commerce," Dec., 1913, and Dec., 1919.
[2] Monthly Summary of Foreign Commerce, Dec., 1919, p. 6.

on the credits advanced to them by the government at Washington; in the case of such purchases as foodstuffs, that use of our Treasury's
advances was formally permitted during eighteen months after the proclamation of peace.[1]
In the twelve months following that event, indeed, these inter-governmental loans were actually increased from $8,171,000,000 to $9,647,-
000,000;[2] a fact which was found to have much
bearing on the subsequent discussion of reducing
or canceling Europe's war debts to the United
States government. In the case of certain other
countries, neutral during the war, large credits
had been accumulated in the United States
through deposit of capital with American banks
for safe-keeping, and these could now be used for
purchase of American goods. The greater part of
the export trade of 1919, however, was financed
on the basis of new bank credits advanced in the
United States; partly through endorsement of
the foreign importer's bills by exporting merchants and the subsequent discount of such
foreign bills at American banks, partly by

[1] Treasury Report, 1919, p. 67, Victory Loan Act of March 3,
1919, Section 7.

[2] Treasury Report, 1918, pp. 36 and 37. *Ibid.*, 1919, pp. 64 and
65.

loans raised directly for account of the foreign markets.

Through these operations, it was estimated by the Federal Reserve Board that the burden of providing cash for not much less than $2,000,000,-000 of the year's American exports had "probably fallen, directly and indirectly, upon the commercial banks throughout the country."[1]   That is to say, our own banks had to that extent virtually advanced to the foreign importer the money to buy the goods from American exporters.   We shall discover, when we come to study the events of 1920, some highly important consequences of this policy.   But in tracing the course of events in the markets of 1919, the essential fact is the enormous volume of merchandise exported in that year by our manufacturers.   Although the early markets of 1919 were curiously oblivious to the movement, it was impossible that such requisitions on the American producer should not have their effect, first upon immediately-available home supplies and next, therefore, on popular ideas regarding trade demand and prices.

It is difficult to determine just when the widespread apprehension in regard to the industrial

[1] Federal Reserve Board, annual report for 1919, p. 25.

future, which marked the early weeks of 1919,
began to change to the totally opposite idea of
general scarcity and a consequent unlimited rise
of prices, absolute belief in which was the outstanding phenomenon of the year's later months.
It was not until May that the board appointed
by the Secretary of Commerce, with a view to
sustaining prices and restoring trade stability in
a supposed emergency, relinquished its undertaking, and it then resigned reluctantly and under
protest.[1] Financial reviews had begun in April
to talk of improving trade; mostly, however, as a
consequence of lower prices;[2] but the rapidity
of the change of feeling, and the outward reasons
for it, are shown by the contemporary trade
reports of subsequent weeks. In the middle of
April, they informed the reader that "uncertainty
of prices is a distinct drawback" to recovery.

Even in May, the best that could be said was
that "merchants are less timid about buying."
By the middle of that month, however, "a large
business is being done both at wholesale and retail" and it was noted, almost for the first time,

[1] Letter of Secretary of Commerce Redfield, May 9. Statement of Chairman George N. Peek, May 12; of Secretary of the
Treasury Glass, May 12.

[2] *Financial Chronicle*, April 5, 1919, p. 1330.

that "export business is on an enormous scale."
At the opening of June the reader of the trade
reviews learned that "wholesalers complain of
scarcity of goods; this is something new." Three
weeks later "there is talk of labor shortage
rather than unemployment; some buyers of merchandise are receiving only a percentage of their
orders." In July "there is a big business in staple
articles as well as luxuries," in which "people do
not haggle so much about the price as they do
about deliveries." At the end of the year "consumption plainly outruns production; in parts
of the country, what might be called a Saturnalia
of buying prevails; the retail holiday business is
said to have been the largest on record."[1]

This talk of scarcity and prediction of an indefinite rise in prices, coming only a month or two after
prevalence of belief in overproduction and in an
era of falling prices, was so unusual an incident of
economic history as to require close examination.
It was all the more extraordinary in that the
notion of scarcity, which became an obsession
when this singular year 1919 drew to a close, was

[1] *Financial Chronicle*, "Commercial Epitome," April 12, May
3, May 19, May 23, June 5, June 13, June 28, July 26, Dec. 27,
1919.

in actual fact complete illusion. It was perfectly true that Europe, after the armistice, had found its retail markets so bare of staple goods for peace-time uses, and even its individual stocks of food, clothing, foot-wear and household utensils so near the exhaustion point, as to require instant replenishment. But in the matter of supplies potentially available in the wholesale and producing markets, statistical evidence should even then have proved a negative on all theories of outright scarcity.[1] By a curious but not unfamiliar economic paradox, the rapid advance of general prices which began in the spring of 1919, and which itself was certain to call forth all the energies of production, also convinced the public that the markets were moving under the influence of wholly inadequate supplies. When once the community at large found itself confronted with advancing prices, it seemed to dismiss from mind all considerations of visible supply. The wheat crop of 1918 had been larger by 280,000,000 bushels, or 44 per cent, than the yield of 1917, and the harvest of 1919 was 51,000,000 bushels larger still; yet wheat sold at Chicago in Christmas week of 1919 for $3.50 per bushel—not only

[1] Annual Report N. Y. Reserve Bank for 1920, p. 8.

higher than any price reached in our Civil War paper-inflation days, but above the highest price reached in the European war. The cotton crop which came on the market in 1919 was the most abundant since 1914, when the high record of American production was reached; yet cotton rose in September, 1919, to a price 6 per cent above the highest of war-time and, although the yield in 1920 also was one of the largest in our history, cotton sold in July of that year for a price, 43¾ cents a pound, which had never been equaled in our agricultural history, outside the three years in the War of Secession when the South was blockaded and its cotton unobtainable.

The Cuban sugar crop of 1919, which usually determines the American price, was 2,000,000 tons above the pre-war average, an increase of nearly 100 per cent;[1] production in the United States was larger than in any pre-war year and the amount retained for consumption, plus the imports, was larger in 1919 than in any year but one of our history;[2] yet the price rose 33 per cent between January and September.[3] In 1919 the

[1] Year book, U. S. Department of Agriculture, 1921.

[2] *Ibid.*

[3] N. Y. Chamber of Commerce, Annual Report, 1919–20, Part II., p.8.

world's production of wool was the largest in eight
years.[1]   The British government had in war-time
bought up the entire Australian clip, which could
not then be exported for lack of ships; in 1919 it
was well known to hold 1,600,000 bales of wool in
England and 800,000 in Australia and New Zea-
land, for which it was anxious to find a market.[2]
Nevertheless, the American price advanced nearly
25 per cent in 1919, to a figure never reached in
war-time.

List prices issued by American makers of woolen
goods were advanced repeatedly and, whereas
between October, 1918, and March, 1919, the
average price of cloths and clothing declined
17 per cent, it was raised no less than 70 per
cent in the next eleven months.[3]   To what extent
all products participated in this marking-up of
prices may be judged from the fact that the general average, having fallen 5¼ per cent between
the high war-time record of the previous September and February of 1919, rose 27 per cent
between that month and April, 1920.   The gov-

[1] Year Book Department of Agriculture.
[2] Secretary of British-Australian Wool Realization Association,
letter to London *Economist* of May 7, 1921, p. 933.
[3] U. S. Bureau of Labor Statistics, "Wholesale Prices, 1890 to
1923," p. 16.

ernment's compilation of prices for 478 commodities, based on 100 as the average of 1913, shows the highest point of our neutrality period to have been 173 and the highest during our participation in the war 204. But in May, 1920, the "index number" had risen to 247.[1]

In the light of subsequent events, we now know that two distinct causes in the markets of the day brought about this economic paradox. One was at the time in plain sight of everybody; the other was not visible and for the most part not suspected. The first was the attitude of home consumers. When prices began to recover from their relapse in the early weeks of 1919, it soon became evident that retail buying was not checked at all; on the contrary, that purchases grew larger as prices rose. Presently, signs of unprecedentedly lavish expenditure appeared,[2] quickly ascribed by merchants to the activities of two very different classes of the population—business men who, in spite of restrictions on prices, had been suddenly and hugely enriched by war contracts, and workingmen who believed themselves

[1] U. S. Bureau of Labor Statistics, "Wholesale Prices, 1890 to 1923," p. 16.

[2] N. Y. Chamber of Commerce, Annual Rep., 1919–20, Part II., p. 82.

to have been similarly enriched by the war-time
rise of wages. The purchases by the so-called
"profiteers," supplemented later by those of Cuban
and South American producers to whom the high
prices now obtainable for their products had
been an unexpected windfall and who presently
visited New York to spend their money, were a
natural incident of sudden wealth. But the outburst of extravagance on the part of the laboring
classes was a more surprising incident.

That extraordinary year was marked, as we have
seen, by a series of movements in finance, production and trade which completely reversed the
expectations with which the year began; but in no
respect was the forecast even of the highest experts
more absolutely discredited than in the matter of
employment. So far astray from the facts had
been the predictions of January regarding "unemployment" and "breadlines" that the industrial problem of 1919 was to obtain sufficient labor
forces and get adequate service from them. This
situation may have resulted partly from the fact
that high pay and full employment during war-time
had left in the hands of the working classes surplus
earnings which led to an independent attitude;
in part from a certain reaction and resentment,

after the war activities, which caused great relaxation of endeavor. Even in Europe, where the necessity of enlarged production was extremely urgent, not only to make good the waste of war but to repair the shattered economic structure, the outstanding fact of the first year after peace was unwillingness of the working classes to exert themselves and inefficiency of those who worked.

It was one of the numerous paradoxical incidents of the day that, although labor was growing much less efficient, its remuneration had to be increased progressively. Wages rose in fairly sensational fashion during the whole of 1919. They had necessarily been advanced during the war, first in recognition of increased cost of living but afterward from a visibly inadequate supply of labor to support our own program of war production. In 1916 the average wage per hour in the United States, as computed by the Department of Labor, stood 7¼ per cent above 1913 and in 1918 it was 32¾ per cent above the pre-war year. But in 1919 it stood 54½ per cent above 1913, in 1920 no less than 99 per cent.[1] In 1919, workingmen who had been getting daily wages of

[1] "Union Scale of Wages and Labor," U. S. Bureau of Labor Statistics, 1925, p. 17.

$3 to $3.50 during the early war period could command $6 to $10.

Yet even the great increase of 1919 over 1913 in the average wage-earner's income was less than the period's increase in cost of living; for that was estimated in June of 1919 to be 77 ⅓ per cent above 1913, in December 99 ⅓ per cent, and in June of the following year 116½ per cent.[1] But that fact the workingman did not grasp. What manifestly appealed to him was the fact that more money than he had ever seen before was pouring into his hands.

His instinct was to spend it; with the resultant curious phenomenon, familiar to all observers in those days, of the laborer not only buying lavishly but insisting that the shopkeepers sell him high-priced goods. As a result of official inquiry into the causes of the high cost of living, it was reported that people of this class were "throwing money right and left with inconceivable recklessness"; that mechanics would ask peremptorily for silk shirts, even when warned that the material would not wear as well as others; that silk stockings costing four times as much as the ordi-

[1] U. S. Bureau of Labor Statistics; "Cost of Living in the U. S."; May, 1924.

nary kind were in great demand by them; that in many instances goods could actually not be sold to such customers unless marked up in price;[1] that, in fact, "there has never been so much spending, such a demand for expensive articles, and such disregard of prices."[2] Department stores, it is true, were already finding orders from their old-time customers curtailed as prices rose. But the new clientage of both sorts more than made up the difference.

This influence on prices was visible to everybody; another, which the public did not see and which even merchants greatly underestimated, was the action of producers and middlemen. At the beginning of 1919, producers who had convinced themselves that shrinkage of home demand and falling prices were not warranted by the actual condition of the home consumer, began to hold back their goods from market. This was designed as a purely temporary expedient. But as soon as that policy, along with the heavy foreign purchases, began to force prices up again in the early spring months, a tendency developed with

[1] Report Massachusetts Commission on the Necessaries of Life. Boston correspondence N. Y. *Evening Post*, Oct. 29, 1919.

[2] N. Y. Federal Reserve Bank, monthly bulletin of November, 1919.

surprising quickness for merchants and even mere individual speculators to accumulate goods at the ruling low prices and hold them against an expected further rise.   Even with such commodities as copper immense amounts, bought up with borrowed money, were stored away where they were not reckoned in the statistical "visible supply."

The resultant advance in prices not only increased the already large speculation in basic raw materials but, as described by the New York Federal Reserve Bank, it "created among merchants and manufacturers a state of mind in which, fearful lest they might not obtain the desired volume of goods, they placed orders far in excess of their real requirements."[1]   This attitude was greatly emphasized as a result of the exceedingly inefficient work of the transportation lines; on which, partly because of the confusion incident to return from war-time to peace-time traffic, partly because of the increasing slackness of labor, and partly because of actual strikes or threatened strikes, the delay in delivering goods was throwing commercial plans into confusion.[2]   The absolute un-

[1] N. Y. Federal Reserve Bank, Annual Report 1920, p. 8.
[2] *Ibid.*

certainty of reliance on the performance of labor was a gravely complicating influence in all producing industries. It actually came to pass that, despite the real abundance of supplies, manufacturers would "allocate" to their customers only a certain percentage of their orders.[1]   Before the year 1919 was over, these numerous influences had so far got control of the entire commercial situation that, as afterward described by the highest banking authority, it presented the picture of "an unprecedented orgy of extravagance, a mania for speculation, over-extended business in every section of the country, and general demoralization of the agencies of production and distribution."[2]

Speculation on such a scale, in practically all the basic commodities, necessitates very extensive use of credit.   To have made possible the later situation of 1919, therefore, not only was widespread belief in the continuous rise of prices essential but abundant facilities of credit.   The periodical bank returns showed what kind of borrowing accompanied the movement.   In the twelve months between the middle of 1919 and

[1] N. Y. Federal Reserve Bank, Annual Report 1920, p. 8.
[2] Federal Reserve Board, Annual Report for 1920, p. 1.

the middle of 1920, that portion of the loans of national banks which included advances on merchandise and warehouse receipts increased $451,-000,000; in the preceding twelvemonth they had increased only $71,000,000.[1] The increase of all national bank loans between March 4 and December 31, 1919, was no less than $2,095,000,000, or 21½ per cent.[2] To sustain this enormous burden, private banks in the Federal Reserve system increased their rediscounts at the Reserve banks, from the low point of the year (in January) to the high point in November, by $1,577,000,000; which was actually a larger increase than was reported in the same account between June, 1917, and the armistice week of November, 1918, during which period bank resources were under the strain of the successive war loan subscriptions.[3]

It therefore seemed logical at the time to describe the rapid advance in prices as an "inflation movement"; not less so in that the outstanding Reserve note circulation of 1919 was also expanded $553,000,000 between January and the year-end. The theory that prices were being driven up solely

[1] Comptroller of the Currency, Annual Report for 1920, Vol. II., pp. 160, 161, 162.
[2] Comptroller's Reports, 1919 and 1920.
[3] Weekly Reports Federal Reserve Board.

by the increase in Reserve note issues—that is to say, by currency inflation pure and simple— was somewhat widely entertained at the time, and was in fact made the basis of a Congressional resolution for inquiry into the question whether the currency ought not to be gradually but arbitrarily reduced.[1]   The enormous inflation of paper currencies of the belligerent European states, the visible and rapid depreciation of those currencies in terms of gold, and the consequent rise of prices during 1920 in France and Italy, for instance, to five or six times what they had been before the war and in Germany to fifteen times the pre-war level,[2] seemed to indicate similar causes at work in the United States.   Responsible banking authorities, however, absolutely rejected this view of the situation; pointing out that most of the European paper money issues were put out wholly in relation to the prodigious deficits of public expenditure and not at all in relation to the requirements of trade, whereas the expansion of our own currency occurred in no respect at the instance of the Treasury and resulted necessarily from the direct application of the business com-

[1] Treasury Report, 1919, p. 17.
[2] Reserve Board, bulletin for February, 1921, p. 195.

munity. It was further answered that, when a member bank had established increased reserves at a Federal Bank, its individual interest would be promoted by making such reserve a basis for additional credit, which could be loaned at a high interest rate, rather than for new note issues paid out to depositors, from which the member bank derived no profit whatsoever.

The governor of the Federal Reserve Board testified to the Senate Banking and Currency committee that the arbitrary keeping in circulation of an excessive volume of reserve notes was impossible under the machinery of the Reserve law, which ensured that new issues could be put out only as a private bank applied for its customers and therefore "only as a need for them develops"; also that outstanding notes, "as soon as they become redundant in any locality," would necessarily be returned for redemption and cancellation to the Treasury at Washington or to a Federal Reserve bank.[1] With this conclusion the Secretary of the Treasury emphatically concurred, stating officially that the currency expansion "is

[1] Letter of W. P. G. Harding to Chairman G. P. McLean of Banking and Currency committee, Aug. 8, 1919; Treasury Report, 1919, p. 18.

an effect and not a cause of advancing prices."[1]
The Reserve Board declared that such changes in
our existing currency always "follow price changes,
they do not precede them," and that therefore
"there is no foundation for the view, still sometimes urged, that changes in the volume of currency are responsible for changes in prices."[2]

But credit inflation was another matter. In
that direction, the circumstances of the day played
directly into the hands of the speculators. Ordinarily, a nation-wide speculation of so large a
scope would have driven up the cost of money,
even at the Reserve banks, but this the Reserve
banks themselves were forced by circumstances
to prevent in 1919. We have seen how, in the
"drive" for the Fourth Liberty Loan of October, 1918, private banks had pledged themselves
for a year to lend unlimited sums to individual
subscribers, at the interest rate borne by the bonds.
The Reserve Board explained officially at the end
of 1919 that the member banks, in order to carry
such a burden, had been obliged to rediscount
their own paper with the Federal Reserve; it
pointed out further that, in order not to inflict an

[1] Treas. Rep., 1919, pp. 17 and 18.
[2] Federal Reserve Board, Monthly Bulletin for October, 1919.

actual loss on the private banks through such
rediscounting, "it was essential that, as long as
the banks were lending to bond subscribers at
coupon rates, the rediscount rate should be related
to the bond rate."[1]   But this meant not only that
private banks in the system could borrow on "Liberty loan collateral" from their Reserve bank at
4 or 4¼ per cent, the official rediscount rate, for
the purpose of "carrying" individual subscribers
to the war loans, but that they might also rediscount government collateral at the low official rate
and lend the proceeds to ordinary customers at
5 or 6 per cent.

Other circumstances of the day enlarged the
scope of this possible operation. In May, 1919,
the floating debt of the United States government,
left over from the war and not yet converted into
longer-term obligations, amounted to $6,467,525,-
000.[2] The "certificates of indebtedness" which
represented that debt were carried by private
banks and, since they usually ran for only six
months or a year, they had to be constantly
renewed. The Treasury naturally wished to
keep down the interest rate upon them, and in

[1] Federal Reserve Board, Annual Report for 1919, p. 2.
[2] *Ibid.*

fact the rate was held at 4½ per cent during most of 1919. But since the private banks were compelled to rediscount a good part of these loans also at the Federal Reserve, it was evident that so low an interest rate could be maintained on such obligations only through an equally low or lower Reserve bank rate. It thus resulted that the Reserve system was making credit artificially cheap at the very moment when its price ought to have risen in the face of the huge requisitions on the general fund by speculators. It was possible for a private bank, which had government bonds or short-term notes in its possession, to use them for obtaining loans at the Federal Reserve and re-lend the proceeds for purely speculative purposes. The Reserve Board itself declared in October, 1919, not only that "the chief factor leading to rediscounting is the expansion of loans and discounts made in favor of customers," but that this loan expansion was suspiciously associated with the "growth of speculative transactions."[1]

It had become evident, indeed, long before the hoarding and forestalling movement of 1919 reached its climax, that the country's credit organ-

[1] Federal Reserve Board, monthly bulletin for November, 1919.

ism was being subjected to a dangerous strain.
The borrowings of speculators in commodities
were superimposed on a series of other exceptionally large exactions. I have spoken of the recourse to bank loans, constantly extended, by exporting merchants to finance the payment by
foreign purchasers for our unprecedentedly large
exports. An import trade, whose increase of
$873,000,000 in 1919 and of $1,375,000,000 more
in 1920 was based largely on the supposed domestic scarcity of goods, called for further and unusually large recourse to the credit fund. That the
banks were carrying billions of dollars of the government's floating debt, we have already seen.
But even these successive strata in the pyramid
of bank debt were only part of the story.

In the first place, it was absolutely necessary
to fund into longer-term loans a part of the Treasury's six-month or twelve-month notes. The new
Secretary of the Treasury, Carter Glass, asked
Congress in February, 1919, for authority to issue
for that purpose additional bonds in amounts not
exceeding $10,000,000,000.[1] Congress granted
authority for the issue of $7,000,000,000 at a rate

[1] Secretary Glass, letters to H. R. and Senate finance committees, Feb. 10, Feb. 13, 1919.

of interest to be prescribed by the Treasury, but it limited the term of such a loan to five years.[1] In April the Secretary announced the offer of a $4,500,000,000 four-year loan, with an interest rate of 4¾ per cent as against the maximum rate of 4¼ on the war loans. Even by the Treasury it was considered doubtful what would be the response to this so-called "Victory loan"; it was recognized that the patriotic fervor created by the presence of actual hostilities had necessarily cooled with return of peace; "a certain apathy among the people"[2] had to be reckoned with.

Nevertheless, the machinery of the "Liberty loan drives" was put into shape again and, after an intensive popular campaign, the $4,500,000,000 for which the Treasury applied was actually over-subscribed by $749,908,000 on the basis of 11,803,-895 separate subscriptions (in this exceeding the record of the first and second Liberty loans) and with all but 13 of the 51 states and possessions asking for more than their allotted quota.[3] This unexpectedly successful operation made possible rapid reduction of the government's floating indebtedness as fast as the obligations matured;

[1] Treasury Report, 1919, p. 44. [2] *Ibid.*, p. 51.
[3] *Ibid.*, p. 253.

from an outstanding total of $6,250,000,000 on April 30 it had fallen to $3,736,352,000 by October 31.[1] But in the case of the national banks, for instance, although their investment in "certificates of indebtedness" had decreased $722,000,000, the same institutions had purchased $384,000,000 of the new United States bonds and had loaned $297,000,000 to individual borrowers against such bonds as collateral.[2]

While this large operation by the government was under way, the money market's position became complicated by two other incidents of the first importance. After return of peace the government had quickly decided, first that extension of credits to European governments for use in supporting their exchange rates should cease; second, that the embargo on gold exports from the United States should also be terminated, and each of these decisions had results of far greater scope than the markets had imagined to be possible. In March, 1919, the New York banking agents of the British government tersely announced that "we have received instructions

---

[1] Treasury Report, 1919, p. 2.

[2] Comptroller of the Currency's statement; Treasury Report, 1919, pp. 946 and 954.

from the British government to suspend purchases of sterling exchange for government account."[1]

Up to that time New York exchange on London had been selling around $4.75¾ for sight bills, a price which had been maintained pretty steadily since 1915 and which represented depreciation in the pound sterling of only 2¼ per cent from gold parity. Before the end of March, however, the rate had fallen to $4.58. Recovering slightly in the later springtime, it went in July below the $4.50 war-time minimum of 1915, broke precipitously when payments for England's autumn purchases of produce came in sight, and by December was carried down to $3.67¼. What happened with the New York valuation of the British currency in 1919 happened also with that of the other European participants in the war. The franc and the Italian lira, whose gold parity was in each case 19⅛ cents and which had been "pegged" respectively at 18⅛ and 15¾ during the war, were down before the close of 1919 to 8⅝ cents for the French exchange and 7⅓ for the Italian.

It might have been imagined that the sweeping movement of exchange rates against those European countries would have resulted in renewal

[1] Statement of J. P. Morgan & Co., March 20, 1919.

of large gold exports to the United States, especially from England.   As a matter of fact, $24,-
000,000 gold was actually sent to us in June
from Canada, largely for British account, and
$44,000,000 in the full calendar year 1919.   But
Europe sent practically no gold directly, and the
imports from Canada were wholly offset by the
results of the next action of our government,
when the Federal Reserve Board on June 9 announced removal of all restriction upon gold
exports.   The sequel was startling, as it is always
apt to be when a period in which such shipments
have been artificially dammed up comes abruptly
to an end.   We have seen in a preceding chapter
that in 1917 the assumption of the obligations
of our European allies in the exchange market
had started an outflow of our gold to neutral
countries, which was checked only by prohibition of gold exports.   But this merely meant that
such obligations had been accumulated in great
amount during the embargo period, whereas now
all restrictions on the draft by neutral creditors
upon our gold supply were suddenly removed.
During the month of June, 1919, no less than
$82,900,000 gold was exported from the United
States.   This abnormally large outflow contin-

ued without interruption. In the twelvemonth beginning with July, the United States actually exported $466,500,000 gold, whereas the largest shipment of any previous corresponding period in our financial history had been the $291,900,000 export of the twelve months ending with June, 1917. In the 1917 period, moreover, gold imports had been so enormous that they exceeded the shipments by $655,000,000, whereas in the period from the middle of 1919 to the middle of 1920 the excess of gold exports was $315,800,000; larger by $150,000,000 than any other twelve months' record in our history.

The destination of the gold exports during and after June, 1919,—they went mostly to Spain, India, China, Japan and South America, countries to which belligerent Europe was heavily indebted on foreign trade account—clearly proved the character of the movement. It is true, a gold export movement of such magnitude seemed a paradox in the face of an excess of merchandise exports over imports, during the same twelve months, of $2,949,000,000. The statistical estimate of the country's whole balance of international payments, including the "invisible items" of exported or imported capital, assigned to the

United States during the calendar year 1919 a net credit balance of $1,091,000,000 as against a net debit of $2,057,000,000 in 1918.[1]   But even this computation left the United States a debtor country to the extent of nearly a billion dollars for the two years combined and, moreover, it is doubtful if any adequate allowance is made in it for the mass of obligations carried in our banks on account of that great part of the country's export trade for which the foreign importers had not paid.   Whatever may be said as to the cause, such rapid reduction in our stock of gold necessarily meant that the banking reserve was being progressively diminished, and at the very moment when the recourse to banking credit was reaching unprecedented magnitude.

Between June 6 and the end of August, 1919, gold holdings of the Federal Reserve system decreased $135,000,000.   Between January and the last weeks of the year, its deposits rose $552,-000,000 as a consequence of the loan expansion and its circulating notes $607,000,000.   The pressure of member banks to relieve the strain on their own credit by rediscounting their paper at the

[1] Harvard University *Review of Economic Statistics*, July, 1920; "The Balance of Trade of the United States in 1919."

Federal Reserve continued without interruption. In armistice week of 1918, the Reserve system's total rediscounts were $1,797,800,000; in the first week of November, 1919, they were $2,189,-400,000, and the motive for that increase appeared in the statement of the national banks, showing that between November of 1918 and November of 1919 their outstanding loans and discounts had been enlarged by $1,463,000,000, or 14¼ per cent[1] —actually twice as great as their percentage of increase during the first twelve months of our participation in the war. By November the system's ratio of cash reserves to liabilities had fallen to 45½ per cent, the lowest in the system's history and only 6 per cent or thereabouts above the legal minimum; the New York Reserve Bank's ratio was down at the same date to barely 40.[2] The time was manifestly approaching when, quite apart from any desire which they may have had to curb a dangerous speculation, the Reserve banks would be compelled to take measures to protect their own position. The history of European central banks had presented plenty of

[1] Comptroller of the Currency, Report for 1920, pp. 299–301.
[2] Annual Report Federal Reserve Board for 1919, pp. 123 and 329.

instances in which those banks had dealt peremptorily with such a situation; they had traditionally done so through raising the bank rate
and thereby forcing reduction of loans. That
happened when the Bank of Germany put up its
rate from 4 to 6 per cent in the autumn of 1905,
avowedly to curb the German speculative mania
of that day, and when the Bank of England,
after the London borrowings by New York speculators had reached abnormal proportions in
October, 1906, raised its rate from 4 to 6 per cent
and threatened 7.[1]

We have seen, in reviewing the incidents of
1919 itself, that the New York Reserve bank rate,
for causes unconnected with sound financial
principles but largely arising from the Treasury's operations, had been kept in 1919 below the
open market. When the strain on the Reserve
system became acute in the autumn, one of those
causes had disappeared; for the private banks had
agreed in 1918 to extend for only one year the
advances made at 4¼ per cent to subscribers to
the Fourth Liberty Loan, and the one-year period
expired at the end of October, 1919. At that
date, the Wall Street open-market rate on four-

---

[1] *Forty Years of American Finance*, pp. 325 and 358.

months' loans with Stock Exchange collateral stood at 6 to 7 per cent and on merchants' paper at 5¼ to 5½; yet the Reserve bank was still rediscounting loans with Liberty bond collateral or on merchants' paper at 4 to 4½ per cent.

An advance in the rediscount rate had in fact been urged by experienced financiers many months before. The Governor of the Reserve Board had himself proposed such a change in August, but he had then been dissuaded by the Treasury.[1] The Advisory Council of eminent private bankers had expressed a similar judgment in September.[2] On the other hand, there had apparently been some hesitation on the part of the Reserve Board itself, especially in the matter of intervention to check the speculative mania. In July, the Board declared of the money market that "there is no necessary connection between rates for speculative purposes and for commercial transactions,"[3] and as late as October its official bulletin asserted that "little desirable restraining influence could have been exercised by Reserve bank rates in

[1] Harding, *The Formative Period of the Federal Reserve System*, p. 157.

[2] *Ibid.*, p. 158.

[3] Statement of Reserve Board, July 9.

recent months."[1]   These admissions had the unfortunate effect of encouraging Wall Street in the
belief that the Reserve Board would take no
stand against the speculative excesses, and in
the autumn the nation-wide speculation, which
now converged on the New York Stock Exchange,
began fairly to run wild.

Between April and November, average prices
of stocks had advanced 25 per cent;[2] shares of
certain industrial companies over which the specu-
lating public had become excited, and in most of
which the season's advance had started from
reasonably high values, were put up in price
250 per cent, 340 per cent, in one case even 500
per cent.   Demand loans on the New York Stock
Exchange, which had risen to 15 per cent in
June, reached 19 per cent in October. With
average prices of commodities also advancing 3
per cent a month under the influence of unre-
strained speculation, and with the New York
Reserve Bank's rediscounts increased from $700,-
000,000 at the end of August to $900,000,000 at
the opening of November, whereas the increase
in the corresponding period even of 1918 had been

[1] Bulletin of Federal Reserve Board for October, 1919.
[2] New York *Times*, Stock Market Averages for November, 1919.

only $116,000,000,[1] it became evident that action could no longer be postponed.

On November 3, 1919, the governor of the New York Reserve Bank announced an advance in that institution's rediscount rate; assigning, as the reason for the advance, "evidence that some part of the great volume of credit resulting from both government and private borrowing which war finance required, as it is released from time to time from government needs is being diverted to speculative employment rather than to reduction of bank loans."[2] The increase of the New York rate, which was followed presently by all the other eleven reserve banks, was not large; it amounted to only ¼ of 1 per cent on some classes of loans and ½ or ¾ of 1 per cent on others, and it still left the bank rate 1 per cent or more below that of the open Wall Street market. Its effect on the Stock Exchange speculation, however, was immediate. The "gesture" of the Federal Reserve, as the advance in the rate was referred to in those days, had accomplished what the mere change in cost of money could not have effected.

[1] Weekly statements N. Y. Reserve Bank, Nov. 7 and Aug. 29, 1919; Nov. 8 and Aug. 30, 1918.

[2] Statement of Governor Benjamin Strong, Nov. 3, 1919.

The furious speculation for the rise in stocks was quickly turned into disorderly decline, in the course of which some of the industrial shares declined sixty, seventy-five and a hundred and twenty-five points in the course of a week or two. At the climax of the crash, furious denunciation of the Federal Reserve became the habit of the day in speculative Wall Street; even in certain newspapers it was editorially demanded that Congress should "investigate" the Reserve Board's conduct. This outburst of unreasoning temper did not last; it quickly subsided when Wall Street began to realize the gravity of the situation that had forced the Reserve authorities to act. But it is worth while to call attention to the demonstration, because, like so many other incidents of the unconsciously prophetic Stock Exchange, it foreshadowed the much more formidable explosion of resentment which came later from the beneficiaries of the same year's speculation in commodities.

That particular field of speculation was not touched by the Reserve banks' action of November, 1919. Long after the inflated stock market had collapsed, the extravagant movement in the commercial markets continued. The average of all commodity prices rose 3 per cent in December and 4 per cent in January, and in May, 1920, when it reached the high mark of the period, it stood nearly 14 per cent above even that of November, 1919.[1] Some staple articles in which speculation had been very wild, such as cotton, did not reach their top price until July of 1920. The rise in cost of living, especially in regard to clothing and rent, outraced even the advance in wholesale prices; labor costs were a source of constantly increasing pressure, for the average wage scale of 1920 was raised nearly 30 per cent above that of 1919.[2] In the retail trade a new phenomenon presently began to be discussed, and even the newspapers talked of the "consumer's strike."

The ordinary thrifty citizen, wearying of what seemed to him to be, and what in many instances actually were, the monstrous exactions of the shop-keeper, simply refused to buy; wore his old clothes and hats for another season, deferred his usual purchase of household utensils, and had his shoes patched for the first time in his life. Nevertheless, for a considerable period the continuance of extravagant purchases by the spendthrift

[1] *Wholesale Prices, 1890 to 1923,* p. 19.
[2] *Wages and Hours of Labor,* p. 17.

part of the community made this attitude negligible. Congress next took a hand and, in view
of the subsequent Congressional attacks on the
Reserve Board for its higher rediscount policy,
its action in the early months of 1920 was noteworthy. In May the United States Senate
adopted a resolution directing the Board "to
advise the Senate what steps it purposes to take or
to recommend . . . to meet the existing inflation of the currency and credits and consequent
high prices," and the debate on this and a similar House resolution was punctured with angry
accusations regarding the use made of bank
credit to hoard and mark up sugar, wool and a
long list of other necessaries.[1]

But this attitude of public protest failed to check
the movement. In March, speculation was resumed on an extravagant scale even on the Stock
Exchange. "Stock dividends" were announced
by a long series of companies. This device con-
sisted of increasing a company's share capital by
transferring to existing shareholders a portion
of the company's undistributed surplus, usually

[1] Senate speech of Medill McCormick, May 17, 1920; of Ellison
D. Smith, May 31, 1920. H. R. speech of E. J. King, May 1;
statement to House Committee, May 7. *Financial Chronicle*,
May 15, 1920, p. 2032.

without increasing the actual amount paid out in dividends. It therefore left the shareholder with exactly the same income from his investment as before, but with a sense of largely increased property, which was translated by the speculators into advances of 150 or 200 points in some of the shares concerned. Two of them were virtually cornered. Along with this returning stock speculation, rates on the Stock Exchange money market rose early in 1920 to 25 per cent for call loans and 9 per cent for time loans, with 6 and 7 per cent paid on Wall Street for commercial paper. At length, on February 21, the New York Reserve Bank reported an actual deficit in reserve below the legally required percentage to notes and deposits.

The Federal Reserve Board was thus forced to act again, in order both to protect the position of the banking system and to curb the growing mania of speculation. The New York Reserve Bank advanced its re-discount rate from 4¾ per cent to 6 on January 22, 1920, and from 6 to 7 on May 29.[1] During that interval the financial disorder had become world-wide. Although British prices had risen 142 per cent between July, 1914, and

[1] Annual Report N. Y. Reserve Bank for 1920, p. 13.

November, 1918, they rose 32 per cent further
between the armistice and the spring of 1920.[1]
In France and Italy the 1920 average was 50 per
cent above that of 1918, and actual cost of living
had risen even faster.[2]   Paper money circulation
in France increased 22 per cent between 1918 and
the end of 1920, although it had been expanded
five times over during the war; even England's
"currency notes" increased 14 per cent during the
two years after the armistice.   In response both
to these confusing influences and to the reaction of
the American situation on the rest of the world, the
Bank of England raised its rate from 5 per cent to
6 on November 6, 1919, and from 6 to 7 on April
15, 1920; the higher rate not having been reached
in nearly half a century, except for eight weeks in
our panic of 1907 and for one day in the London
"war panic" of 1914, when the rate went to 10 per
cent.   This meant that the whole world's situation
had now duplicated that of 1906 and 1872.   To
any one familiar with economic history, these
signs of the times unmistakably portended the
approach of a financial crisis.

[1] London *Economist*, Feb. 19, 1921, p. 349, "Commercial History and Review of 1920."
[2] League of Nations, monthly bulletins of statistics.

CHAPTER VII

THE BEGINNING OF "DEFLATION"

THERE is no evidence that the business community, or any considerable portion of it, entered the year 1920 with a clear idea of the very grave situation which was immediately ahead. It is true, as we have seen, that uneasiness existed among bankers over the money market's condition, and that even merchants were confessing their dislike at the altered character of retail purchases. But at the beginning of the year, doubt was seldom expressed over continuance of an immense home demand for goods and an unprecedented export trade. Neither had given any sign of reaction. During the closing month of 1919, indeed, after all the Wall Street turmoil, our shipment of merchandise to the outside world had been larger by nearly $70,000,000 than in any month prior to that year, and a further increase at the beginning of 1920 was correctly predicted.

The Christmas trade at the end of 1919 was described in the press as "enormous," with "supplies of merchandise in very many lines inadequate to meet such a call from consumers."[1] At the beginning of 1920, mercantile reviews reported retail trade as "remarkably heavy," with the full output of some industries "sold ahead for the first and even the second quarter."[2] During January the wholesale trade reported buyers as "clamoring for goods both for prompt and future delivery," the steel trade as "jammed with orders" and "some kinds of steel bringing high premiums." In February the mercantile reviews were still of opinion that "there is under-production, all over the country, of the things that modern civilization most needs."[3]

In a carefully-selected symposium of financial forecasts for 1920, published at the end of 1919 and including the views of four well-known economists, three high experts in financial branches of government service and fifteen presidents of banking institutions, a substantial majority expressed belief in continued American prosperity

[1] N. Y. *Financial Chronicle*, "Commercial Epitome," Dec. 20, 1919, p. 2367.

[2] *Ibid.*, Jan. 2, 1920, p. 87.

[3] *Ibid.*, Jan. 10 and 17, Feb. 7; pp. 176, 271, 570.

throughout the New Year, while eight predictions of falling commodity markets were opposed by nine judgments in favor of sustained or even higher prices.[1] One official discussion of the question by the head of a statistical bureau of the government, after arguing that the high prices early in 1920 were the result of inflated paper currencies, concluded that there was "no prospect of any considerable fall in prices for several years to come" but, on the contrary, that prices were certain to go on advancing.[2] As a matter of fact, the increase of paper-money issues was not checked during 1920. All European paper issues were greatly enlarged, and our own Reserve note circulation rose from $2,844,000,000 on January 23 to $3,405,000,000 on December 30.[3]

The markets themselves, at the beginning of 1920, distinctly and at times emphatically indicated that they shared in such expectations. Even on the Stock Exchange, where the fall in prices which began in the previous November continued intermittently during the first two

[1] N. Y. *Evening Post*, Dec. 31, 1919.

[2] Statement of Royal Meeker, U. S. Commissioner of Labor Statistics, Jan. 5, 1920.

[3] Annual Report Federal Reserve Board for 1920, p. 43.

months of 1920, an advance of great violence
occurred in March, shares of a long list of manufacturing enterprises rising 25 per cent or more;
some of them doubling or trebling in price.   Until May, the rapid advance of commodity prices
did not halt at all; on the contrary, their rise in the
first five months of 1920, from the already very
high average of December, 1919, was 17½ per
cent.[1]   Dozens of large industrial companies
increased their cash dividends or distributed
"stock bonuses" to shareholders.   On the surface,
the signs seemed to point to uninterrupted prosperity.   In Wall Street, even the 7 per cent rate
on merchants' paper and the 9 and 10 per cent
charged for loans on Stock Exchange collateral
were commonly discussed as being merely evidence
of the scope of that prosperity and of the market's
willingness to pay high for the means of exploiting
it.

This confidence was suddenly shaken by two
unexpected occurrences.   The warning came first
from the outside.   Precisely as doubt over our own
economic condition had been created, early in 1907
and before the autumn crisis at New York, by
outbreak of financial panic in Germany, South

[1] *Wholesale Prices, 1890 to 1923*, p. 18.

America, and the Far East,[1] so in April, 1920, much uneasiness was aroused when the cables reported the sensationally disastrous collapse of the speculative craze in Japan. The markets of that country had been moving on parallel lines with our own; prices for Japanese merchandise had been rushing upward, since the peace, with the same furious momentum and under the same ideas and influences as were simultaneously prevailing in America. The average of commodity prices in Japan, reckoning 1913 as 100, had in 1918 ranged below 196; in 1920 it was 259⅝.[2] Our own prices, whose average, similarly computed, had been 194 in 1918, reached 247 in May of 1920.[3] A single bank failure at Tokio on April 18, 1920, started the crumbling of the whole speculative structure, and this was immediately followed by a panic of such proportions as to compel every financial and commercial exchange in Japan to stop business. It brought all trade to a halt and, under the forced sales of hoarded merchandise by holders struggling to escape bankruptcy, drove down prices of staple Japanese commodities

[1] *Forty Years of American Finance*, pp. 360–363.
[2] Statistical Bulletins, League of Nations, 1920.
[3] *Wholesale Prices, 1890 to 1923*, pp. 9 and 19.

17 to 35 per cent in the space of five or six weeks.[1]

The analogy between the Japanese situation on the eve of this formidable reckoning, and our own, was too close for even the careless speculator to avoid entirely a shiver of anxiety. The New York stock market turned to a disorderly decline, and merchants began to express rather more openly their own misgivings over the "consumer's strike"; which was now, American-fashion, taking the shape of country-wide organizations known as "Overall clubs" and "Old-clothes clubs," whose membership was pledged to buy no more new wearing apparel until prices should come down.[2] This demonstration often assumed spectacular shape; it went so far as to copy the methods of the Liberty loan drives. In April, New Yorkers watched an "Economy parade" up Broadway,[3] in May the city government of New Orleans undertook to proclaim a special holiday which it called "Old Clothes Day," on which speeches should

[1] Statement of Japanese Financial Commissioner at New York, April 22, 1920. London *Economist*, Tokio correspondence, June 12, 1920, p. 1298; July 17, p. 100. N. Y. *Financial Chronicle*, Apr. 24, 1920, p. 1699.

[2] *Financial Chronicle*, Apr. 24, 1920, p. 1763, "Commercial Epitome."

[3] N. Y. *Times*, April 16, 17, 18, 20, and 25, 1920.

be made to urge suspension of buying. Extravagant purchases of goods by the newly-enriched traders and the highly-paid laborers were indeed continued, but retail stores were growing uneasy over the departure of old-time customers, with the frank declaration that they proposed to restrict their buying to the smallest possible minimum so long as the price for clothing, shoes, hats, and household utensils was kept at what they considered a preposterous figure, often double the prices of war-time. The spread of this movement had begun to alter the viewpoint even of the wholesale trade, whose glowing reports of the year-end had already gradually been replaced by references to the "note of conservatism," the "slowing down of trade," the tendency of merchants and middlemen "to pick their way cautiously."[1]

At precisely this moment a single incident in the American retail trade brought apprehension to a focus. Those large-scale traders in merchandise which we call our department stores are peculiarly sensitive to any shrinkage of popular demand, for the reason that their own financial security depends on making a "quick turn-over" of their heavy stocks of goods. In ordinary times,

[1] *Financial Chronicle*, Feb. 21, 1920, p. 776; Feb. 28, p. 882.

announcement by such concerns of "bargain sales" or "marked-down prices" attracts no attention in the markets, which assume that the department store is only, in the trade vernacular, "clearing out old stocks."   But the announcement of John Wanamaker on Monday morning, May 3, 1920, came at a psychological moment; it was also of unusually sweeping character. Widely displayed in the newspaper advertising columns, it set forth that, at a time "when the highest financial authorities point out the probability of still higher prices," the establishment would "put at the disposal of the public . . . $20,000,000 of the best merchandise . . . by offering the full retail stocks of both our stores in New York and Philadelphia at 20 per cent reduction from actual prices."   The language was that of the clever advertiser; it resulted in the return, temporarily at least, of a mass of regular customers; but the action itself was startling and, to the army of uneasy speculators, very ominous. It was recognized as the outstanding event of the day even by the Stock Exchange, which watched with keenest concern the immediate sequel in the trade; a series of announcements of reduction in retail prices running to 10, 25, sometimes even

50 per cent.[1] The rapidity with which three unfamiliar and unpleasant words were now coming into use to describe the situation is illustrated by the remark of a sober and conservative trade review published in May, 1920, to the effect that "deflation seems to be gathering momentum; liquidation of stocks and bonds is extending to commodities; there are further cancellations of goods."[2]

As a matter of fact "deflation," of which the markets were destined to hear a vast deal more in the next few months and years, was actually and visibly under way. Average prices of commodities, which reached high-record for the period in May, 1920, fell 2 per cent in June and nearly 14 per cent before autumn, the percentage of decline in clothing being twice as great.[3] But the movement of prices was irregular; although the general average reached in May its highest point of 247, as against 203 in November, 1918, and 100 in 1913, some important groups of commodities, such as house furnishing goods, fuel and building

[1] Advertising columns of New York newspapers, May 5, 6 and 7, 1920.

[2] *Financial Chronicle*, "Commercial Epitome," May 22, 1920, p. 2208.

[3] *Wholesale Prices, 1890 to 1923.*

materials, continued to rise until July or September.[1] Cotton, whose average price in 1913 was 12⅞ cents a pound, whose highest war-time price was 38¼ cents and which had averaged 32½ in 1919, went to 43¾ on July 22, 1920; that price being the highest reached since the years immediately following the Civil War blockade of the cotton states.[2] Belief that important or continuous reaction in prices was improbable found some encouragement in the exorbitant prices for food and clothing asked by many retail dealers even in the summer of 1920. Perhaps it found still more in the extremely rapid advance of rents as the autumn season approached—an advance which proceeded with such violence as to occasion something like panic in the ranks of tenants, who were led to suppose that "under-construction" of housing facilities in war-time had left the supply of residence and office buildings wholly unequal to demand.

Whatever its ground of reasoning, a great part of the business community refused to believe that the end of the rise in prices had come. There is "no real uneasiness as to the future of American

[1] *Wholesale Prices, 1890 to 1923.*
[2] *Ibid.* Shepperson, " Cotton Facts."

business," one highly conservative financial journal wrote, during that month.[1]   In the face of the cut in prices at the retail stores there were well-known instances of New York bankers advising Western mercantile clients that, as a result of the "consumer's strike," the consuming public would be forced to replenish its supplies in autumn, when merchants, because of their fright over "deflation," would have entered the busy season with empty shelves.   The sagacious trader, therefore, would be he who should buy heavily in the spring and thus have the autumn market in his hands.   The advice was somewhat widely taken; it resulted, later on, in a struggle of the unlucky clients to escape insolvency; but for the moment there seemed to be no doubt that the argument was allaying the worst of the apprehension.

The stock market did not recover, but that was because financial observers now had other things to watch than declining retail prices.   The extreme tension in money rates was one.   It was on May 29 that the New York Reserve Bank's rediscount rate, which had previously been raised from 4¾ per cent to 6 on January 22, was advanced to the abnormally high figure of 7 per

[1] *Financial Chronicle*, May 29, 1920, p. 2304.

cent. When the first advance of 1920 was made, the New York Bank's ratio of cash reserve to deposits and note circulation had fallen to 38½ per cent, which was virtually the statutory minimum; the bank had in fact been compelled, as the Reserve Board subsequently reported, to put $100,000,000 of its mercantile paper collateral "under rediscount with other Federal Reserve banks in order to maintain its legal reserve percentage."[1] This was pretty nearly a signal of distress. The 6 per cent Reserve bank rate of January checked the process of impairment only momentarily. The reserve ratio recovered to 42¼ per cent in March, but by the end of May was down again to 40⅛ per cent;[2] for which the main cause was recourse of hard-pressed private banks, on a wholly unprecedented scale, to the facilities of the Federal Reserve. When the New York bank rate was first advanced, in November, 1919, the institution's discounts had stood at $958,000,000, or $146,000,000 more than in the armistice week of 1918. But by the end of February, 1920, they had reached $1,132,000,000. Note circulation of the bank, whose maximum was

[1] Annual Report Federal Reserve Board for 1920, p. 386.
[2] *Ibid.*, p. 396.

$736,500,000 in 1918 and $824,900,000 in 1919, stood at $854,800,000 on May 14, 1920.[1]

With money commanding 7 and 8 per cent on the Wall Street open market, it was out of the question to leave the Reserve bank rate at 6. Such a margin of difference would mean that private banks in the Federal Reserve would be able continuously to increase their own loans to customers, while throwing the burden on the Reserve banks and making a double profit to themselves— through the very high open-market rates and through the opportunity of getting the necessary money for much less than the individual borrowers paid them. The 7 per cent Reserve bank rate, fixed at the end of May, was a measure of plain necessity; it was followed or preceded by a similar rise at nearly all the European central banks, while bank rates even on such distant markets as Bombay and Tokio went to 7 and 8 per cent. For short-dated government borrowings the United States Treasury had been paying 4½ per cent per annum up to the last week of 1919, and as late as February, 1920, it put out a loan for a very short term at the same rate. But in May it had to offer 5½ per cent for a six-months' loan;

[1] Annual Report Federal Reserve Board for 1920, p. 396.

by October it was paying 5¾ and by December 6 per cent.[1]

It was impossible for this to happen without profound influence on the price of outstanding government bonds. In armistice week of November, 1918, the 4¼ per cent Liberty bonds had sold on the Stock Exchange for slightly less than 99, or barely 1 per cent below the subscription price. Early in 1919, largely because of the higher interest rate fixed for the Victory 4¾ per cent loan of May, they ranged between 93 and 96. The raising of the New York Reserve bank rate in November of 1919, and the expiration of the one-year term for which private banks had engaged in October, 1918, to lend on Liberty bond collateral at the rate of interest paid by the bonds themselves, caused further decline to 91 and 92; yet they ended that year with fairly steady values.

In 1920, however, the market for these bonds was very severely shaken; first through the direct influence of the high Reserve bank and open market money rates, next through heavy realizing sales by business men and companies that had been large subscribers to the Liberty loans and now needed the money to conduct their own expensive

[1] Treasury Report for 1920, pp. 12–17.

trade and, finally, through an outpour of the bonds from discouraged individual investors who had either taken fright at the already large decline or who, not having paid off the bank loans with which they had raised the purchase-money, were confronted with a charge of 6 per cent or higher to carry the 4¼ per cent investment. It was now, indeed, that the market had to pay the reckoning for the immense mass of subscriptions on borrowed money to the war loan of October, 1918, and the loss fell on the men and women who had been urged to make subscriptions in that way for patriotic motives. Some idea of the scope reached by the closing-out of such bank loans may be obtained from the fact that whereas in November, 1919, rediscounts by all the twelve Reserve banks of private bank loans secured by government bonds stood at $1,771,028,000, the amount had fallen to $1,444,175,000 in the first week of May, 1920, and to $1,231,841,000 in the middle of June.[1]

Under the pressure of these various kinds of liquidation, the price of the Liberty 4¼ per cents, which had been subscribed at par, fell in May, 1920, as low as 82; even the Victory 4¾s, with

[1] Annual Report Federal Reserve Board for 1920, p. 44.

their maturity only three years off, sold below 95.
The market's rating of the government's credit
was on an interest basis higher than 5 per cent.;
something which could not have been said even
in the panic of 1873. These prices of May were
the lowest ever reached; but in actual fact the
decline was checked only by the action of institutions such as savings banks, which were by instinct
so convinced of the great intrinsic undervaluation
of United States bonds at prevailing prices that in
many instances they sold some of the best "gilt-
edged" investments from their strongboxes to
reinvest the principal in Liberty bonds.[1] Necessarily, what happened to United States government bonds happened in even more formidable
shape to the investment bond market in general.
At the time of the armistice a published average of
prices for typical selected bonds was higher than
that of December, 1914, and only 3 or 4 per cent
below December, 1913. From that 1918 average
of 82⅓ the figure declined to 79 in June of 1919,
to 71 in December and to 65½ in May of 1920[2].
That it went no lower, but on the contrary rose to

[1] Report of committee on investments to New Jersey Savings
Banks Association, May, 1920.

[2] New York *Times*, daily Stock Exchange averages.

73 in the autumn of 1920, when the agony of forced liquidation was dominating every other market, can be explained only by the supposition that great masses of capital, withdrawn in complete distrust from investment in stocks or commodities, were seeking refuge in the higher grades of fixed-revenue securities.

This spectacular movement in the investment market was watched both by Wall Street and by the general public with something like bewilderment, and the confusion which surrounded it was not diminished by the fact that the crumbling-away of bond values in the early part of 1920 occurred almost simultaneously with the fall of sterling exchange to $3.18 in February, representing a discount of 34½ per cent from gold parity —apparently a greater depreciation than had occurred even in the sensational fall of sterling when Napoleon returned from Elba in 1815.[1] Beyond any question, an important contributory cause for this sweeping decline in the exchange value of the British currency was recall of their European credit balances, wherever possible, by American bankers and merchants who were now trying to safeguard their own position. But the rapid de-

[1] Tooke's *History of Prices*, Vol. II, p. 33, note.

preciation of sterling reflected also economic conditions in England, whose paper currency issues
had increased £54,000,000 during 1919, or 13 per
cent, and whose foreign trade in 1919, even with
the year's great increase in exports as compared
with war-time, had shown an excess of imports
over exports £535,000,000 greater than that of the
pre-war year 1913.[1]   Along with the precipitous
fall in sterling, the French franc broke at the beginning of 1920 to $5\,7/8$ cents, as against gold parity
of $19\,1/3$ cents and a price of $18\,1/4$ at the armistice.
A feeling prevailed that the whole financial situation was in the grip of abnormal forces whose scope
and direction it was impossible to measure.   In the
public mind, misgiving began to a certain extent
to show itself as to whether the fall in the war
bonds might not mean that the credit of the United
States government itself was undermined and that
the prospect for maintenance of the public faith
had been impaired.   But even while all this was
happening, the markets themselves were preoccu-
pied with other and more definite problems which
called for immediate solution.

Among the long list of troublesome legacies
left by war finance, two were regarded with par-

[1] Report of British Board of Trade for December, 1919.

ticular anxiety. Government operation of the railways and government control of the wheat trade had sustained those two great industries, during our own participation in the war, through the pledging of the public credit for the support of each. The time had now arrived when each would in the natural course of events have to be returned to private auspices. But basic conditions in both industries had in the meantime been so completely altered by war-time influences that it was difficult to see how the transfer of responsibility could now be made without great hazard to the industries themselves. With the railways, partly because of the immensely increased war-time traffic but largely also because of a 25 per cent advance in freight rates, made early in 1918 by the Federal Railway Administration, gross revenue rose from $4,014,142,000 in the calendar year 1917 to $5,184,064,000 in 1919; an increase of $1,169,922,000.[1] But the vastly more rapid advance in cost of material and fuel, supplemented by several sweeping additions to the railway wage scale and undoubtedly emphasized by the period's decreased efficiency of labor—a world-wide phenomenon of the day—

[1] Statistical reports, Interstate Commerce Commission.

had far overtopped the increase of revenue. Even during 1916 and 1917, railway wages in the United States had been raised in the aggregate by the private managements upwards of $300,000,-000,[1] and in May of 1918, on the recommendation of the Wage Commission, the Railway Administration had further increased wages from the $1,917,419,220 total of December, 1917, to $2,205,-432,938.[2]

The Wage Commission's report set forth that, while their own increase of railway wages, $288,013,718, represented an addition of 15.021 per cent, the total increase of $593,865,544 since the middle of 1915 amounted to 36.85 per cent.[3] This happened in the first year of government operation; Mr. McAdoo's successor as Director-General summed up the railway situation, a year after the wage advances of 1918, as one in which rates had been increased approximately 25 per cent while cost of materials, wages, and other necessary railway expenditures had gone up from 50 to 70 per cent.[4] The result was that, as against

[1] Report of Railway Wage Commission, May, 1918. *Financial Chronicle*, May 18, 1918, p. 2086; June 1, pp. 2307–2309.
[2] *Ibid*.   [3] *Ibid*.
[4] Statement of Walker D. Hines, cited in Washington correspondence of New York *Journal of Commerce*, May 28, 1919.

the increase of $1,169,922,000 in railway gross revenue for 1919 compared with 1917, these increasing costs had simultaneously added $1,590,-000,000 to operating expenses, so that annual net earnings had shrunk by nearly half a billion dollars.[1]

What that meant, in the matter of earning power under the conditions of 1919, was suggested by the subsequent report of the second Director-General to President Wilson. In his recapitulation it was shown, first, that during the entire period from January 1, 1918, to March 1, 1920, operating expenses had exceeded operating revenues by $715,500,000; second, that the footing of this loss, together with meeting the government's guarantee to the companies of compensation equivalent to their pre-war net earnings, had resulted during those twenty-six months in a net outlay by the government of $1,886,322,000.[2] That did not indicate a condition of solvency, if the properties were to be thrown back overnight into the hands of their owners. It is true that most of this huge loss was due to a guarantee based on peace-time earnings; also that, as the

[1] Statistical reports, Interstate Commerce Commission.

[2] Report of Director General Walker D. Hines to President Wilson, Feb. 28, 1920.

Director-General took pains to point out, "the railroads like other industries were subject to the conditions growing out of the war," which "would have been the same if the railroads had been in private control."[1] But on the other hand, although the war was now over, war-time dislocation of industry was not, and actual results of railway operation in 1919 were much worse than those of 1918.

The Federal Control Act of 1918 had provided that the period of the federal guarantee should not be extended further than "the one year and nine months next following the date of the proclamation by the President of the exchange of ratifications of the treaty of peace." The President was also authorized, however, to relinquish all federal control "at any time he may deem such action needful or desirable," and it was stipulated that, in case he were so to decide, "no right to compensation shall accrue to such owners from and after the date of relinquishment."[2] The date for return to private operation, with all these complex conditions surrounding it was therefore

[1] Report of Director-General Hines.
[2] Act to Provide for the Operation of the Transportation Systems while under Federal Control, March 21, 1918, Section 14.

really optional with the Executive. In December of 1918 Secretary McAdoo, then also railway director-general, after considering all possible alternatives regarding date of relinquishment, formally advised a five-year extension of the period of Federal control. His argument was that such action would "take the railroad question out of politics," "would admit of a comprehensive program of improvements" and would make possible the discovery, by longer consideration, of "the permanent solution of the railroad problem."

Mr. McAdoo did not recommend public purchase and ownership of the roads; but he believed it "impossible, after return of peace, to restore the competitive conditions of pre-war days" and he recommended, if the five-year extension were not granted by Congress, that the railways should be immediately returned to private operation.[1] This unquestionably hazardous advice was not followed in either particular. Although McAdoo had stated, ostensibly for the president, that "this conclusion accords with his own view of the matter,"[2] Mr. Wilson's first

[1] Letter to Senate and H. R. Interstate Commerce committees, Dec. 11, 1918.

[2] *Ibid.*

formal declaration of purpose, in his message to
the extra session of Congress in May, 1919, set
forth that "the railroads will be handed over to
the owners at the end of the calendar year."[1]
This was, however, on the presumption that
Congress, during the seven-months' interval,
would have prescribed the status for the transfer.
But the House and Senate were unable during 1919
to agree on any program of railway legislation;
therefore the date of relinquishment was further
extended to March 1, 1920.[2]

Unfortunately, the vacillating attitude of the
government had other results than postponement
of return of the railways; it called into life the
slumbering propaganda for government ownership.
That proposal, which had never greatly com-
mended itself to the highly individualistic American community, had assumed a different aspect in
the eyes of railway labor, whose petitions for
increased wages had been conceded without debate
by the Federal Railway Administration and to
whom, therefore, government ownership made a
powerful personal appeal. It should be observed

[1] Message cabled by President Wilson from France, May 19,
1919.
[2] Proclamation of Dec. 24, 1919.

that the whole civilized world was echoing, in the early months of 1919, with the demand of labor for a direct and often for a controlling share in the management of industry. In Russia the Communist revolutionary leaders had utilized the movement to seize control not only of industry but of government itself, in the alleged behalf of labor. Elsewhere in Europe, the attitude of organized labor had been openly menacing. In some countries, dictation of the Soviet type was uppermost in politics; in several, notably Italy, success appeared already to have been achieved in ousting the owners of industrial plants from individual control. It was under these circumstances that a Chicago corporation lawyer, Glenn E. Plumb, previously unknown to the general public outside his own city but who had once been president of a street railway company and had conducted some railway litigation, submitted in August to the committee of Congress which was considering the railway question a radical proposal.

He urged that the Federal government should buy all the railways from their owners for "the amount actually necessary to secure their investment," and that thereafter the whole railway system of the country should be managed by

fifteen directors, of whom five should be elected by
what he called the "classified employees" and
five by the "official employees," with five appointed by the President of the United States.
After fixed charges and operating costs should
have been met, the surplus earned by the railways
was to be divided equally between the government and the railway employees.[1] This extraordinary proposal was at once incorporated into a
bill submitted to Congress by Representative
Thetus W. Sims of Tennessee, which provided
for Plumb's ideas of operating management and
division of surplus profits, which based the terms
of government purchase on "a valuation as determined finally by the courts," and which stipulated "automatic reduction of rates when the
employees' share of the surplus is more than 5 per
cent of gross operating revenue."[2]

Had this sweepingly Socialistic proposal been
sponsored only by its individual authors, it would
probably have attracted merely the curious attention bestowed upon scores of other fantastic bills
and memorials on economic questions which at

[1] Testimony before H. R. Interstate Commerce Committee,
Aug. 7, 1919.
[2] *Congressional Record*, Aug. 2, 1919; Statement of T. W. Sims,
Aug. 4.

such times always go to fill the waste-baskets of Congressional committees. But it immediately developed that the responsible heads of the railway labor organizations were members and officers of the "Plumb Plan League," one of them being its president; also that the submitting of the Sims bill to the House had been dictated by the National Brotherhoods of railway engineers, trainmen and firemen, by the Order of Railway Conductors, and by the executive council of the American Federation of Labor.[1] The labor chieftains presently put in personal appearance at Washington, where they proceeded to issue declarations of their purposes which amounted to open threats. "We are walking on a very thin crust," the head of the Locomotive Brotherhood and president of the "Plumb League" asserted.[2] "The railway employees," the joint manifesto of the railway unions declared, "are in no mood to brook the return of the lines to the former control."[3]

Thus suddenly came the anxiously-awaited test of the question, what underlying political and

[1] Statement of T. W. Sims, Aug. 4, 1919.
[2] Warren S. Stone, interview of Aug. 3.
[3] Statement of Warren S. Stone, W. G. Lee, Timothy Shea, L. E. Sheppard, B. M. Jewell at Washington, Aug. 2.

social situation had actually been left in America by the war. We have seen what was happening in Europe. During the nine months after the armistice, organized labor seemed in one way or another, varying with the political temper and traditions of the different European states, to have seized the reins. It was issuing ultimatums of wholly unprecedented arrogance in regard to political procedure, and neither governments nor employers appeared to have the courage to resist. In the challenge to Congress regarding railway legislation, the stage was set dramatically. The statements for labor were defiant and precise. Not only were all the railway unions committed unreservedly by their officers to the revolutionary program, but the declarations of policy carried the names of more than one labor leader previously esteemed for conservatism—Samuel Gompers, for instance, President of the American Federation of Labor and member during the war of the Advisory Council of National Defense, of the War Industries Board, and of the War Labor Administration. Probably the American public was for the moment wholly unable to guess what would be the outcome. As for the potential scope of the new economic proposal, its author, when asked at a Congressional hearing whether his plan, if logical for the railways, was not equally logical for commercial enterprise in general, replied that he could see no barrier "if it was for the public benefit."[1]

This, then, was a fairly crucial test of American public sentiment and of the temper of our public men. The response was immediate and emphatic. It not only proved unmistakably that Plumb and the so-called "Big Four" railway brotherhoods had wholly misinterpreted the American situation and the temper of the American people, but it went far toward fulfilling the prediction of an eminent American economist, early in the war, that whatever should happen to any other nation as a result of the political and social upheaval, the United States would emerge from the conflict the most conservative nation in the world.[2] Responsible public men at Washington answered the appeal of the labor organizations for their personal support promptly and sternly. Senator Pomerene of Ohio wrote in reply that the Plumb plan was "the most vicious piece of legislation that has been presented to Congress since I

[1] Testimony of Glenn E. Plumb before H. R. Interstate Commerce Committee, Aug. 8.

[2] William A. Dunning, Columbia University, statement in 1916.

have been in the Senate."[1]   Senator Hitchcock of Nebraska stated his absolute opposition, adding that Congress would not be warranted even in touching "such radical legislation without a mandate from the people."[2]   Senator Smith of Georgia declared the proposal "so unreasonable that its unfairness should be clear" even to the railway workers.[3]   Governor Cornwell of West Virginia denounced the plan as "not Socialism but chaos," adding that "they are trying to run things that way in Russia, and we know the result."[4]

Even the original defenders of the project began to waver.   Plumb himself, while insisting that his plan would be "a big issue in the next campaign," admitted that "there is no hope of getting the so-called Plumb bill through Congress this session."[5]   Bryan, an habitual advocate of government ownership, opposed the plan, although characteristically offering a fantastic and unwork-

[1] Atlee Pomerene, Letter to Committee of Ohio railway employees, Aug. 11.

[2] Gilbert H. Hitchcock, telegram to Nebraska railway brotherhoods, Aug. 11.

[3] Hoke Smith, letter to Savannah Chamber of Industry, Aug. 28.

[4] J. S. Cornwell, letter to West Virginia Federation of Railway Employees, Aug. 23.

[5] Interview at New York, Aug. 27.

able alternative of his own.[1]   Gompers, returning from Europe and being told by the reporters that they had been "waiting to hear him come out for the Plumb plan," replied that "you will have to wait a little longer."[2]   A few days later, he announced for the executive council of the American Federation of Labor that action on the plan would be deferred until a sub-committee "examining into all the facts" could report.[3]

The postponement was indefinite, and Plumb's dream of a "big issue in the next campaign" was never fulfilled.   It was in fact quickly discovered that overtures by railway labor to win co-operation even of the farmers had failed.   At first, the agricultural organizations merely kept silence on the proposals; but evidence presently appeared, not only of dissatisfaction among the farmers at actual results of the war-time government operation of the roads but of dislike at the whole idea of public ownership.   In December, the New York State Federation of County Farm Bureaus, through a convention resolution, urged restoration of the railways to their owners under conditions

[1] Testimony before H. R. Interstate Commerce Committee, Aug. 29.

[2] Interview at New York, Aug. 27.

[3] Statement at Washington, Aug. 30.

which "will insure reasonable returns on the value of the properties and reasonable rates"[1] and, a month or two later, a memorial to President Wilson in behalf of a dozen national farmers' unions described government ownership or operation as "costly, inefficient and inadvisable"; "against good public policy and the principles of sound Americanism."[2] Even before this condition of public sentiment had become distinctly visible, the chairman of the House Committee had declared frankly and publicly that the Plumb plan "will not be adopted by the Interstate Commerce Committee"; whose deliberations, he went on to say, were concerned with "questions of credit, of labor, and of financing the roads through the period of transition back to private ownership."[3]

That the American business community was in favor of the program thus set forth had been pretty plainly indicated, even before the controversy over the "Plumb plan" reached its climax. The public hearings by the railway

[1] Resolution at Syracuse Convention, Dec. 19, 1919.

[2] Memorial to President by W. I. Drummond, Chairman International Farm Congress and T. C. Atkeson, Washington representative National Grange, Feb. 25, 1920.

[3] J. J. Esch; speech to conference of H. R. Republicans, Aug. 26, 1919.

committees of House and Senate, in advance of
the formulation of a railway statute, had reflected
strongly the wish for early return of the roads to
their owners. Several members of the Senate
committee were individually committed to government ownership, and it attracted attention that,
in the committee's public hearings, they made
little or no effort to cross-question witnesses with
a view to disparaging the wisdom of restoration
of the railways to their former management.
This hesitancy was frankly ascribed by their
colleagues to the fact that the constituents even
of these government-ownership Congressmen held
the opposite view. As early as January, 1919,
a very careful newspaper canvass of public opinion
at half a dozen typical centres of transportation,
in widely separate parts of the country, had
elicited the fact that those communities were
wholly dissatisfied with the war-time government
operation and anxious for return to the pre-war
status.[1]

For this attitude, the American instinct for
individual rather than governmental achievement

[1] Special dispatches from Kansas City, St. Paul, Boston, St.
Louis, Philadelphia, Memphis, San Francisco, Pittsburgh, Seattle
and Cincinnati; N. Y. *Evening Post*, Jan. 23, 24, 25, 27, 28, 29,
30, 31, Feb. 1 and 3, 1919.

was in many respects the clearest explanation.
But it also unquestionably resulted from discontent of shippers of merchandise over some
actual results of state operation of the railways.
For one thing, they had lost the old-time advantage of prescribing the route for freight consignments, of selecting the most advantageous plan of
shipment, of keeping track of the location of their
goods at a given moment.[1] The change in such
matters was perhaps an inevitable consequence of
the particular war-time problems of transportation,
but the shippers had ceased to make allowances
when the same conditions continued to prevail
during 1919. In that year and in 1920 the
"freight blockades," the absence of any assurance
of prompt delivery of goods from producer to
consumer, were believed by many merchants to be
an essential cause for the abnormally high prices
of 1920 and the abnormally large amount of money
tied up in merchandise.[2] Behind all these considerations there existed, especially among the
farmers, great dislike at the much higher transportation rates under government operation.
Those advances were considered to be largely

[1] *Evening Post* dispatches.
[2] N. Y. Federal Reserve Bank, Annual Report for 1920, p. 8.

a consequence of the still greater advance in wages for railway labor. But the farmer got no compensatory benefit; on the contrary, the great rise of wages in mechanical industries, including railway operation, had drawn away labor from the farms on such a scale that the average pay of agricultural workers in the United States had by 1920 increased 120 per cent as compared with 1915 and 62⅜ per cent as compared even with 1917.[1] It was not surprising that the farm organizations should have refused to indorse the railway plan of the "Big Four" brotherhoods.

The railway committees of the two houses of Congress had been holding public hearings on the question throughout 1919; in September a completed bill was submitted to the Senate, in November to the House. The two measures differed widely; the so-called Cummins Bill, proposed by the Senate committee, taking much the more advanced ground of the two, especially in the matters of prescribing rates sufficient to yield a fair return on property investment, of dividing with the government earnings in excess of a stipulated rate, and of providing, so far as possible, for the compulsory consolidation of existing rail-

[1] Yearbook U. S. Department of Agriculture, 1921, p. 785.

ways into a stated number of larger systems.
The House passed the Esch Railway Bill November
17 and the Senate on December 20 adopted the
Cummins Bill. Irreconcilable as the two measures seemed to be in principle, the conference
committee managed, by modifying the Senate bill
and bringing the House bill closer in line with its
provisions, to reach agreement. The compromise
measure was reported to both houses by the committee on February 18, 1920; it passed the House
on February 21 by a vote of 250 to 150, and the
Senate on February 23 by 47 to 17.

The first provision of the new Transportation
Act was that government control and operation
should terminate on March 1, 1920, but that for
six months after that date the government should
continue the guarantee of income on the basis
prescribed during Federal control. The Interstate Commerce Commission was to establish such
rates as would enable the railways as a whole,
"under honest, efficient and economical management" and with "reasonable expenditures" for
keeping up the property, to "earn an operating
income equal, as nearly as may be, to a fair return
upon the aggregate value of the railway property"
used in transportation. The commission was to

determine both the property value and what percentage of that property value was a "fair return," but for the two years beginning with March, 1920, the law provided that the earnings thus made an objective should be 5½ per cent per annum, to which the commission was authorized to add ½ of 1 per cent for property improvement. These stipulations of the law gave rise to a more or less prevalent popular belief that the government had explicitly guaranteed a 5½ per cent income to the carriers; but that belief was erroneous.

No provision was made, beyond the six-months' extension of the war-time guarantee, for making good even a deficit in earnings below expenditure in the case of any individual railway. The rates actually fixed by the commission did not in any of the next five years produce for the carriers as a whole as much as 5 per cent earnings on their tentative valuation.[1]   Furthermore, the Act provided that, if any railway were to earn a yearly net operating income in excess of 6 per cent, one half of that excess was to go to the company's reserve fund and the other half to be paid over to the government for use in necessary loans to other

[1] Bureau of Railway Economics, "Railway Revenues and Expenses," annual statements.

carriers. A Labor Board was established, with the duty of passing on questions of higher or lower wages which were under dispute between the companies and their employees, but the original plan, compelling submission to its decree under penalty, was abandoned. Finally, acquisition of one railway by another was authorized, if approved by the commission, and the commission itself was directed to frame a plan for general consolidation into a "limited number" of larger systems. No hint at compulsory consolidation was however incorporated into the Act.

Thus was begun an entirely novel experiment in regulation of the American railway industry. The decision of the law-makers was accepted by the railway managements and by investors in railway securities—not certainly with enthusiasm or without misgiving, but with a sense of great relief, arising from the fact that not only had the extravagances of the "Plumb plan" been decisively rejected but that railway labor, relinquishing its threat of action in case the plan of Congress was enacted, had submitted.[1] The two main

---

[1] Statements Railway Union delegation to President Wilson, Jan. 27, Feb. 26, 1920. Proclamation American Federation of Labor, Feb. 8. Statement in behalf of railway unions, March 2.

doubts of the railway managers concerned the
questions, first, whether uniform rates that
would yield a "fair return" on the average to
carriers in the district to which those rates applied
would ensure a living profit to the weaker lines;
second, whether the "recapture clause" for earnings in excess of 6 per cent would not injure the
prospects even of the stronger lines.

Opinion varied on the plan of consolidation.
Such a plan was already being rapidly mapped out
in England; in that country it was put into actual
operation three years later. But in England
an Act of Parliament was supreme, there were no
restrictions of a written constitution on Parliamentary authority, and it was possible to declare
that, unless the railways combined voluntarily on
the lines prescribed by the Parliamentary commission, they would be compelled by law to do so.
In the United States, on the contrary, it was recognized that compulsory consolidation would amount
to invasion of property rights under the constitution, and would probably be so interpreted by the
courts. Judgment was therefore quite suspended
on that proviso of the Transportation Act. As
for the rest of it, every one waited now to see what
the commission's policy on rates would be, how

that policy would affect the different railways,
and how far their productiveness would be influenced by good or bad times in American trade.
We shall presently see to what extent the problem
was complicated by the subsequent course of the
country's industrial history. Between March 1
and September 1 of 1920, however, continuance
of the government's pledge to make good for that
period a shortage in any railway's income below
the pre-war average relieved immediate apprehension. The private managements, resuming
operation of their several roads, busied themselves
with disentangling each railway from the network
of diverted traffic and of widely-scattered equipment which had necessarily attended war-time
operation of them as a unified single system.

Long before the six-months' "guaranteed-
earnings period" of the railways had elapsed,
markets were watching with even greater perplexity the sequel to removal of the government's
guaranteed price on wheat. Since this guarantee
had been made in war-time for the purpose of
ensuring maximum preparation by the farmers for
the next season's wheat crop, the price that the
government's Grain Corporation engaged to pay,
for all wheat offered to it, covered the period up to

the beginning of the next crop's harvesting; which would occur in the subsequent July. Thus the guaranteed price of $2.20 on the wheat crop of 1917, fixed by the President in August of that year,[1] held good until the middle of 1918. In the early weeks of 1918, bills had been introduced into Congress to raise the guaranteed price to $2.50 or $2.75 per bushel; but in February of that year the President had anticipated Congressional action by proclaiming continuance of the $2.20 guarantee until July, 1919, with a subsequent extra allowance, because of higher freight rates, making the guaranteed price $2.26 at Chicago. When Congress, in July, 1918, passed a compromise bill granting a guarantee of $2.40,[2] the President vetoed it,[3] presently following that veto by an order fixing the basic price for the 1919 wheat crop, a year ahead, at $2.20.[4] That action explains why the government guarantee was still in force during 1920, and why it applied to a wheat crop which was not only harvested after the war had ended but was largely planted after the armistice.

It was perfectly evident, however, that the

[1] Proclamation of President Wilson, Aug. 30, 1917.
[2] *Congressional Record*, July 6, 1918.　　[3] *Ibid.*, July 12.
[4] Proclamation of President Wilson, September 2, 1918.

guarantee could not be continued during another season. In May, 1920, the President proclaimed that on June 1 all government control of the wheat trade should terminate, and with it all purchases of wheat by the Grain Corporation.[1] The market, therefore, now faced the test as to whether or not the price of wheat could hold at anything like the existing figure without the government's purchases at the guaranteed price. Even in the grain trade, there were curiously divergent ideas upon the question. The director of the Grain Corporation, an experienced dealer in wheat, expressed great apprehension; he described the impending situation as one in which withdrawal of the government as the main buyer and distributor of wheat, and recourse for such services to private capital as in the days before we went to war, threatened "not only the grain-handling but the credit structure of the country," and opened the possibility of "agricultural demoralization."[2]

This view was certainly plausible. The estimated value of the period's annual wheat crop on the farm was around $2,000,000,000.[3] In

[1] Proclamation of President Wilson, May 25, 1920.
[2] Statement of Julius H. Barnes, May 8, 1920.
[3] Agricultural Department's estimate, December, 1919.

order to prevent the submerging of the market at
harvest-time by the offer of all available wheat at
once to actual consumers, it had always been
necessary, in pre-war days, either for farmers to
hold back a great part of their grain or for middlemen to buy and store it.   In the second process
the grain-market speculator played an essential
part, because he had personally to "carry" grain
in storage.   But for either of these expedients,
the use of immense amounts of capital or credit
was required.   Ever since the Grain Corporation took control of the market in 1917, the
government had raised the necessary money.
Now it was about to return the grain market,
nearly at harvest-time, to the auspices of private
capital, and it was doing this at a moment when
credit was hard to get, when time loans and
merchants' paper were bringing 7 to 9 per cent
even on Wall Street and when the Federal
Reserve rediscount rate was going to 7 per
cent.

It might be supposed that this prospect would
have aroused intense and widespread uneasiness in
the grain trade, as the similar suggestion of
immediate return to private operation had aroused
it in the railway industry.   But in a year when,

as we have seen, ideas of intrinsic values were perverted in the entire business community, the grain trade had not escaped the prevalent illusion. The idea had obtained great vogue, even in Congress, that the government's guaranteed price established, not a minimum but a maximum;[1] in other words that, without the intervention of the Grain Corporation on its arbitrarily established basis of valuation, all wheat would have sold after August, 1917, far above $2.20. This notion was encouraged by the fact that in May of 1917, before the government's "stabilized price" was fixed, sales had been made for $3.45 a bushel at Chicago; also that, in December, 1919, and January, 1920, the best grades of wheat brought $3.50, a high record for our time. When it was selling at $3, in the spring of 1920, a very careful and conservative grain-market publication, discussing the government's expected withdrawal from the market, wrote that "one man's guess appears quite as good as another's regarding what wheat prices will do after the market influence of the Grain Corporation is removed," and asserted that, in the trade itself, "predictions range all the way

[1] U. S. Senate speech, Arthur Capper of Kansas, March 23, 1920.

from $1.50 to $4 per bushel, without convincing arguments in either direction."[1]

The grain trade did not have to wait long to learn the truth. Although the government withdrew from the market on June 1, 1920, the Chicago Board of Trade postponed to July 15 resumption of open trading for future delivery, which had been suspended since August, 1917. As late as the middle of June, 1920, the cash price at Chicago was $3.13; on July 15, when trading in "futures" began, the first transactions ranged between $2.75 and $2.72. Falling then to $2.48 but recovering to $2.86 in August, the wheat market thereafter pursued a downward course along with other commodities. This happened notwithstanding a September estimate on the wheat crop nearly 200,000,000 bushels less than the yield of 1919 and a final harvest 135,000,000 under it. In October the price went below $2, for the first time since 1916; it got to $1.62 in November. The decline was destined not to stop until, in November, 1921, wheat sold at $1.00½ or 50 cents a bushel below the figure which, as we have seen, the wheat trade in the spring of 1920 had named as the lowest imaginable price.

[1] *Northwestern Miller*, April 24, 1920.

This series of events in finance and industry had inevitably thrown every American market into confusion. Financial bewilderment was not lessened by the fact that, even with the approach of autumn, always the critical period in a disordered economic situation, the impressions of the business community were still conflicting. One highly conservative authority reported that, in the later months of 1920, "a slowing-up of the drop in commodities, an upturn in securities, and a better inquiry for certain lines of goods, gave rise to some encouragement."[1] Qualified hopefulness was also based on "realization that the unprecedented price declines and the losses, the shutdowns and the unemployment they occasioned, had all taken place without deranging the financial machinery of the country."[2]

In talk of general trade, an idea became somewhat prevalent that, "if the pendulum had swung too far upward" in 1919, it might also have swung too far in the other direction under the reaction that had already occurred in 1920.[3] Furthermore, while wholesale prices had been falling

[1] N. Y. Federal Reserve Bank, Annual Report for 1920, p. 19.
[2] *Ibid.*
[3] *Financial Chronicle*, Oct. 2, 1920, p. 1382, "Commercial Epitome."

rapidly, there had been little reduction in retail prices since the department-store cuts of May, and this gave some basis for belief that the "consumers' strike" might be losing force.[1] On the other hand, however, these gropings after reassurance were offset not only by the continuing fall in staple prices but by unpleasant prediction from high financial quarters, where it was declared that "we are touched by the waiting period which always precedes reaction";[2] that "it might take a year or two to get back to a normal condition of stability";[3] that the country was probably entering "a period of readjustment which will mean losses on accumulated stocks of merchandise and loss of time to the working classes."[4] But the general tendency of the business community was to grasp at consoling considerations and to hope that the worst was over—an altogether usual attitude on such occasions.

It was under these confusing circumstances, and with the public mind in the perplexed condition caused by them, that the presidential election was held in November, 1920; it resulted in a major-

[1] N. Y. Federal Reserve Bank, Report for 1920, p. 8.

[2] Henry Ford, statement of Sept. 21, 1920.

[3] A. B. Hepburn, interview in Brooklyn *Eagle*, Sept. 24.

[4] Julius Rosenwald, interview in N. Y. *Times*, Sept. 25.

ity of wholly unprecedented magnitude against
the party which had been in power since March,
1913, and which had shaped the country's policies
both in the period of neutrality and during our
own participation in the war. The explanations
of the day for that emphatic electoral verdict were
very numerous, and most of them were correct;
it was, in fact, a very unusual combination of
adverse influences which the Democratic party had
to face in its campaign. The cost of living, which
was still more exorbitant and oppressive than in
the memory of living men, was alone sufficient,
in the light of political precedent, to overthrow a
party in power. But at the same time, resentment arising from exactly opposite considerations
prevailed in the farm communities because of the
autumn fall in wheat and cotton; for which that
part of the electorate was beginning to blame the
government at Washington and the Federal
Reserve.

The Democratic party could indeed claim
recognition for conducting an immensely successful and triumphant war. Its own national platform of July, 1920, hailed "with patriotic pride
the great achievements for the country and the
world, wrought by a Democratic administration,"

and described the "imperishable honor, . . . the plaudits and gratitude of all free nations," which that administration had brought to the American people. But nothing is more familiar in political history than the insecurity of reliance on popular gratitude thus inspired. The high-pitched enthusiasm with which a nation follows the successful public leader in war-time is extremely apt to be followed, on return of peace, by reaction of feeling proportioned to the violence of war-time sentiment. Political reaction of that nature became a historical fact of high importance with England after 1815 and, in a measure, with the United States after 1865. This very year 1920 had witnessed in January the downfall of the French war premier who carried that country's campaigns to its successful conclusion and in May the defeat of Italy's war executive. The political débâcle of the war minister of England was shortly to follow, and in the case of Clemenceau, Orlando and Lloyd George, the adverse political verdict was in its way as decisive as with the Democratic party in America.

President Wilson's physical break-down after the war had practically removed him from the activities of politics, but his personality and

record were none the less a factor in the acri-
monies of the campaign of 1920, because of angry
division of opinion over his effort to bring the
United States into the League of Nations.
The Republican platform of May had utilized
with much adroitness all these elements making for political reaction.   The League coven-
ant signed at Paris by President Wilson, it set
forth, "contained stipulations. . . . intolerable
for an independent people"; nevertheless (since
the ultimate feeling of the electorate on the general
question was not certain), the platform pledged
its candidate "to such agreements with other
nations of the world as shall meet the full duty of
America to civilization and humanity."   But it
was necessary also to dispute the claim of the
other party to reward for its successful prosecution
of the war.   "Unpreparedness" when the country
went to war was attacked in the Republican platform as a blunder which, but for the help of our
European allies, "would have been punished with
disaster."   The war had been largely "financed
by a policy of inflation through certificate borrowing from banks and bonds issued at artificial rates
sustained by the low discount rate established
by the Federal Reserve Board."   The Reserve

Board's policy towards credit and money rates had been "frankly dominated by the convenience of the Treasury" and had inflicted great losses "on the millions of people who in good faith bought Liberty bonds at par." The high cost of living was "due to a gross expansion of our currency and credit," which had been brought to pass by "the unsound policies of the Democratic administration."

Any one who has read the narrative of the preceding chapters will recognize at once that all these indictments of the government's fiscal policy from 1917 to 1920 had at least an arguable basis. Considered as a contribution to historical judgment, their weakness lay in the fact, of which every statesman was perfectly well aware, that if the Republican party had itself been in power during our period of war, it would unquestionably have adopted precisely the fiscal policies which the Wilson Administration pursued. But considered as an appeal to an electorate already disposed to hostile judgment, the platform was exceedingly effective. Its criticisms and accusations were repeated in the party's campaign oratory, with the result, on November 2, of a popular plurality of 7,004,847 votes for Mr.

Harding and the Republican ticket, whereas even Roosevelt's victory of 1904, unprecedented at the time, brought a plurality of only 2,544,333 and whereas Wilson polled in 1912 only 2,160,194 more votes than the strongest candidate of the divided Republican party. The magnitude of Mr. Harding's plurality resulted largely, it is true, from an influence not necessarily connected with changed political alignment of previous voters; for the Woman Suffrage amendment to the constitution had been ratified in August, 1920, and the total vote cast in November exceeded that of 1916 by slightly more than 8,000,000, or 44 per cent. Supposing that increase to have resulted wholly from the women's vote, and supposing that vote to have been divided between the parties in exactly the same ratio as the men's, it would obviously have enlarged to precisely that extent not only the total poll, but the plurality of the successful party. Even so, however, and in the face of the probability, shown by earlier tests in state experiments with woman suffrage, that the women's vote was distributed in much the same way as the men's, the essential fact remained that Mr. Harding polled more votes by 6,602,364 than Mr. Hughes in 1916, while his opponent, Governor

Cox, polled only 17,747 more than the same year's vote for Mr. Wilson.

Whatever else might have been inferred from this remarkable result, it was at least beyond dispute that a candidate committed to conservative policies had been returned with huge majorities, backed by the largest Congressional plurality in the party's history. The American business community has never lost the habit of imagining that a business situation may be vitally changed overnight, for better or worse, by a national election. It therefore watched next day, with very exceptional interest, for the verdict of the Stock Exchange. The response in that quarter was in all respects disheartening; it indicated that the large investors were in a mood of great apprehension and that, although confident of Harding's election, they had been postponing sales of their securities only with a view to selling out on the better market which they thought the news should bring. During the rest of election week, shares of the great industrial companies fell 2 to 10 points; in the following week the decline ran in many of them from 10 to 50 points. Shares of the railways rose momentarily, then they also plunged downward; between election day and Christmas week the average price of fifty stocks selected as representative had fallen almost 25 per cent. [1] The decline became disorderly, at times even panicky, before the year had ended, and watchers of finance and industry were soon made aware what the crash on the Stock Exchange foreshadowed.

N. Y. *Times*, daily "market averages."

CHAPTER VIII

THE CRISIS OF 1920

A GREAT financial crisis usually comes to a climax in the spring or autumn; the reason being that in those two periods of a year the actual trade position is definitely tested, while at the same time demand for necessary credit reaches its highest point. We have seen to what extent the markets received in April and May, 1920, the warning of an approaching crisis; but trade, finance and industry unquestionably failed to comprehend the actual situation until autumn. Most of the phenomena which preceded and foreshadowed older financial panics had, it is true, been in evidence earlier in 1920; a midsummer 8 per cent rate on discounts of merchants' paper, for instance,[1] and a sweeping fall of 30 per cent

[1] Report N. Y. Reserve Agent; Annual Report Federal Reserve Board for 1920, p. 379.

in prices of commodities, between May and December, to the lowest average reached since our entry into the war.[1] But in all previous episodes of the kind, the actual signal for financial panic and acute commercial distress had been unexpected confession of insolvency by important banks or business houses.

The New York panic of 1907 is still associated in historical reminiscence with the Knickerbocker Trust Company's failure,[2] the panic of 1893 with the downfall of the Milwaukee Bank and the Erie Railway,[3] the panic of 1884 with the failure of Grant & Ward and the Metropolitan Bank.[4] London's panic of 1890 is identified with the embarrassment of Baring Brothers[5]; its panic of 1866 with the Overend-Gurney insolvency. There was no such outstanding event in 1920 and, although the condition of several large commercial houses and of one important banking institution became very critical during the four or five subsequent months, the crisis of 1920 could at no time be described as an old-time

[1] *Wholesale Prices, 1890–1923.*
[2] *Forty Years of American Finance,* p. 366.
[3] *Ibid.,* p. 194.
[4] *Ibid.,* p. 99.
[5] *Ibid.,* p. 157.

"credit crisis."[1]   No run on the banks occurred in the larger cities.   With a few exceptions, the bank failures which ensued affected mostly small interior institutions whose embarrassment was due to special causes.

The reasons for this immunity from a "money panic," under circumstances of the severest economic strain, we shall presently examine.   But even without visible evidence of collapsing credit the business situation of autumn, in its other aspects, took extremely alarming shape.   It had by that time become evident, not only that sweeping trade reaction and deflation were absolutely world-wide phenomena and not only that huge supplies of goods accumulated by merchants, middlemen and exporters had become difficult to sell, but that some of the largest wholesale purchasers of merchandise, home and foreign, were unable to pay for the goods which had been sold to them and unwilling to accept the goods which they had ordered and which were already on the way to them.   In other similar periods of American trade reaction, notably after 1907 and 1893, there were foreign markets whose buying power had been little impaired and to which our mer-

[1] Annual Report Federal Reserve Board for 1920, p. 2.

chants were therefore able to sell their goods in
great quantity at the lower prices. But in the
later months of 1920, the commercial machinery
of the entire outside world came virtually to a stop[1]
—not only in Japan, whose markets had sounded
the first signal of distress, but throughout Europe and South America, where merchants had
up to that time been buying our exported merchandise on a scale limited only by the credit
obtainable.

The whole commercial world had in point of
fact been conducting its transactions under a series
of illusions—first, that the supply of necessary
goods was far short of requirements, whereas the
apparent shortage was actually attributable only
to slowness of producers to sell, to the holding
back of goods by speculators, or to delay in delivery by railway; second, that purchasing capacity
of consumers was unlimited, whereas the war had
left a great part of the world in poverty[2]; third,
that the credit resources whereby accumulation
of goods by home and foreign merchants (not to
mention speculative operations) was conducted,
could be indefinitely extended, whereas the credit

[1] Annual Report Federal Reserve Board for 1920, p. 10.
[2] *Ibid.*, pp. 2, 8 and 10.

organism of practically every country in the world was already strained to the limit.[1] It was the coincidence, during the spring of 1920 and on every market in the world, of an utterly abnormal rise in prices with an equally abnormal advance in money rates which revealed how completely artificial the supply-and-demand position was. High prices had greatly stimulated production, and they had done so at the moment when hoarded goods were being brought rapidly upon the market as a result both of the tempting price and the prohibitive cost of credit. Thus a seeming under-supply became visible over-supply, and apparently inadequate production was transformed into over-production; this when the retail markets were suddenly discovering how blindly the real consumer's buying capacity had been overrated.

Although the American market was almost the last to face the dilemma on its own account,[2] it was deeply concerned with the foreign situation because of the unprecedented magnitude both of our exports and our imports. It should be observed that, partly in consequence of holding-

[1] Annual Report Federal Reserve Board for 1920, p. 10.
[2] *Ibid.*, p. 11.

back of merchandise by speculators and partly because of delay in contracted deliveries, due to industrial strikes and railway blockades in the United States, even the foreign customers of our exporting merchants had been placing orders much larger than they expected to be filled.   American exporters had therefore been active quite beyond precedent in the South American trade.   An increasingly large absorbent of our merchandise in war-time, that market was believed in 1919 to be capable of indefinite expansion.   As late as in May of 1920, the London *Economist's* correspondent had written from Argentina that, in the "wave of prosperity" which was sweeping over that country, "the question of prices is a secondary consideration," but that there was "no speculation or overtrading."[1]   The same idea was expressed in March of 1920 in a still more responsible quarter, when the annual report for the $50,000,000 company, organized at New York in 1915 to finance and extend our new foreign trade, stated that "the South American nations have been materially enriched by the war" and that, since "the wide and profitable market for their

[1] London *Economist*, June 12, 1920, p. 1299, letter from Buenos Ayres.

natural products" had kept up their exchange rates, "to the great benefit of their purchasing power," the situation "spells opportunity for the United States." [1]

The inference was correct, but events proved that the effort to grasp the opportunity—in Wall Street's favorite phrase, to "capitalize" it—had been rashly overdone, both in the export and the import trade. To South America we shipped in the calendar year 1920 $182,000,000 more worth of goods than in 1919 and $477,000,000 more than in 1913; our imports also from that Continent increased over the same two years $73,000,000 and $562,000,000 respectively. Only a small part of that immense increase could be ascribed to the 100 or 150 per cent rise of average prices compared with the pre-war year; the combined exports and imports in 1920 were greater by 300 per cent than in 1913. [2] Not only had American exporters and importers been heavily engaged in the South American field, but American banking concerns had invested on a very large scale in South American and Cuban producing enterprises. Our banks

[1] Annual Report for 1919, American International Corporation.
[2] Monthly Summaries U. S. Foreign Commerce, December, 1913, p. 507; December, 1920, p. 6.

had established branches in South America, for
the most part hastily arranged and imperfectly
equipped but confident of easy commercial success.
While the importing merchants of Cuba and South
America were placing orders on a wholly unprecedented scale for the products of our manufacturers, there had seemed to be no limit to the
demand for the export products of those countries
or to the price which could be exacted for them.
Holders of such commodities as sugar, production
of which was believed at the end of 1919 to be so
far short of consumers' needs as to threaten actual
"famine,"[1] stood out for constantly mounting
prices. The paper wealth acquired by native
dealers in those markets was so great that, at the
climax of the price-inflation movement, the lavish
expenditure in New York hotels and shops by
Latin-American visitors became subject of remark
equally with the extravagance of our own profiteers
and workingmen.

It was impossible that either home or foreign
banks should continue to increase indefinitely
their loans for the conducting of this highly
speculative business. The shape which the situ-

[1] Annual Report N. Y. Chamber of Commerce, 1920–1921,
Part II, p. 3.

ation had begun to take in the spring of 1920 was that banking institutions were asked to provide progressively larger sums of credit for commodities held in storage;[1] to do so when prices already seemed to prudent bankers dangerously high and when signs were becoming visible, both that the hoarded goods were coming on the market, and that the sales were finding extremely poor response from consumers. No banker in his senses would have neglected to guard his credit facilities carefully under such circumstances. American banks were in fact hardly in a position even to continue their existing advances to such borrowers, when the prospect of selling the merchandise at a profit and paying off the loans was visibly growing more remote. In the autumn, loans and discounts of all American banks were officially reported to have increased between October, 1919, and the middle of 1920, no less than $5,805,000,000, or more than 23 per cent.[2]

But the attempt of banks to reduce or limit the credit had the effect of making the speculator's position untenable. Hoarded merchandise was

---

[1] Annual Report Federal Reserve Board for 1920, p. 12.

[2] Comptroller of the Currency, statement of Oct. 15, 1920, N. Y. Reserve Bank, Annual Report for 1920, p. 7.

pressed for sale in greatly increased quantity;
the market literally crumbled. This change affected first the export market for South American and Cuban products, in which the position had
already been weakened from other causes. When
the Cuban sugar trade had fixed, some months
before, what even the New York consuming
market deemed an exorbitant price, our own refin-
ers bought supplies from Java, India, Japan and
Australia; countries which had never previously
been regarded as practicable sources of supply for
the United States, but in which the rise of prices
during 1919 had been less violent.[1] When the
Argentine wool market reached its highest price,
the British government removed restrictions on sale
of the war-time accumulations of Australian wool.[2]

As a result of these numerous influences, wool
prices fell in the consuming market from 66 cents a
pound in March, 1920, to less than 40 in October,
rubber from 39 cents to 19, coffee from 17 ⅛ cents
to 6 ⅛, or less than the pre-war price, sugar from
21 cents to 8.[3] This meant that the Southern

[1] Annual Report N. Y. Chamber of Commerce, 1920–1921,
Part II, p. 3.

[2] Annual Report Federal Reserve Board, 1920, p. 10.

[3] Chamber of Commerce Report 1920–1921, Part II, pp. 2, 3,
and 13. Federal Reserve Board Report for 1920, p. 9.

producing countries could not now sell their merchandise in the export market except at a heavy
sacrifice, and that native dealers who had been
accumulating and hoarding produce were confronted with heavy losses. Importing merchants
on those markets were simultaneously finding
unexpected difficulty in selling to the home trade
goods bought from the United States; yet this was
the very moment when speeding-up of production
was enabling the American export trade to deliver
all the goods against orders which had been
placed in expectation of getting only half. When,
along with these other difficulties, the increased
bank credit on which the South American merchants had been reckoning began to fail them, a
very critical situation was inevitable.

In the middle of the year, cable dispatches
from Buenos Aires began to revive the anxiety
that had been caused by the Japanese news of
April; they described such congestion of the
Argentine market for imported merchandise that
not only were warehouses packed to capacity
with unsold goods but the sidewalks piled with
boxes and bales of goods which were still coming
in. Up to that time, American exporters had
received with reasonably satisfactory regularity

remittances in payment of their consignments to these Southern markets; but in that regard, the position changed very suddenly. What happened was not even recourse to deferred remittances; the South American importer sent outright cancellation of his previous orders for goods which at the date of cancellation were in the exporter's hands, or on the sea, or in many cases actually at the port of delivery.[1] This repudiation of contracts, practiced as it was on a wholly unprecedented scale, may conceivably have been suggested by memory of the world-wide adoption of "moratorium" on debts in 1914, or it may, like that expedient, have been provoked by the sudden emergency with which the importing merchant found himself confronted when his own market for the goods had failed him and their price had fallen 20 or 30 per cent. Since, however, the individual credit of the American exporter was engaged in the merchandise already bought or shipped, the necessary result was the shifting of the crisis to American business houses.

Not only in Argentina but in Brazil, Para-

---

[1] Annual Report Federal Reserve Board for 1920, pp. 54, 55, 56. Proceedings N. Y. Chamber of Commerce, Jan. 6, 1921; Annual Report for 1920–21, Part I, pp. 176–180.

guay and Cuba, great masses of goods already exported were thus thrown back on the hands of the American shippers, who had to appeal to their own banks for help.[1] At the end of 1920 it was estimated that resultant actual losses had run to not less than $150,000,000.[2] From its total net operating profits of $5,969,000 in 1920, mostly derived from foreign trade, the American International Corporation wrote off $4,750,000 for "losses in accounts receivable and inventories"; in 1921, although operating profits had declined to $3,499,000, it had to write off $6,000,000. Its surplus earnings after all deductions in 1919 had been $7,569,000, in 1921 it reported a deficit of $5,899,000.[3] There was no recovery to make good these losses. The paralyzing reaction that came in this foreign trade on top of the cancellations of 1920 is illustrated by the record privately compiled for a large American exporting house, showing that its orders for Brazil fell from $3,294,000 in 1920 to $114,000 in 1921, for Cuba from $3,576,-000 to $680,000, for Mexico from $1,465,000 to $362,000, even for Africa from $1,353,000 to $226,-

[1] Annual Report Federal Reserve Board for 1920, p. 54.
[2] Annual Report N. Y. Chamber of Commerce, 1920–21, p. 179.
[3] Annual Reports American International Corporation for 1919, 1920, 1921.

000. For a time, at the end of 1920 and in the
early months of 1921, the position of numerous
strong exporting concerns in the United States was
extremely critical; the banking reviews of the year
reported "a certain amount of mortality" among
them.[1] That the "cancellations" were not an
utterly destructive influence in the credit situation
of the moment was due to the generally sound
position of the banks and their leniency in dealing
with maturing credits.[2]

The leniency was severely tested in other ways.
The large exporting houses that were left in debt
to American manufacturers, on account of goods
ordered for the South American trade but which
the South American consignees had refused to
accept, were carried over by their banks. But
meantime the very numerous smaller concerns
which had been drawn into the export trade by
the prospect of large profits began to copy the
methods of the foreign importers; they refused
to take the goods which they had ordered from
merchants and manufacturers. In December, a
report to the New York Chamber of Commerce
described a "wave of cancellations of buying

---

[1] Annual Report Federal Reserve Board for 1920, p. 54.
[2] N. Y. Reserve Bank, Annual Report for 1920, pp. 8 and 9.

orders and contracts of sale" by both home and foreign buyers, "which at present is sweeping the world and is menacing also the United States."[1] A special inquiry by the Chamber found that, in many trades, cancellation of orders had been recognized as allowable up to a reasonable point, but that all precedent had been surpassed in 1920. The clothing trade characterized the season's practices as "very menacing to the industry." The leather trade reported cancellation of orders as much larger than at any time in its history. The furniture trade stated that it was only in 1919 and 1920 that dealers had got into the habit of ordering far more goods than they really required, and canceling orders when deliveries had met their requirements.[2]

The policy had originated largely at the time when, in 1919, a seemingly insatiable demand for goods had compelled manufacturers to allocate to customers only a prescribed percentage of their orders.[3] The first of the cancellations had actually been received with a feeling of relief, as

[1] Annual Report of the N. Y. Chamber of Commerce, 1920-21, Part I, p. 138.

[2] Monthly bulletin N. Y. Chamber of Commerce, November, 1920.

[3] N. Y. Federal Reserve Bank, Annual Report, 1920, p. 8.

reducing the commitments for delivery of goods
which circumstances seemed to make impossible.[1]
But these considerations cut little figure when the
movement to repudiate contracts spread; it
merely shifted the losses in a falling market from
the merchant to the middleman or the manufacturer. As early as July, it was reported in the
markets that cancellations of domestic wool orders
had reached $100,000,000,[2] and it was officially
stated that $40,000,000 of such orders had been
canceled at one manufacturing concern.[3] Large
holdings of almost every kind of merchandise
became virtually unsalable; the uninterrupted fall
of prices seemed only to make consumers more
distrustful of the market. One of the largest
American "mail-order houses," whose sales for
1920 were $101,745,000, had to report for the whole
year a loss of $7,855,000, and in 1921 had to write
off $5,615,000 for "loss on inventory, loss on
accounts receivable, and depreciation."[4] It was
not strange that failures of American business

[1] *Financial Chronicle*, Dec. 11, 1920, p. 2293.
[2] *Ibid.*, "Commercial Epitome," July 31, 1920, p. 507.
[3] Annual Report N. Y. Chamber of Commerce for 1920-21, Part
II, p. 83.
[4] Annual reports Montgomery Ward Co. for 1920 and
1921.

houses in the third quarter of 1920 should have
been greater by 1,903 in number and by $104,194,-
705 in liabilities than in the same months of
1919[1] or that, with the inevitable curtailment of
production, the number of unemployed laborers
should have increased 3,473,000 over the previous
year-end.[2]

It can hardly be doubted that the situation
which existed at the close of 1920 and the beginning of 1921, had it arisen under our pre-war banking system, would at some point have resulted in
an old-fashioned "Wall Street panic" of the most
formidable scope.   In the speculative markets,
in home and foreign trade, in the entire field of
American credit, the stage was set for such an
outcome as plainly as it had been set in 1907 or
1873.   The sweeping decline in commodities,
which carried down the general average of prices
nearly 43 per cent between May, 1920, and the
middle of 1921,[3] had caught the whole merchant
community with exceptionally large stocks of
goods on its hands, purchased at much higher

[1] *Dun's Review* statements. *Financial Chronicle*, "Commercial Epitome," Dec. 11, 1920, p. 2337.
[2] Report U. S. Labor Department's employment service;
Financial Chronicle, Jan. 29, 1921, p. 479.
[3] *Wholesale Prices, 1890–1923*, p. 19.

prices and on the basis of large indebtedness to the banks. Those loans were now falling due. In a normal market they would have been paid off through sale of merchandise to consumers. But in the existing situation the proceeds of such a sale would not have covered the loans and, furthermore, a great part of the goods thus carried were in fact virtually unsalable, either because prospective buyers on foreign markets had canceled their orders for merchandise actually delivered or because of the outright disappearance of the home market.

The Stock Exchange also had to face a credit crisis; it had been confronted in March, 1920, with an overwhelming fall of prices for stocks which had been advanced with the greatest recklessness through very large accumulation of stocks by speculators. Continuance of the decline in the autumn months had carried the general average nearly 26 per cent below that of November, 1919, with shrinkage of 50 to 60 per cent in a long list of shares which had led in the speculation for the rise. The banking position was indicated by the fact that, instead of reducing the enormous loan account necessarily put out in war-time, the eight thousand national banks had enlarged their

loans and discounts, between the middle of 1919
and September, 1920, by $1,840,924,000, or 17
per cent[1]—actually a greater increase, both in
amount and percentage, than had occurred in
a period of equal length after our declaration of
war in 1917.[2]   A very large part of this heavily
expanded loan account could not be met by the
borrowers at maturity.   The banks had begun
by "taking over" the stocks held by large speculators for the rise in the disastrous spring market
of 1920; in the autumn, they practically took over
the unfortunate ventures in merchandise by importing or exporting merchants.

But in both cases they necessarily curtailed
their individual power of granting credit for other
hard-pressed business men.   Just as the words
"deflation" and "cancellation" had made their
first appearance in the markets of 1919 and 1920,
a third new term, "frozen credits," now became
the familiarly descriptive phrase of the banking
situation.   It meant, the Reserve Board officially
pointed out, advances which "had been carried
beyond the time when the transactions which gave

---

[1] Annual Report of the Comptroller of the Currency for 1920,
Part II, pp. 301 and 303.
[2] *Ibid.*, pp. 299 and 300.

rise to the credit should normally have liquidated
themselves."[1] There was no way of knowing
when such indebtedness could be paid off; nor was
it possible, then or afterward, to say how large a
part of the country's entire credit facilities was
tied up in such irredeemable loans. But there was
reason to believe, the Reserve Board reported, that
at the end of 1920 "they constituted an alarmingly
large proportion of the total loans and discounts
carried by the commercial banks of the country."[2]

Nor was even this the end of the blockade of
credit. The sudden and sweeping "deflation" of
agricultural prices brought a great part of the
farming districts, West and South, to a condition
where loans granted by banks to farmers either had
to be closed out when the security was not now
worth half the face of the loan, or else had to be
indefinitely extended. The farming population's
attitude, as the sweeping fall of prices continued in
the autumn, was first an expression of incredulity,
then of consternation, and next of angry and
futile rebellion against the situation. When
cotton had fallen from 43¾ cents a pound in
July to 23 in October, the Southern growers

[1] Federal Reserve Board, Annual Report for 1921, p. 6.
[2] *Ibid.*, p. 6.

demanded that the ginners should cease altogether turning out cotton in marketable form until the price had recovered to 40 cents. "Night riders," reviving the Ku Klux activities of Civil War reconstruction days, nailed threatening notices to that effect on the doors of warehouses and ginneries; it was reported in early autumn that 25,000 bales had been actually destroyed by these vigilantes, and there were instances where houses were burned and defiant cotton-ginners killed.[1] But this did not even momentarily arrest the fall in the price.

The wheat growers fought against "deflation" with equal futility, though in a more orderly way. When wheat went below $2 a bushel on the Chicago market in October, the Wheat Growers Association of the United States, claiming a membership of 70,000, issued at Wichita, Kansas, a proclamation ordering farmers to sell no wheat after October 25 until the price had returned to $3 at the growers' terminal market.[2] So far were this

[1] News dispatches from Georgia, Alabama, South Carolina, Tennessee, Arkansas and Texas; Oct. 7, 12, 14, 15, 16, 22, 1920. *Financial Chronicle*, "Commercial Epitome," Oct. 9, 1920 p. 1482; Oct. 16, p. 1581; Oct. 23, p. 1670.

[2] N. Y. *Times* dispatches, Oct. 10, 13, 27 and 28, 1920. *Financial Chronicle*, Oct. 16, p. 1524.

and other similar demonstrations from helping the
market that contract wheat had fallen to $1.50
four weeks after the order of the growers' association had been declared effective. It reached in
the autumn of 1921 the price of one dollar per
bushel, which was a pre-war valuation and which,
in the case of many farmers, did not meet the still
greatly increased cost of the necessary material
and of farm labor; the average monthly wage paid
Western farm hands in 1920 having been $73.36
against $33.51 in 1915, an increase of 126 per cent. [1]

But this was not the only factor in the farming
West's financial embarrassment. During the high
grain prices of the war years, the western farmer
had commonly invested his profits in additional
acreage, for which he paid prices far above any
precedent; few of them had established reserves of
cash or available assets against a possible turn of
fortune. [2] Mortgages on the farms of the four
Northwestern grain states had in 1920 risen to a
total value nearly 200 per cent above that of 1910,
and the greater part of the increase was based on

[1] Department of Agriculture, bulletins on average prevailing
farm wage rates.

[2] "Economic position of agriculture in the Northwestern grain-
raising areas," report to Reserve Board, Nov. 12, 1923, by John
H. Rich, Federal Reserve Agent at Minneapolis, p. 2.

wartime wheat prices of $2.25 and upward. When wheat fell below $1.50 per bushel at the end of 1920 and below $1 in 1921, the bank loans of the farmers became simply unpayable. Some of this farm debt was foreclosed; in the four years beginning with 1920, out of 203,040 Northwestern farmers 5,388 went thus into actual bankruptcy.[1]

That number, however, was largely made up of inefficient farmers who had rushed into the district under the stimulus of the war prices. In the area of heaviest failure, it was officially ascertained afterward, 51 per cent of those who went upon the land were without previous farming experience and 30 per cent had no capital.[2] But the greater number of competent farmers were "carried" by their banks, which meant not only that older loans already due for payment were extended indefinitely but that new credit had to be granted to make possible the planting of the new crop. Precisely the same condition existed in the cotton-belt, where the sweeping decline in cotton from 43¾ cents a pound in July 1920 to 10⅞ in June, 1921, left the planter wholly unable to meet his maturing debts. The lower price was less than the pre-war average; it was quoted for a crop the cost of pro-

[1]Rich, p. 7.   [2] *Ibid.*

ducing which, as measured by average prices of
materials, seed, fertilizer and farm labor in the
cotton district, had been more than double pre-
war cost.[1]   Although the yield of 1920 had been
greater by 2,000,000 bales than that of 1919,
its value on the farm in December was estimated
to be less by $1,101,000,000 than the previous
year's harvest. The Agricultural Department
subsequently calculated that, as a whole, farm
production in the United States resulted, during
the twelve months ending with June, 1921, in a
net loss of $486,000,000.[2]   The agricultural West
and South were in fact insolvent; the resources of
their banks were tied up in non-collectible loans.

This chain of financial calamity, stretching
from the Wall Street speculator to the wholesale
and retail merchant and thence to the agricultural
producer, embodied in extremely aggravated shape
the very elements which brought the country's
credit structure of 1873 and 1893 to the breaking-
point. That nothing in the nature of a "money
panic" resulted from them in 1920 or 1921 cannot

[1] *Wholesale Prices, 1890 to 1923.* Agricultural Department,
bulletins on average prevailing farm wage rates, by geographical
divisions.

[2] Department of Agriculture, bulletin of August, 1924, "Income from Agricultural Production in the U. S., 1919–1924."

be explained except by the use made of the Federal banks' reserve of credit resources.[1] A rule established as sound by all previous experience in financial crises is that banking institutions should lend freely at such times, but at rates so high as to make sure that the borrower who really needed the additional credit would obtain it. This procedure the reserve banks followed. Although their rate for rediscount went to 7 per cent in June, 1920, in the five subsequent months their holdings of paper rediscounted for member banks, instead of decreasing, had been increased $262,567,-000; the increase in such takings of paper based on purely commercial obligations being $485,273,000.[2]

Without this support from the powerful central credit organization, it is probable that the private banks would have had to choose between throwing their delinquent individual debtors into insolvency, or facing insolvency for themselves. In the crisis of 1893, when 153 national banks suspended in the West and South, some of the unlucky "country banks" had to suspend payments when reserve money was actually on the way to them from

[1] Comptroller of the Currency, Annual Report for 1920, p. 2. Annual Report Federal Reserve Board for 1920, pp. 2, 11, 12, 13, 14.

[2] Annual Report Federal Board for 1920, p. 130.

distant depositories.[1] In 1920, the Federal Reserve Bank of such a country institution's district could arrange to take over its commercial paper almost immediately for rediscount, thereby establishing for it a fresh reserve or placing at its service Reserve note issues with which to meet a run. With that support, judiciously and promptly granted to member institutions, it was possible for the private commercial banks of the Federal Reserve system to extend the debt which merchants and farmers could not meet, and at one critical juncture to take over by united action upwards of $50,000,000 obligations contracted in the foreign field by a single institution.

At no time during this period of shaken credit and strain on bank resources was there any such run on the banks as occurred in 1907, 1893 and 1873. With the Federal Reserve's machinery of note-issue on commercial paper operative, there was no panic of bank depositors, no hoarding of money, no issue of clearing-house certificates, no "premium on currency." In the twelve months ending with June, 1921, actual failures of national banks (all of which were members of the Reserve system) numbered only 28, and these

[1] *Forty Years of American Finance*, pp. 192 and 193.

were in every instance small institutions with less than \$100,000 capital, mostly located in sparsely settled districts of the West and South.[1]   But with the state banks, private banks, savings banks, and loan and trust companies, most of which were not affiliated with the Federal Reserve, the mortality following the crisis of 1920 was very heavy. The number of these institutions which suspended in the twelvemonth was 330, with aggregate liabilities of \$96,124,000.   In number, all records were exceeded except 1893; in liabilities, all except 1908.

In particular, the small state banks of the agricultural regions suffered severely; out of the 263 failures of such banks in the period, (comparing with only 32 in the preceding year) 52 occurred in Georgia, 51 in North Dakota, 25 in Texas and 16 in Nebraska;[2]   there were none outside of the Western and Southern States. The average liability involved in the 263 suspensions was only \$94,300[3] and in most cases, notably in North Dakota, insolvency was a consequence, not only of the agricultural situation but of defective state

[1] Annual Report Comptroller of the Currency for 1921, pp. 102 770, 771.
[2] *Ibid.*   [3] *Ibid.*

banking laws or inefficient management. Nevertheless, the Western and Southern bank suspensions emphasized the scope of derangement in
the country's credit structure, which was further
indicated by 26 failures of loan and trust companies with total liabilities of $65,534,907, the
greater part of which loss was incurred in Massachusetts as a result of the textile complications.[1]

The attitude of the hard-pressed West and
South towards the Federal Reserve, however, was
by no means that of gratitude or approbation.
One matter of controversy, which came immediately into the foreground as the nation-wide
financial strain approached its culmination, requires notice because of its political after-conse-
quences. It had to do with the policy of the
Federal Reserve before the general crash began.
A meeting of delegates from agricultural associations, covering the wheat, cotton, live stock and
tobacco industries, was held at Washington in
October of 1920. The report submitted to the
conference began by declaring that, in the desperate condition of American agriculture, "producers
of all crops have come to feel that the hand of the
government is against them." The agricultural

[1] Comptroller of the Currency, Report for 1921.

distress, it proceeded, was a direct result of various official actions, particularly the "restricting of credits," "raising the rate of discount on farm products," and "the statements given out by the Secretary of the Treasury, the Governor of the Federal Reserve Board and the Federal Reserve banks," which "have been construed to the effect that commodity prices, especially prices of farm products, were too high and that a pre-war basis, or an approximation of a pre-war basis of prices, must be reached in a short time."[1] These assertions, and the angry declaration by delegates to the conference that the Reserve Board was engaged in a deliberate "drive to force wheat from $2.55 to $1.60,"[2] became the basis of widespread political unrest in the farming states, which had much to do with the breaking of party lines in the next two Congresses, and which doubtless contributed also to the vote against the existing administration, polled by those states in November, 1920.

The intimation in the conference report, that responsible government officials had predicted early return to pre-war prices, was quite unfounded.

[1] Report of special committee to Agricultural Conference, Oct. 13, 1920.

[2] N. Y. *Times*, Washington dispatch of Oct. 12.

No such expectation was held or expressed in any official quarter; indeed, the farmers' conference report itself guarded its assertion by merely saying that statements actually made had been thus "construed." But official statements had certainly been made with emphasis, earlier in the year, to the effect that prices in general were oppressively and dangerously high—a fact which was publicly recognized in the United States Senate's resolution of May 17—and the Governor of the Federal Reserve had spoken with perhaps more frankness than discretion in declaring at a Southern cotton conference that "it is not the function" of the Reserve system "to aid any one section of the country to maintain a high price for its products."[1] In reply to the accusation that the Reserve Board had caused the agricultural distress by "restricting credit," the Board itself pointed out that between January and October, 1920, the twelve reserve banks had increased their holdings of agricultural and commercial paper by $500,000,000 and the member banks by more than $1,800,000,000.[2] In a subsequent report, it produced figures to show that rediscounts by

[1] W. G. P. Harding, speech at Birmingham, Ala., Oct. 8, 1920.
[2] Statement of Federal Reserve Board, Oct. 17, 1920.

the reserve banks, of agricultural and live stock paper alone, had been so largely increased in every month of 1920 that the $246,938,000 thus held at the end of the year compared with $140,-691,000 in May and with only $51,068,000 at the end of 1919.[1]

The policy of lending with the greatest possible freedom, but at rates sufficiently high to limit the fresh grants of credit to borrowers in urgent need of it, was in fact consistently pursued throughout the crisis, both by the Federal Reserve and, with its assistance, by the private banks. Neither rediscounts nor circulating notes reached their high point until December, 1920, when the one account stood $225,000,000 higher than at the beginning of deflation during May and the other $321,000,000. The reduction which then ensued was merely evidence, always present at that stage of a great commercial reaction, of the rapidly waning activities of trade. Notwithstanding absence in 1920 of the spectacular phenomena of a financial crisis, the scope of forced economic readjustment which followed was possibly wider than in any American "panic period" since 1873. The fall in prices of commodities did not cease until January, 1922,

[1] Annual Report Federal Reserve Board for 1920, pp. 17 and 18.

when the average stood 44 per cent below its
high point of May, 1920.

Prices on the Stock Exchange at the end of 1920
stood 33 per cent under the average of April.
The country's production of steel fell from 42,132,-
000 tons in 1920 to 19,783,000 in 1921; the smaller
figure being less than the output of any year since
1908, when the trade depression following the
panic of 1907 was at its worst.   Checks drawn on
American banks in 1921 were less in aggregate
value than those of 1920 by $113,000,000,000.
or 25¼ per cent, a ratio of decrease three times as
great as had occurred in the year after the panic of
1907, and half as large again as that of the year
after 1893.[1]   Mercantile failures of 1921 were not
only numerically more than double those of 1920,
but in liabilities involved they exceeded by
$269,500,000, or 74 per cent, the highest previous
yearly figure.[2]   The year's movement of freight
on the country's railways during 1921 was less than
in 1920 by 618,786,000 tons, or 25 per cent; the
gross receipts from freight declined $395,716,000.[3]
In one month of 1921 the total operating revenue

[1] *Financial Chronicle*, annual figures.
[2] *Dun's Review*, annual reports.
[3] Annual reports, Interstate Commerce Commission.

of all the railways fell below working expenditure, and for the year as a whole only 3⅛ per cent was earned on property valuation.[1]   American export trade in 1921 fell $3,743,000,000 below that of 1920 and the imports $2,769,000,000; so that, although the shrinkage in the figures was largely a matter of falling prices, our surplus of merchandise exports was reduced by nearly a billion dollars.

The "deflation process" was as complete as it was swift; it left American finance and industry, by the middle of 1921, in a condition which rendered prediction of the future extremely difficult.   As we have seen, the collapse of the hugely inflated financial, commercial and industrial organism had been as sudden and far-reaching in the rest of the world as in the United States; no help in the task of rebuilding the shattered structure could be expected from other countries.   Only one financial movement in the American markets of the day stood out in contrast with the rest.   During the twelve months ending with June, 1920, our gold exports had been $466,420,000, exceeding the period's gold importations by $315,880,000.   In

[1] Bureau of Railway Economics, "Railway Revenues and Expenses for the 12 months ended Dec. 31, 1921."

May of 1920, however, when American deflation
really began, the large outflow of gold was abruptly
checked; by autumn, monthly gold imports were
rising again to the war time figures.   In the twelve
months ending with June, 1921, our gold export
was only $133,537,000 and our gold import
$638,559,000; the surplus of imports, $505,022,000,
having never been matched in any fiscal year
except 1917.

Large gold importation at an hour of crisis in
the home credit market was nothing new in
American financial history; it was in fact a familiar
incident of all our panics.[1]   It had occurred on
those earlier occasions, however, either because of
heavy borrowing by our bankers in the European
money markets to relieve the American market, or
because of sudden and great increase of the American merchandise export surplus.   But in 1921, as
we have seen, the "trade balance" in this country's
favor was enormously reduced, and Europe was in
no position to make loans to any other country.
The gold movement of the period was therefore
striking proof of the commanding position of the
United States in international finance and of its
power, in case of necessity, to draw on a vast

[1] *Forty Years of American Finance,* pp. 196 and 375.

reservoir of existing foreign credits of its own. In that respect, the course of events at the climax of our trade depression pointed to facts in the situation which were certain to affect our subsequent economic history.

CHAPTER IX

IN THE RECONSTRUCTION PERIOD

THE after-war "deflation" which had been predicted in 1915, constantly apprehended
during the "peace rumors" of 1916, awaited with
nervous apprehension in the early months of 1919
and then dismissed as a financial probability in
the subsequent commercial speculation, may be
said to have run its course by the end of 1921 or
the beginning of 1922. That was the term of the
spectacular deflation movement even in Europe,
except for Germany and one or two other of the
central states where continued inflation and
depreciation of the currency, on a scale quite
unprecedented in human history, prolonged for a
year or two after 1921 the fictitious financial and
industrial activities. Between May of 1920 and
February of 1922, average prices declined 49 per
cent in England and 47 per cent in France; after
the later of those dates, recovery ensued which by

the end of 1923 had brought the British average nearly 8 per cent and the French 18 per cent, above the low points of 1922.[1] The American average, based on the 1913 figure as 100, having fallen from 247 in May, 1920, to 138 in January, 1922, had got back to 159 as early as March of 1923, and did not vary greatly from that figure during the next three years.[2]

With the post-war episode of rapid deflation completed in this country, the story of American finance in war-time might properly end. The chapter of economic history which followed was necessarily made up, in the world at large, of the prolonged and trying task of reconstruction; in the United States it was marked by readjustment of American finance and industry to the changed conditions of the outside world. All past experience in the aftermath of other wars had taught that the double process would be long-continued; it may still be many years before it is possible to say that the world or any part of it has absolutely regained economic equilibrium. When nearly twenty years had elapsed after our own War of

[1] Estimates of French Statistique Générale. London *Economist*, monthly index numbers.

[2] *Wholesale Prices, 1890 to 1923.* Monthly reports Bureau of Labor Statistics, 1924–1925.

Secession, economic reconstruction continued to be discussed as the problem of the Southern States. Not until 1878 did the South raise as large a cotton crop as that of 1859;[1] it was in 1886 that Henry W. Grady's speech on "The New South" attracted nation-wide attention for its evidence that industrial reconstruction had at last been effected in the defeated states. One of the most eminent English economists, reviewing Europe's reconstruction after the Wars of Napoleon, has held that the process actually occupied the thirty-nine years between the Battle of Waterloo and the Crimean War of 1854. During that interval it was England alone which had been able to accumulate capital for large-scale investment in enterprises of deferred profit and it was British capital which provided, for the industrial rehabilitation of the outside world, the resources which the markets of other countries were unable to procure in adequate amount at home.[2]

The part which England played in the world's economic reconstruction after 1815 has unmistakably been the rôle of the United States since 1918.

[1] *Financial Chapters of the War*, p. 197. Shepperson, *Cotton Facts*, edition of Oct. 1918, p. 30.
[2] Thorold Rogers, *Economic Interpretation of History*, p. 292.

Notwithstanding the immense outflow of gold in 1919 and 1920, an evident result both of our assumption of England's foreign obligations in 1917 and 1918 and of the advancing by our own banks of the money to finance our own huge exports of merchandise in the first year after the war, the position of the United States as creditor of the outside world was steadily emphasized. It was not merely a question of the war debt by foreign governments to the United States Treasury based on advances of money for the war. That of itself amounted on the books at the end of 1918 to $8,171,976,000,[1] but no payment of interest or principal on these intergovernmental loans was asked in the four years immediately following the armistice.

A careful and thorough computation by economic experts, however, conducted under the auspices of the United States Department of Commerce, found that, when all actual payments on international account had been allowed for— balance of trade in merchandise, gold and silver, interest on our own foreign loans, actual exports of United States currency to countries whose citizens wanted a stable medium of exchange or basis for

[1] Treasury Report, 1918, p. 36.

hoarded money, American tourists' expenditure abroad, remittances to Europe by immigrants in America, freight charges of foreign steamships, and American investments in European markets— the calendar year 1919 resulted in a credit balance of $1,082,000,000 in favor of the United States against the outside world, and that 1920 produced a similar credit of $1,143,000,000.[1] The shifting of the gold movement in favor of the United States was not surprising, under those circumstances.

It is true, the financial and industrial depression which followed the great deflation on every foreign market, coupled with the much lower price of merchandise, cut down the American export trade of the calendar year 1921 $3,742,900,000 as compared with 1920. But the simultaneous severe reaction in the internal trade of the United States curtailed our importations also; they were $2,769,-300,000 less in 1921 and that year's surplus of exports, although greatly reduced from the year before remained at $1,975,800,000, or vastly larger than in any year before 1916. More important as an immediate influence, American bankers and merchants were now engaged in call-

[1] U. S. Department of Commerce, "Balance of International Payments of the United States," September, 1923.

ing back home the capital loaned to Europe rather
than in advancing new loans and, as a consequence,
there was no way for Europe to meet its rapidly
mounting current obligations to the United States
except by shipping gold. In 1921 this country
received from abroad $667,300,000 more gold than
it sent out; in the four-year period after 1920, our
gold imports exceeded exports by $1,457,800,000,
of which $601,700,000 came from England and
$261,000,000 from France.[1] Whereas the gold
holdings of the United States were reckoned at
$1,887,000,000 when war broke out in August,
1914, and at $3,079,000,000 on the signing of the
armistice in November, 1918, they had reached at
the end of 1924 the sum of $4,547,000,000.[2] At
the end of 1923 the United States Mint estimated
the whole world's monetary stock of gold at
$9,407,761,000, out of which total $4,247,201,000
was held by the United States alone.[3]

The ending of the war and the completing of the
immediate post-war deflation had left three very
different problems on the hands of the United

[1] Monthly Summary of Foreign Commerce, U. S. Department
of Commerce.

[2] U. S. Treasury, monthly statements of U. S. money circulation, Aug. 1, 1914, Nov. 1, 1918, Dec. 31, 1924.

[3] U. S. Mint, Annual Report, 1924, pp. 216 and 219.

States. One was the adjustment of this extraordinary balance of trade in favor of the United States, without perpetually heaping up gold on top of an accumulation which had long before been recognized as unnecessarily large. The second was the avoiding of such inflation of credit and prices as seemed to be threatened by use, for a banking reserve, of the huge amount already accumulated. The third, a very different matter, was the adjustment of the mutual relations of home trade and industry after the always uneven and irregular working of the deflation process.

The position of the United States in the field of international finance was in some respects the most remarkable ever presented in economic history. All past experience had indicated that, in the long run, so immense an accrued and accruing indebtedness by other countries to a single creditor state must result in greatly increased shipment of merchandise by them in payment. That kind of settlement had transformed England's habitual surplus of exports, nearly two decades after 1815, into a permanent and very large annual excess of imports. Nothing of the kind was in sight for the United States when the deflation episode terminated.

Our position differed radically from that of England after the Napoleonic wars. Whereas England in that reconstruction period took payment from the outside debtor countries in food and raw material of manufacture which were not produced in the British Islands, the United States was itself in 1921 the world's largest producer of such commodities for its own use and that of the outside world. It is true that, with the country's increased wealth, credit and purchasing power, its import trade increased very rapidly when it had emerged from the depression following the crash of 1920. Evidence of such recovery had become visible during 1922 in that surest of industrial indications, iron production; which had fallen from a daily average of 108,900 tons in March, 1920, to an average of 27,889 in July, 1921, but which by the end of 1922 had risen again to 99,577 and in May of 1923 to 124,764, thereby surpassing all previous monthly figures.[1] It was similarly reflected in the checks drawn on the country's banks, whose face value had decreased from $123,564,000,000 in the fourth quarter of 1919, the highest quarterly record at that time, to $83,791,-000,000 in the third quarter of 1921, but whose

[1] *Iron Age*, monthly estimates.

rapid increase after the second date brought the total to $102,234,000,000 in the last three months of 1922 and to $138,050,000,000 in the same months of 1925.[1] Freight loaded for transportation on the country's railways decreased from 45,118,000 cars in 1920 to 39,323,000 in 1921, but it had increased to 43,713,000 in 1922 and to 49,812,000 in 1923.[2] The trade revival thus indicated expressed itself by increase of $603,000,-000 in merchandise importations during 1922, of $679,000,000 in 1923, and by a further increase of $435,000,000 in 1925 as compared with 1923.

Since exports, mostly because of the hard times in Europe, remained in the two years after 1921 below the total of that year, the annual surplus of exports decreased; it amounted in 1923 to $375,000,000, as against $1,975,000,000 in 1921. During four months beginning with March, 1923, indeed, the government reported an actual excess of imports amounting to $151,800,000; the largest surplus of the kind on record for a period of that length, and in the seven months from December of 1924 to June of 1925 inclusive, the United

[1] *Financial Chronicle*, quarterly reports of bank clearings.
[2] American Railway Association, statements of weekly and yearly loadings of revenue freight.

States exported more gold by $179,600,000 than it imported in the period. This had the appearance of a movement towards readjusting in a normal way, the double problem of an unwieldy annual credit balance on international account and an utterly superfluous domestic stock of gold. But the process did not continue. Disastrously short American cotton crops in 1921 and 1922 and low prices of grain were partly responsible for the smaller export trade. In 1924 and 1925, however, the cotton yield was exceptionally large and European spinners bought heavily to replenish their reduced supplies, and in 1924 a shortage of wheat in Europe and Canada, during a season when our own farmers had raised one of the three largest crops since war time, caused both rise in grain prices and immediate increase of our export trade, which brought the surplus of exports over imports, in the twelve months ending with June, 1925, above $1,000,000,000.

Only one means had appeared of meeting the resultant heavy current indebtedness of the outside world to the United States; this was the lending of American capital to Europe in particular and the foreign markets in general, on the basis of new securities of such foreign countries taken by American investors. Prior to the war, that expedient would have been hard to imagine; but war-time necessities, as we have seen, had accustomed the thrifty American to placing his surplus funds in bonds of foreign governments. The economic condition of Europe after 1920 was not in itself such as to stimulate the movement; but on the other hand, the change in the American money market after the immense reduction of credit commitments in 1920 and 1921, had influenced the investment market profoundly. Between May, 1920, and May, 1921, the New York Reserve Bank rate remained at 7 per cent; but at the later date it was lowered to 6½, from which subsequent reductions brought it to 4½ before the end of 1921, to 4 in the middle of 1922 and in the last half of 1924 to 3 per cent, the lowest in the Reserve system's history.

As against the correspondingly low rates to which loans declined on the open market, the new securities offered by European and other foreign markets bore interest rates ranging from 6 to 8 per cent; practically all of them were made payable in gold, and it was already evident, from the course of the market for domestic bonds, that the available supply of American investment capital required some other outlet even than the large new offerings of home securities. The foreign offerings were taken with great readiness. Department of Commerce experts estimated that in 1921 such new foreign investments by the American market aggregated $1,092,000,000, in 1922 $963,000,000, in 1923 $417,000,000 and in 1924 $909,000,000. The result, when all other items of international transactions had been estimated and included, was to balance the whole account in each of those years except 1923—in fact, to leave an annual net debit against the United States, which meant the establishment of foreign balances in America.[1]

Current obligations of the outside world to the United States were therefore fully met. To what extent this recourse of long-term loans to Europe and the rest of the outside world would permanently meet the situation, if not accompanied hereafter by a large and continuous excess of merchandise imports into the country over its export trade, continued to cause conjecture and perplexity in all the markets. That question was left in all the greater obscurity, because of the prospect that payments would now be resumed on

[1] "The Balance of International Payments of the United States in 1924," p. 26, U. S. Department of Commerce

the enormous war-time debt of our European allies and other states to the United States government. At the end of 1922 those obligations, plus accrued and unpaid interest up to that date, amounted to no less than $11,656,932,737.[1] Negotiations were now begun with the twenty foreign governments concerned, to refund the debts into formal long-term bonds, pledging payment of annual interest and of such yearly instalments on the principal as should extinguish the indebtedness at maturity.

In June, 1923, the American Debt Commission reached such a settlement with England, whereby the debt of $4,600,000,000 was converted into a 62-year loan, bearing interest at 3 per cent until 1932 and of 3½ thereafter. Yearly payments then began, not only of the stipulated interest but of amounts on principal account rising from $23,000,000 in the first year to $175,000,000 in the sixty-second.[2] Funding of Italy's debt of $2,042,000,000 was arranged with the commission in 1925 on a similar interest basis, but with annual payments on principal rising from $5,000,000 to $79,400,000;[3] Belgium, although large concessions were made in the adjustment, pledged payments

[1] Treas. Rep., 1922, p. 281.   [2] Treas. Rep., 1923, p. 262.
[3] Treas. Rep., 1924, p. 318.

rising from $2,100,000 in 1926 to $12,500,000 in 1986,[1] and there were left unsettled, at the end of 1925, numerous debts of other countries—including France, whose indebtedness for principal and interest accrued was then $4,304,012,277.[2]   In all the funding arrangements made, a new and large annual debit against the outside world was bound to be created, offsetting the expedients which had thus far balanced the yearly international account.

The accumulation of gold in the United States, only briefly interrupted at the end of 1924 and the beginning of 1925, was a problem by itself; but it was aggravated by the considerations which I have just set forth.   In Europe, and to a great extent in the United States also, the "gold movement" was discussed as an influence making inevitably for progressive inflation of credit and prices.   The London financial community very generally expressed the view that such advance in American prices, as a result of "gold inflation," would solve the problem of international finance by rapidly increasing our imports and decreasing our exports because of the higher scale of prices

[1] Treas. Rep., 1924, p. 288.
[2] Treas. Rep., 1925, p. 265.

in the United States.[1]   But that did not happen.
We have seen how immense was the addition to the
American stock of gold between 1920 and the end of
1924.   Yet average American commodity prices,
after reaching in January, 1922 (on the basis of 100
for 1913) their low point of 138 and recovering in
March of 1923 to 159, declined to 145 in June of
1924 and advanced no further than 161 in the very
active trade of 1925.[2] This was very far from
"inflation of prices"; it still left the margin
between the 1913 and the 1925 valuations practically the same as that of the British average.[3]

There were various explanations. One was
based on the fact that the Federal Reserve did not
increase its holdings of gold in proportion to the
increase of the whole country's supply. Not only
was that supply enlarged by the great gold imports
of the period, but something like $50,000,000
annually was added from American production.[4]
Between the middle of 1922 and the end of 1924,
the total stock of gold in the United States

[1] John Maynard Keynes, "Monetary Reform," 1924. Regi-
nald McKenna, chairman's report to annual meeting Midland
Bank of London, Jan. 27, 1925.
[2] Monthly statements, U. S. Bureau of Labor Statistics.
[3] Monthly index number, British Board of Trade.
[4] U. S. Mint, Annual Reports.

increased $761,800,000.[1] Yet the gold in the Reserve banks decreased $84,300,000 during the same period.[2] This resulted partly from the fact that private banks in the system, having largely paid off with imported gold the excessively large rediscounts incurred at the Reserve banks in 1919 and 1920, were no longer under the necessity of paying over the gold now received on import. But the larger cause was the policy deliberately adopted by the Reserve banks of paying out as ordinary cash, in the form of gold certificates, part of their own existing and accruing gold reserve.[3] While the gold in the Federal Reserve was falling during the period just cited, in the face of a huge increase in the country's total gold holdings, gold coin and certificates in general circulation, outside the Treasury and the Federal Reserve, increased $838,000,000.

Whether this movement of reserve money into general circulation was sufficient of itself to arrest what otherwise might have been a tendency to excessive inflation of the credit or currency, with the expected influence on prices, may possibly

[1] Monthly money circulation statements, U. S. Treasury.
[2] Weekly reports, Federal Reserve Board.
[3] Annual Report Federal Reserve Board for 1923, pp. 22 and 23.

be doubted. Even with this releasing into general circulation of superfluous gold reserves (a process which had been anticipated, even in pre-war days when the Treasury kept the gold reserve against the currency[1]), the Reserve system's cash reserve remained at a height sufficient to have supported, under the minimum percentage prescribed by law, double the combined amount of note circulation and deposits resulting from rediscounts which were then outstanding; yet there was no attempt at such expansion. The private banks at times increased their own loans very largely (as in the increase of a thousand million dollars during the year of excited stock exchange speculation, 1925,) in loans of member banks in the Federal Reserve.[2] But that expansion in credit was based in no important measure on recourse to the Reserve bank facilities;[3] and, furthermore, it had no visible effect on prices outside the stock market, for the average prices of commodities actually moved slightly downward during the same year.[4]

[1] Annual Report Federal Reserve Board for 1923, pp. 23 and 24.

[2] Reserve Board, weekly statement of Jan. 7, 1926, on "Principal Resources and Liabilities of Member Banks."

[3] Reserve Board, weekly statement of Dec. 31, 1925.

[4] Monthly reports, U. S. Bureau of Labor Statistics.

The problem of American agricultural distress, after the deflation of prices following 1920, stood pretty much by itself.   It was not, like the others which I have examined, an unfamiliar incident of the period after a great war.   Hard times in the farming country had been a sequel of great importance, economically and politically, to our own Civil War.   In the "deflation period" after the great European war, the cause for the distress was the same—abnormally large production in war-time on the basis of inflated prices, and a heavy burden of indebtedness left to be dealt with on the footing of a 50 per cent decline in prices. The farmer's difficulties between 1920 and 1924 were aggravated by the fact that competitive production of grain, in the European countries during the first years of reconstruction, increased much faster than competitive production of other commodities.   The world's annual production of wheat increased from 2,997,000,000 bushels in 1919 to 3,742,541,000 in 1923, or more than the aggregate harvest prior to 1912.[1]   Since the American yield had not increased during the interval, it was clearly a new and trying world-market in which the American farmer had to sell his wheat.

[1] Year-book U. S. Department of Agriculture for 1924, p. 569.

Not only did wheat at Chicago fall during 1923 as low as 96½ cents a bushel, but this reversion to the pre-war price occurred while the price of commodities which the farmer had to buy had recovered substantially from the low point reached in 1921 or 1922. Reckoning 1913 prices as 100, the average of 1919 for agricultural prices had been 221 while the non-agricultural average was 199. Even in 1920, however, the agricultural average went below the other; in 1922, while the price of non-agricultural commodities averaged 168, that of agricultural products averaged only 136¼.[1] The resentment of the farmer made itself felt, as usual, in politics; but the paralysis of buying power in a great part of the farming district was even more formidable as an economic problem.

It was a difficult question for the economic future. Although fortune favored the American grain-producer in 1924, when the world's wheat-production decreased more than 400,000,000 bushels from the year before, yet when the American crop increased 75,246,000, there was no assurance that the happy accident would be repeated. The harvest of 1924 was a very timely windfall; sold as

[1] Calculations of U. S. Labor Bureau's statistical department.

the wheat crop was for an amount $400,000,000 greater than the valuation of the crop of 1923, and bringing much the largest aggregate return of any wheat yield since 1920,[1] it released the greater part of the agricultural "frozen credits" left after 1920. Yet the next year's world-harvest was some 250,000,000 bushels larger while our own decreased 193,262,000. Nevertheless, the results in 1924 had the result of narrowing the discrepancy between agricultural and non-agricultural prices; which, indeed, for a time in 1925, were nearly on a parity.

These are the special difficulties and uncertainties which have beset the United States in the early stages of the post-war reconstruction period. Others will doubtless follow, as the economic world adjusts itself to its new conditions. Yet the larger view of the economic and political world as it has emerged from the European War is certain to emphasize first of all what has been perhaps the most dramatic transformation of economic history; the change since 1914 in the international position of the United States. That event and its consequences will necessarily provide

[1] Year-book of U. S. Department of Agriculture for 1924, p. 560.

the key to the financial future, in America as in Europe; the course both of political and economic history will be largely shaped by the capacity of our bankers, merchants, investors and statesmen to meet the resultant new responsibilities.

LIST OF AUTHORITIES CITED

GOVERNMENT PUBLICATIONS

U. S. Treasury, annual reports.
U. S. Treasury, monthly circulation statements.
U. S. Comptroller of the Currency, annual reports.
U. S. Department of Agriculture, annual reports and monthly bulletins.
U. S. War Department, annual reports.
U. S. Department of Commerce, annual reports. *Monthly Summary of Foreign Commerce.* "Balance of International Payments of the U. S.," special bulletins, 1922–1925.

"Wholesale Prices, 1890 to 1923," U. S. Bureau of Labor Statistics, 1925.

"Union Scale of Wages and Labor," *Ibid.*, 1925.

"Cost of Living in the U. S.," *Ibid.*, 1924.

Federal Reserve Board, annual reports, monthly bulletins, weekly statements of condition.

N. Y. Federal Reserve Bank, annual reports and monthly bulletins.

Interstate Commerce Commission, annual reports. *Congressional Record.*

"History of the National Bank Currency," National Monetary Commission, 1910.

"War Time Profits and Costs of the Steel Industry," U. S. Federal Trade Commission, 1925.

"The Stabilization of the Price of Wheat during the War," U. S. Grain Corporation, 1925.

Report of Massachusetts Commission on Necessaries of Life, 1919.

Report on Prices, Wages and Transportation, U. S. Senate, 1893.

British Board of Trade, monthly bulletins.

League of Nations, monthly bulletins of statistics.

PERIODICAL LITERATURE

The Economist, London.
Commercial and Financial Chronicle, N. Y.
Iron Age, N. Y.
Railway Age, N. Y.
Dun's Review, N. Y.
Engineering & Mining Journal, N. Y.
Northwestern Miller.
N. Y. Chamber of Commerce, annual reports.
Railway Revenues and Expenses, Bureau of Railway Economics, Washington.
Review of Economic Statistics, Harvard University.
American Iron and Steel Institute, annual reports.
U. S. Steel Corporation, annual reports.
Bethlehem Steel Company, annual reports.
American International Corporation, annual reports.

OTHER PUBLICATIONS

American Industry in the War, Bernard M. Baruch, report of War Industries Board, 1921.

Industrial America in the World War, Grosvenor B. Clarkson, 1923.

The Formative Period of the Federal Reserve System, W. G. P. Harding, 1925.

The World Crisis, 1915, Winston S. Churchill, London, 1925.

The First World War, Col. C. à C. Repington, London, 1920.

War and Lombard Street, Hartley Withers, London, 1915.

British War Finance, W. R. Lawson, London, 1915.

Monetary Reform, J. M. Keynes, London, 1924.

History of Prices, Thomas Tooke, London, 1838.

Public Debts, H. C. Adams, 1887.

Economic Interpretation of History, Thorold Rogers, London, 1889.

Investigations in Currency and Finance, Stanley Jevons, 1884.

Forty Years of American Finance, A. D. Noyes, 1909.

Financial Chapters of the War, A. D. Noyes, 1916.

INDEX

Brewer, David J., Associate Justice U. S. Supreme Court, interpretation of Anti-Trust Law, 22, 23

Bryan, W. J., Secretary of State, disapproves war loans to belligerents, 111; authorizes sale of munitions, 113; opposes Plumb railway plan, 357

C

Canada, Bank of England agrees to receive gold in, 84; U. S. gold exports to, in 1914, 85

"Cancellations," in export trade of 1920, 394; in home trade, 394

Churchill, Winston S., remark on British gold resumption and American finance, 7; describes shortage of British war munitions, 110

Clearing house loan certificates, issue of, during 1914 war panic, 74, 75

Congress, U. S., change in composition of, in 1910, 11; in 1912, 18; appoints "Money Trust committee," 42, 43; discusses Federal Reserve Law, 46–48; passes Reserve Act, 49; favors plan of Roosevelt war unit, 164; appropriations of 1917 of, for the war, 165; passes war finance bill, 167; opposition to draft, 168; passes bill for loans to European Allies, 169; supports President's attitude, 169–170; passes war finance bill, 175; authorizes war loans, 175; conditions of loan by U. S. to European allies, 176; tax legislation of 1917, 195; asks

investigation of high 1920 prices, 325

"Conservation" while U. S. at war, applied to manufactured goods, 270; to food and fuel, 271

"Consumer's strike," first appearance of, in 1919, 324; organized demonstrations of 1920 in, 333

Cooke, Jay, his "drive" to float Civil War loans, 181

Copper, demoralization of 1914 market for, 67; great rise in output and prices of, in 1915, 121; price reduced in 1917, on army orders, 269

Cotton, yield of 1912 breaks past records, 16; huge production of 1914, 64; export stopped by outbreak of war, 64, 65; rapid fall in price, 65, 66; demand of planters for government relief, 66; assistance offered by bankers, 67, 122; very low price for, early in 1915, 95; no borrowings by planters from relief fund, 122; rapid recovery in market for, 123; increase of textile exports, 123; home demand later in 1915 absorbs surplus of 1914 crop, 123; high value of 1917 and 1918 crops, 223; decline in price of, immediately after war, 286; violent rise of, late in 1919, 296; sweeping break in, at end of 1920, 401; "night riders" warn producers not to sell below 40 cents, 402; price falls from 43¾ to 10⅞ cents, 404; short crops of, in 1921 and 1922, 426; large crops of 1924 and 1925, 426

Cummins, Albert B., U. S. Senator, disapproves U. S.

Forty Years
of
American Finance

Being the Second and Extended Edition of "Thirty Years of American Finance"

By Alexander D. Noyes

A NEW edition of the same author's "Thirty Years of American Finance," originally published in 1898. The new book carries the story of the American financial markets down to 1908, describing and examining such episodes as the industrial revival after 1898, the great boom of 1901, the history of the Steel Trust, the promoters' mania, the "rich men's panic" of 1903, the "millionaire speculation" of 1905 and 1906, and the panic of 1907.

This is the first complete and thorough history that has been published of this extraordinary dramatic and interesting chapter in finance.

G. P. Putnam's Sons

New York   London

The
Theory and History
of Banking

By

Charles F. Dunbar

Fourth Edition, Revised and Enlarged

With Supplementary Chapter Presenting the
Record of the Federal Reserve System

By

Henry Parker Willis
Professor of Banking in Columbia University;
Former Secretary of the Federal Reserve Board

This work has firmly established its place in the
literature of banking. It gives a clear-cut statement
of ordinary banking operations, supplemented by a
series of historical chapters, on certain of the great
banks and banking systems.

To the new edition exceedingly important material
has been contributed by Prof. Henry Parker Willis.
The new chapters deal with Foreign Exchange,
Central Banks, and the Federal Reserve Banking
System. Many changes have also been effected in
the existing text in order to make the volume
thoroughly applicable to the needs of the reader.

G. P. Putnam's Sons

New York   **London**